W9-AIR-685

HITLER'S WAVE-BREAKER CONCEPT

Hitler's Wave-Breaker Concept

AN ANALYSIS OF THE GERMAN END GAME IN THE BALTIC

BY

HENRIK O. LUNDE

CASEMATE
Philadelphia & Oxford

Published in the United States of America and Great Britain in 2013 by
CASEMATE PUBLISHERS
908 Darby Road, Havertown, PA 19083
and
10 Hythe Bridge Street, Oxford, OX1 2EW

ISBN 978-1-61200-161-6
Digital Edition: ISBN 978-1-61200-162-3

Cataloging-in-publication data is available from the Library of Congress and the British Library.

10 9 8 7 6 5 4 3 2 1

Printed and bound in the United States of America.

For a complete list of Casemate titles please contact:

CASEMATE PUBLISHERS (US)
Telephone (610) 853-9131, Fax (610) 853-9146
E-mail: casemate@casematepublishing.com

CASEMATE PUBLISHERS (UK)
Telephone (01865) 241249, Fax (01865) 794449
E-mail: casemate-uk@casematepublishing.co.uk

CONTENTS

Maps

Preface and Acknowledgments

The idea for this book goes back several decades, to when I was a student at the US Command and General Staff College in Fort Leavenworth, Kansas. I became curious about the question of how and why the better part of three German army groups became pinned against the Baltic Sea towards the end of World War II, and thus not available for the final defense of Germany.

I discovered in my initial exploration and numerous subsequent visits to the National Archives while stationed in Washington, D.C., and Carlisle Barracks, Pennsylvania, that it was an exceedingly complex issue, thoroughly interrelated with other subjects—particularly those pertaining to the German northern theater of operations. While I took copious notes, I decided not to attempt to do anything more on the subject until I had more free time. Several folders containing some of those old notes were destroyed or damaged to the point of being virtually unreadable when our home in Florida was flooded in a storm in March 1993.

The free time I was looking for took a long time coming since I entered the business world following my retirement from the US Army. When spare time finally appeared, I concentrated first on writing about the German operations in Norway and Germany's co-belligerency with Finland. This had the great advantage of making me familiar with many of the issues involved in the withdrawal from Leningrad. In addition, several articles written over the past few years also focused on the German northern theater of operations or on operations on the Eastern Front. I have been able to use much of the research that went into the earlier books and articles in this project.

I was also intrigued by the excellent and thought-provoking writings of Professor Howard D. Grier in his 2007 book.[1] Although I arrive at different conclusions, I have relied on his research throughout this work. As in the past, I have depended on the research of Earl F. Ziemke on the German northern and eastern theaters of war. I learned a long time ago to trust the accuracy of his meticulous research. Finally, a number of outstanding books have appeared in the last decades that made my research much easier than it would have been in the 1970s. I have also used several works in Swedish and German that have not been translated into English.

It is hoped that this book, by building on the research of others, will provide useful information for the student of military history on a confusing and controversial part of World War II, the outcome of which had profound consequences. I owe a special debt to those who have written about World War II on the Eastern Front—especially covering the last two years of that war—and they are frequently referenced in text and notes.

I am grateful to a number of libraries and archives. I wish to give a very belated thanks to the extremely helpful staff at the National Archives. After all these years, I don't recall any names but they went to great length to help this novice find what he was looking for. When in doubt about what to look for and where, they gently steered me in the right direction. I also want to give specific mentions to the staff of the Coyle Free Library in Chambersburg, Pennsylvania, and the Collier County Library system in Naples, Florida. The friendly and helpful staff at these two library systems worked tirelessly to locate references, some of them rather obscure, which were then provided to me through the excellent interlibrary loan program.

I am very grateful to my old friend Dr. Enoch Haga in California, who has again offered invaluable assistance. He has tirelessly served as an editor and advisor for every part of the book. Dr. Haga provided many helpful suggestions and gave encouragement whenever I encountered seemingly insoluble problems—and that was quite often. Dr. Loislane Lowe, also in California, has also assisted in the proofing and editorial process.

I am also grateful to the Publisher, Mr. David Farnsworth, and his excellent staff at Casemate for showing confidence in me by accepting this book for publication and also for their assistance by taking over the map making and photo selection chores when it became obvious that I was going to encounter problems in meeting the publication schedule because of major events in my own life. I am particularly grateful to Mr. Steven Smith, the Editor Director, and to Ms. Tara Lichterman, my point of contact, who patiently listened to my many gripes and cleared administrative hurdles.

Finally, it is obvious that this work could not have been completed without the understanding and support of my immediate family members. My debt to them is immense. My wife Florence died on June 3, 2012, as I was in the middle of writing this book. For almost 50 years she was loyally at my side through good and bad times. Knowing of my deep interest in military history, her encouragement was a driving force in my writing. This book is therefore dedicated to her.

Despite the diligence of those who provided assistance, comments and advice, I must stress that I take full responsibility for all conclusions and such errors as this book may inadvertently contain.

NOTES

1. Howard D. Grier, *Hitler/Dönitz and the Baltic Sea: The Third Reich's Last Hope, 1944–1945* (Annapolis: Naval Institute Press, 2007)

Introduction

In order to examine and hopefully understand Hitler's decision to defend the Baltic States at all costs this book attempts to tackle five exceedingly complicated and interrelated subjects:

1. Military strategy;
2. Hitler's strategic thinking;
3. The progressive changes in the military environment, especially those involving the opposing forces on the Eastern Front;
4. Hitler's fascination with the northern theater of war, including both Scandinavia and the Baltic region;
5. The validity of the reasons given by Hitler for refusing to withdraw in the Baltic.

The many reasons given by Hitler for his rigid forward defense in the Baltic States include:

1. Fear that a withdrawal would lead Finland to make a separate peace with the Soviets. The loss of Finland could lead to:
   a. The entrapment of the German Twentieth Mountain Army in northern Finland;
   b. The loss of the nickel supply from Finland;
   c. Breakout of the Soviet Baltic Fleet from Kronstadt, which would endanger German naval control of the Baltic and jeopardize the transport of iron ore and finished products from Sweden.

2. The threat to the submarine training area from both east and west.
3. Swedish intervention in the war on the side of the Allies. This outcome would:
   a. End the transit of German troops through Sweden;
   b. End the import of iron ore and finished products from Sweden;
   c. Pose a serious threat to the German hold on Norway;
   d. Strategically outflank the Germans from the north.
4. The protection of the Latvian oil fields.
5. An assumption that holding "fortified places," including enclaves along the coast, would slow the Russian advance and frustrate their drive into Germany.
6. An assumption that it required more forces to encircle and destroy a "fortified place" than it did to defend it—in other words it was an economy of force measure.

Some of these issues are examined within the chronological chapters ahead, while others, because of their complexity, are addressed in separate chapters. It is easy to see, however, that these subjects don't lend themselves to a strict chronological organization within this book. In fact, a sizable portion pre-dates the actual start of the German withdrawal from the Leningrad area. A retrospective position is therefore necessary to ensure that the reader understands subsequent operations on the Eastern Front, and to illustrate Hitler's handling of a situation that had changed from a string of victories before the invasion of the Soviet Union to a series of major setbacks from the winter of 1941/42. Basil Henry Liddell Hart (1895–1970) notes that by the summer of 1940 Hitler's successes, many of them bloodless, had resulted in his being viewed as a brilliant political/military strategist.[1] How did this person become by 1944–45 a paranoid and irrational individual who refused to listen to the advice of his military leaders and who increasingly involved himself in minute operational matters?

While I purposely avoided the details of the many bloody battles fought as Army Group North withdrew from the Leningrad area, it became necessary to devote a good portion of this book to a chronological review of the flow of fighting not only in the Army Group North's area, but also in the adjacent area of Army Group Center. This coverage may assist the reader in following the progressive changes in the military environment and Hitler's conduct of the war. Deliberations are kept at corps level and above. Hopefully this structure has resulted in a more orderly presentation of the chaotic events discussed.

Chapter 1 deals with Hitler as a strategist, a subject appropriate for a separate book. We look at the origins of his ideas with particular emphasis on the *Wellenbrecher* (wave-breaker) concept, his early successes, his continued emphasis of the importance of Scandinavia and the Baltic, and his growing overconfidence in his abilities in the military arena. The planning for Operation *Barbarossa* (the invasion of the Soviet Union), the seeds of failure we find in that plan, and a brief review of its early phases are examined in Chapter 2. We also consider the effect that Hitler's views of Finland had on shaping strategic goals. These views were important at the time of the German invasion of the Soviet Union in 1941, and they continued to be at the center of Hitler's strategic thinking until after Finland's withdrawal from the war.

Chapter 3 is a summary review of the failures of Army Group North in the period 1941–43. Again, we find that Hitler was driven by concerns for Finland, and that all operations on this front were anchored on those concerns. Chapter 4 then addresses the beginnings of the German retreat from Leningrad, Germany's troubled co-belligerency with Finland, Hitler's last strategic directive, the Soviet offensive against Finland, and that country's withdrawal from the war. The loss of Finland voided several of the stated concerns that drove Hitler's operations in the Baltic.

Chapter 5 is an overview of Germany's summer of disasters on the Eastern Front in 1944, particularly the Red Army's Operation *Bagration.* That operation completely outflanked Army Group North. Also addressed is Hitler's growing insistence on rigid defense and designation of "fortified places." Hitler's continued insistence on not making any withdrawals until it was too late must be ranked as perhaps the most illogical behavior by a supreme military leader during World War II.

Chapter 6 is devoted to an overview of Army Group North's withdrawal from the Narva front, an action that Hitler took with his eyes wide open, and its subsequent entrapment in the Courland Peninsula. The various pros and cons of this decision are evaluated. With the withdrawal, only two of Hitler's many reasons for holding onto the Baltic coast remained—

the possible effect on Sweden and the potential loss of the Baltic training areas for the new submarines.

Chapter 7 reviews the very accommodating policy adopted by Sweden following the German occupation of Denmark and Norway. Neither Germany nor Sweden feared an attack from the other but there were signs that this policy was about to change in accordance with the world-wide military situation. These signs led the Germans to plan and assemble forces for an invasion of Sweden in 1943. This was a foolish idea in view of Germany's strained resources and military setbacks. As Sweden concluded, like Finland, that Germany would lose the war, the country began to change its earlier accommodating policies. Hitler was forced to accept this change in attitude for fear that to do otherwise would drive Sweden into the arms of the Allies.

Chapter 8 assesses the influence of the German Navy on Hitler's operational concept in the Baltic States. The development of new submarines is summarized, as are Karl Dönitz' (1891–1980) repeated assurances to Hitler that a decisive turn in the naval war was just around the corner. This chapter also looks at the various reasons for that turn never appearing, including heavy British mining of the submarine training areas starting in August 1944, before Hitler allowed Army Group North to be trapped in Courland.

Chapter 9 is an overview of the Soviet winter offensive in 1945 up to the Red Army's appearance along the Oder River. At the beginning of the winter offensive two German armies and a portion of a third were isolated in Courland and Memel. By the time the Soviets reached the Oder River the equivalent of four more German armies were trapped against the coast in East Prussia and Pomerania due to Hitler's refusal to allow them to withdraw behind the main lines. The defense of the Oder/Neisse Line was left in the hands of four armies, mostly consisting of a motley collection of hastily raised units. These faced a total of 21 armies in the First Belorussian and First Ukrainian Fronts (a front was essentially equivalent to an army group) when reserves are counted. Chapter 10, the last chapter, deals with Soviet efforts to clean up the enclaves along the Baltic coast. Courland was left to surrender at the end of the war.

Military Strategy

I have been an avid reader of military history for more than 60 years. As a result I have drawn some simplified and generalized conclusions that place military historians into one of three categories.

The first category is composed of those who deal with military operations in considerable detail, but don't analyze concepts and strategy. Although these writers focus on the trees at the expense of the forest, they provide an indispensable service to the student of military history in providing otherwise difficult to obtain details of operations. The second category is composed of writers who take a broad view of events, but often neglect some of the very important details. These writers focus on the forest at the expense of the trees. They provide an important service by conceptualizing the study of operations. The third category comprises those who combine the first two categories. These writers include necessary detail while they at the same time provide a rich coverage of concept—they analyze wars or campaigns by putting events into an existing strategic framework. This group is small in comparison to the other two.

With this work I make a full entry into the often murky waters of military strategy, a term often misused. Some writers shy away from this term since it is often difficult to deal with properly. Furthermore, it leaves the writer open to controversy and criticism. One of my favorite military historians, John Keegan, expresses his own frustration and that of many of his colleagues when he writes:

> "Strategy," as we have come to understand the word, may well have been given too wide a meaning. I am increasingly tempted towards the belief that there is no such thing as "strategy" at all, and that international relations and military affairs would prove more manageable callings if it could be banished from their vocabularies. Certainly, if "strategy" means what military academies have taught these last 150 years, it is a crippled concept of distorting effect.[2]

This is a very damaging conclusion by such an excellent scholar and writer, damaging to any systematic study of military operations. When one speaks about military academies in the United States we are focused on the basic level of military training and education. The academies there provide an excellent liberal arts and engineering education. However, in the field of military training and education the focus is on the essential tools a young lieutenant needs when he (or she) graduates. This is supplemented by a one-year basic course in the branch of service to which the graduate is assigned (i.e. infantry, armor, engineers). The training focus is on tactics, weapons, and equipment. After about four or five years in service, a person returns to his branch school for additional training, now focusing on staff work at brigade and division level. Except for specialized courses such as airborne and ranger, this is normally the last training an officer receives at his branch of service.

The next step in the education of an officer is at Command and General Staff level, where he is trained for a battalion-level command or staff duty at division or corps level. The final step in the learning experience of an officer is at a War College, which is more of an educational than a training experience, reserved for those who may go on to become flag officers or to high positions in the military establishment. At this level the student focuses on strategy—both military and national—as well as logistical operations at corps level and higher. This is the level at which practitioners become deeply involved in what Keegan refers to as "military strategy," and his conclusion is not reflected in my years of experience at the War College.

To disregard the theory of war in exasperation is to throw out the "baby with the bathwater." Liddell Hart wrote, "When a Chief of the Imperial General Staff wrote that 'he had never had time to study the details of military history' . . . it was as if the President of the Royal College of Surgeons said he had never had time to study anatomy, or do any dissection."[3] It is true that the United States has a dismal record when it comes to the application of strategy in our wars since World War II. In Vietnam, for example, we failed to understand the nationalistic nature of the Vietnamese form of communism and faultily concluded it was part of the global communist threat. In Iraq (the 2003 war), we unwisely took the "cork out of the bottle" by dismantling a political/military balance of power strategy that had served the West well for over half a century. Despite what history should have taught us from British and Soviet experiences, we allowed ourselves to become involved in a drawn-out land war in Afghanistan. There are several explanations for such failures. Immediately after World War II, our military and economic power was so great that policy makers and strategists thought that they could disregard some of the principles that were codified over centuries.

The importance of judicious use of military strategy and principles grows in importance as power—military and economic—declines. Later, policy makers who were not at all well versed in those principles, forced tasks down the throats of military practitioners with predictable results. Military strategy must be subordinate to national or grand strategy and thus governed by political objectives, but it must be understood by policy makers that they can't demand from the military what is practically impossible.

We must have a framework by which to analyze military operations by nations, and "strategy" and "principles of war" provide that framework. Since they are fundamental tools of the military profession it is necessary to have a commonly accepted definition that can be used as a reference point throughout this book. This is a definitional issue that will have an impact on every part of this book.

Some writers refer to Germany's military operations in the Baltic during the last 18 months of World II as the "wave-breaker strategy." Most German writers don't call it a strategy. Percy Ernst Schramm, for example, calls it a doctrine.[4] We will consider whether it is proper even to give it this description, since a doctrine is most often defined as a theory based on carefully worked out principles.

While most modern military strategic concepts evolved from the writings of Karl von Clausewitz (1780–1831) and Antoine Henry Jomini (1779–1869), they in turn relied not only on earlier military history but upon prior writers on strategy: Sun Tzu (c. 544–496 BCE) more than 2,500 years ago, Flavius Vegetius, Marshal Maurice de Saxe (1696–1750), the instructions of Frederick the Great (1712–86) for his generals in 1747, and the military maxims of Napoleon (1769–1821). These have served as guiding principles for military commanders over the centuries and have had enormous influence on the conduct of war and the course of history.[5] The most prominent writers on military strategy in the 20th century were undoubtedly J. F. C. Fuller, who died in 1961, and the controversial Liddell Hart, who died in 1970. After World War I, Liddell Hart developed a set of basic principles which he thought should serve as the basis for all good strategies and which he claimed were ignored by most commanders in World War I. His strategic thinking can be boiled down to one single principle—the indirect approach—based on two fundamentals: 1) direct attacks almost never work; 2) the indirect approach upsets the enemy's equilibrium. He also believed that working on the opponent's mind was the key to victory and that an elastic defense was far superior to rigid or fixed defenses. While his ideas may not have been fully original or adopted by the Germans, as he claims, there is little doubt that his writings were more influential in Germany than in Great Britain. His books on the indirect approach became a textbook in staff colleges throughout the world after World War II.

There are many other books published by theorists and practitioners besides those mentioned above, and some had considerable impact on military theory and operations. These include Caius Julius Caesar's *War Commentaries*, Niccolo Machiavelli's *The Prince*, and Helmuth von Moltke's (the elder) *Militärische Werke*, to mention only a few.

There is no universal consensus as to the exact meaning of the term military strategy. Various definitions abound. The US Army War College Glossary of Military Terms makes reference to no less than eight definitions.[6] This lack of consensus illustrates the first and perhaps the most serious problem one encounters in the study of this complex subject, comprising a grave challenge for both the student and writer of military history. The term "military strategy" is invariably used too loosely nowadays and this muddles the understanding of events. The most common of several fallacies is to confuse national strategy with military strategy. Military strategy is only one component of national strategy. The other components include, but are not limited to, political, economic, and psychological strategies. They are all part of national strategy and should be supportive of each other, but there are frequent examples of where they are not, or where the instrument (military, political, or economic) chosen for the attainment of a national objective is not the most appropriate.

The various elements of national power need to be orchestrated at the highest levels both nationally and within a specific theater of operation to keep them from being contradictory. If they are not properly spelled out, orchestrated, and explained, those who carry out the strategy as well as the public are left in such a state of confusion that support for the national or military strategy is often undercut. Colonel Arthur F. Lykke, Jr., who served as Director of Military Strategy at the US Army War College, writes the following:

> Some call a line drawn on a map a strategy. Others believe a laundry list of national objectives represents a strategy. The problem is not just semantics; it is one of using competently one of the essential tools of the military profession. In trying to decide between alternative strategies, we are often faced with a comparison of apples and oranges, because the choices do not address the same factors. Only with a mutual understanding of what comprises military strategy can we hope to improve our strategic dialogue. There needs to be general agreement on a conceptual approach to military strategy: a definition; a description of the basic elements that make up military strategy; and an analysis of how they are related.[7]

The US Department of Defense definition of military strategy is found in Joint Chiefs of Staff (JCS) Publication 1: "The art and science of employing the armed forces of a nation to secure the objectives of national policy by the application of force or the threat of force." This definition has remained rather consistent over the years and is the one that will be used in this work with the understanding that it will be limited to German military strategy within a specific theater of war.

Military strategy, to be complete, must specify the ends—military objectives to be achieved—the ways in which these objectives are to be achieved (military strategic concepts), and finally adequate means to achieve the objectives (military resources). The reader can tell already that it is going to be difficult to apply this to the German withdrawal through the Baltic States, but it is worth a try. What makes the analysis exceedingly difficult is that while many of the objectives frequently referred to by Hitler may have had some validity at the beginning of the withdrawal, they were no longer valid later in the operation. Some of these objectives were real while others were subterfuges or based on wishful thinking rather than cold hard logic.

The noted military historian and theoretician Trevor Nevitt Dupuy writes that the principles of war or military operations may be defined as the fundamental truths governing the execution of both strategy and tactics. The collection of concepts going back many centuries is as close as we have come in the formulation of an acceptable theory of war. Dupuy calls these fundamental features the "timeless verities of war," and they remain valid despite changes in weapons and characteristics of armies. This leads to a recognized theory of war which has as its foremost element "that every military operation must be directed toward a decisive, obtainable objective."[8]

The list of principles is not immutable, like the laws of physics, and not all need to be applied in every situation but serves as a practical checklist to assist sound judgments by practitioners. It is through these prisms that Hitler's wave-breaker concept will be examined.

NOTES

1. B. H. Liddell Hart, *Strategy* (New York: Praeger Publishers, Second Revised Edition, 1972) p.3.
2. John Keegan, *The Mask of Command* (New York: Penguin Books Ltd, 1987) p.7
3. US Army War College, *Military Strategy: Theory and Application*, ed. by Colonel Arthur F. Lykke, Jr. (Carlisle, PA: US Army War College, 1986) pp.2–17. This publication is a compilation of essays by military and civilian leaders dealing with military and national strategy.
4. Percy Ernst Schramm, *Hitler: The Man & The Military Leader*, edited, translated and introduction by Donald S. Detwiler (Chicago: Academy Chicago Publishers, 1999) p.158.
5. Those who write or study military history should be familiar with some of the most popular books dealing with military theory and strategy, such as Liddell Hart's cited work in note 1 above; Thomas R. Phillips (ed.), *Roots of Strategy* (Harrisburg: Military Service Publishing Company, 1955); Jay Luvaas (ed. and translated), *Fredrick the Great on the Art of War* (New York: Free Press, 1999); Edward Mead Earle (ed.), *Makers of Modern Strategy: Military Thought from Machiavelli to Hitler* (Princeton: Princeton University Press, 1973); and J. F. C. Fuller, *The Conduct of War 1789–1961.* (New Brunswick: Rutgers University Press, 1962).
6. US Army War College, *op. cit.*, pp.1–2.
7. *Ibid*, pp.1-2 to 1-6.
8. Trevor N. Dupuy, *The Evolution of Weapons and Warfare* (New York: The Bobbs-Merrill Company, Inc., 1980) pp.323 and 326. Trevor Dupuy was a prolific writer, authoring more than 50 books. His best known works include *Military Heritage of America*, a 12-volume *Military History of World War I*, a 19-volume *Military History of World War II*, and *A Genius for War: The German Army and General Staff, 1807–1945*.

1
Hitler's Strategic Thinking

Early Life and World War I Experiences

Hitler, as is true for most of us, was a product of his life experiences. His military and strategic thinking was based on multiple factors: his personal service as a soldier in World War I; his sometimes warped view of history; the turbulent social, economic, and political scene in Germany in the 1920s; the years of struggle as a party leader; his own personality as it had developed over the years; and the intoxicating years of triumphs from 1933 to 1941. He claims to have read and studied some of the military theorists mentioned in the introduction, and there is no reason to doubt this claim. For the most part, however, rather than use these theories as a framework for arriving at a strategy, he selectively used what he read to support actions already chosen.

It would be surprising if Hitler was not, like some of the Soviet leaders—particularly Vladimir Lenin—influenced by Clausewitz' writings, as was the German General Staff. Walter Görlitz' book on the history of the German General Staff has a whole chapter titled *The Philosopher of War.*[1] A reading of Hitler's *Mein Kampf* reveals a number of similarities to Clausewitz' thoughts. Karl von Clausewitz was not always the ultimate rationalist that we associate with his main work—*On War*. After Prussia's defeat by Napoleon he wrote a much lesser-known essay titled *I Believe and Profess*. It is worthwhile quoting a passage from this essay as it may throw some light on Hitler's behavior in the closing period of World War II:

> I believe and profess that a people never must value anything higher than the dignity and freedom of its existence; that it must defend these with the last drop of its blood; that it has no duty more sacred and can obey no law that is higher; that the shame of a cowardly submission can never be wiped out; that the poison of submission in the bloodstream of a people will be transmitted to its children, and paralyze and undermine the strength of later generations; that honor can be lost only once; that, under most circumstances, a people is unconquerable if it fights a spirited struggle for its liberty; that a bloody and honorable fight assures the rebirth of the people even if freedom were lost; and that such a struggle is the seed of life from which a new tree inevitably will blossom.... Danger must be countered with virile courage joined with calm and firm resolve and clear conscience. Should we be denied the opportunity of defending ourselves in this manner, I hold reckless despair to be a wise course of action.[2]

Hitler was apparently an avid reader and there are reasons—direct and indirect—to indicate that he had read a number of military theorists and practitioners, including Clausewitz, Frederick the Great, and Napoleon. Hitler's biographer Ian Kershaw writes that the shelves in his sparsely furnished room in Munich were loaded with books on history, geography, mythology, and especially war.[3] Ernst Hanfstaengl, who befriended Hitler in the early days after World War I, makes a similar observation.[4]

Books by or about the German existentialist philosopher Friedrich Wilhelm Nietzsche (1844–1900) are often mentioned. Nietzsche challenged the foundations of Christianity and traditional morality, but he was not an anti-Semite. Nietzsche believed that a person should be guided by the world we live in and not by the world beyond. Although Hitler never met Nietzsche, his thoughts were compiled and espoused by the Nazis, such as justification for war, aggression, and domination based on national and racial grounds. Nietzsche's influence on Hitler is partly due to Hitler's friendship with Elisabeth Förster Nietzsche (1846–1935), Friedrich Nietzsche's sister. She established the Nietzsche Archive in 1894. She had been married to a strident anti-Semite named Bernhard Förster (1843–89) and she was obviously influenced by both her brother and husband.

What Hitler learned from his readings and how he used what he read are different matters entirely. He seems to have applied ideas selectively and when it suited his purposes, disregarding them when it was inconvenient. John Keegan relates one such incident from August 1941, when Hitler lectured his generals during the pause on the Eastern Front.[5] Referring to Clausewitz' writings, he observed that one must first destroy the enemy in the field and then occupy their capital. While I don't know the date of this statement, it was made after the partial failure of several encirclements and was probably a defensive argument for stripping Army Group Center of its armored strength and sending it to the flanks, particularly the southern flank, against the wishes of most of his generals. Hitler was arguing what his generals had maintained during the *Barbarossa* planning period and during the pause, but for different reasons. They had argued for a drive to Moscow—not because it was the capital—but because it was the political and economic epicenter of the Soviet Union. They assumed that the Soviets would commit their full armed strength to defend this geographic locality and give the Germans the opportunity to inflict a decisive military defeat that could, for all practical purposes, end the war.

After the two very successful encirclements at Kiev and Vyazma, Hitler decided to go for Moscow, despite what he had said earlier and the lessons from Napoleon's campaign. Again, most generals argued against it because of the lateness of the season and the requirements to regroup. The arguments between Hitler and his generals during the pause is a perfect example of Hitler's selective use of what he had absorbed from his earlier readings.

Hitler's interest in Nordic mythology is testified to by other books on his shelves. He often referred to a verse from the Norwegian Eddas that reads: "All things will pass away, nothing remains but death and the glory of deeds."[6] Hitler was deeply influenced by another 18th-century German, the famous composer Wilhelm Richard Wagner (1813–83).[7] Wagner was also an ardent nationalist and a leading polemicist. The difference between a debater and a polemicist is that unlike debaters, who try to seek a common ground, a polemicist intends to establish the truth of a controversial point of view while refuting the opposing point of view—there is no room for compromise. We find this a main trait throughout Hitler's adult life. His dogmatic attitude and stubborn refusal to compromise or make concessions can be traced directly to this trait and probably to the influence of Wagner. It would be surprising if Hitler's behavior, military strategy, and operational concepts, particularly in the last years of World War II, were not heavily affected by his earlier learning experiences.

There were few things in Hitler's early life that would make one think he would become a leader of a great nation and one of the most influential men of the 20th century. He came from a family of very modest means, had a meager education, was a drifter and unemployed neurotic who lived from hand to mouth in the slums of Vienna. He failed at his ambitions of becoming an artist or architect. However, Hitler had some qualities that fitted well into the tumultuous times of Germany in the 1920s—just as Napoleon fell into his opportunity at the end of the French Revolution. Sometimes fate brings men and events together either for good or evil.

It is beyond the scope of this work to examine Hitler's personal traits, education, and abilities in detail.[8] However, a few comments are in order. Hitler excelled in the political arena. He was a strong and mesmerizing orator who spoke to the masses in terms they understood. As a populist he was adept at combining nationalistic and down-to-earth social and economic sentiments. He found the necessary scapegoats for Germany's dilemma in Communists, socialists, Jews, and the Versailles Treaty. He promised that Germany could regain its greatness and the people their prosperity, and that he was the man to bring those achievements to fruition. Hitler exemplified the potential danger of falling victim to a spellbinding orator who exploits social and economic problems by promising to cure their ills through radical approaches.

When Hitler came to power he set out to keep his promises. In the 1930s he gave the Germans a string of bloodless achievements on the international scene (the occupation of the Rhineland, the annexation of the Sudetenland and take-over of Czechoslovakia, and the *Anschluss* with Austria). Those successes addressed the "nationalist" part of the party name. He also undertook massive public works projects—roads, canals, dams, airports, and harbors—that not only helped solve the unemployment problem but brought about a sense of prosperity and well-being to the working classes. This action addressed the "socialist" part of the party name. His rearmament program served the same purpose, while also achieving the support of industrialists and the military.

Many of Hitler's views on both strategy and relations with the military were influenced by his service in World War I. Ian Kershaw writes that World War I was a godsend for Hitler.[9] His quest to become an artist came to an end with his 1907 failure at the Art Academy. Also, he soon realized that he would not become a great architect. Hitler had no credible prospects for a career and did not have the personality to make lasting and close friendships. He sunk into the doldrums, drifted without any realistic hopes for the future, and grew increasingly angry at a society that had rejected him.

Although he failed to register for military service in Austria in 1909 he was nevertheless liable for service when he turned 21 in a state (Austria) that he detested. He managed to avoid the call-up until 1913 and it appears that the danger that he would be caught was one of the motivations for him to leave for Germany that year.[10] Despite his earlier reluctance to serve in the Austrian military, Hitler, like so many of his generation, reported to the colors in August 1914. In the 1920s the question was raised of how it was that a person of Austrian nationality was allowed to join the Bavarian military rather than being sent back to Austria. The nationality issue appears never to have been raised. Although he volunteered on August 5 for service in the 1st Bavarian Infantry Regiment, he was not called to service until August 16, and assigned to the 2nd Bavarian Infantry Regiment.

In the beginning of September 1914 he was transferred to a newly formed regiment, the 16th Bavarian Reserve Infantry Regiment, also known as the "List Regiment," after Colonel Julius List, its first commander. It was sent to Flanders on October 20, and quickly received its baptism of fire. Hitler wrote that the strength of the regiment dropped from 3,600 to 611 men after four days of fighting. Kershaw writes that the losses in the regiment were confirmed at 70 percent.[11] Colonel List was among the fallen.

Hitler found the sense of purpose and friendships he had been looking for in the List Regiment. He considered it his home and the comrades his family. His early elation soon turned to embitterment, however. It was a decisive period in forming his personality.

John Keegan deplores that almost all of Hitler's biographers have missed or passed over Hitler's years of service on the Western Front. Keegan writes that Hitler's experience and service had been honorable and he goes on to succinctly summarize that experience and notes that any German of his generation would have been proud of that service:

> Thrice wounded—once by shrapnel in the face, once by a shall fragment in the left thigh, once by gas which temporarily blinded him—he took part in twelve battles, served twenty-five other spells of duty in the trenches and was five times distinguished or decorated, finally with the Iron Cross First Class. Two spells of home leave and five months in hospital apart, he was continuously with his regiment, the 16th Bavarian Reserve, at the Western Front from October 1914 to October 1918.[12]

There is little doubt that Hitler's experience in the bitter positional/trench warfare of World War I had an influence on his fixation for holding onto occupied terrain. In December 1941, General Heinz Guderian (1888–1954), then commanding the Second Panzer Army, advised Hitler to retreat, but was overruled. Hitler told him that he should use his howitzers to blast craters in the frozen ground as was done in Flanders during World War I. He ignored Guderian's statement that the winter conditions in Russia could hardly be compared to those in Flanders.[13] Thomas Weber also claims that a reason for Hitler's increasing tendency not to listen to his generals after the tide of war had begun to turn had its roots in his experiences in World War I.[14] Hitler spent much time living in close proximity to the officers of the List Regiment. Familiarity is often a breeding ground for lack of respect, and the officers of the regiment may have lost some of their aura of superiority in Hitler's eyes. He realized that they, like others, "put their pants on one leg at the time" and that he, as a mere soldier, may have concluded that he had a better understanding of the conditions at the front.

Gitta Sereny reports Albert Speer (1905–1981), Minister of Armaments and War Production, making the following statements on Hitler's failure to listen to his generals:

> Hitler and Stalin were very alike in some dreadful respects, but there is one fundamental point in which they differed absolutely. Stalin had faith in his generals and, although meticulously informed of all major plans and moves, left them comparative freedom. Our generals, on the contrary, were robbed of all independence, all elasticity of action, even before Stalingrad. All decisions

> were taken by Hitler and once made were as if poured in cement, whatever changing circumstances demanded. This, more than anything else, lost Germany the war.
>
> The central problem was between Hitler and the generals. Except for Keitel, who was "his" man and only told him what he wanted to hear, and Jodl, whose activities were soon severely curtailed precisely because he showed some independence of thought, he accepted information but never tactical advice, and was increasingly surrounded by what I came to call *Nickesel* (nodding donkeys).[15]

As the war went on it was virtually only the "nodding donkeys" who were admitted into Hitler's presence. His schedule was increasingly controlled by Martin Bormann (1900–45), Chief of the Party Chancellery, General Wilhelm Keitel (1882–1946), and Hans Heinrich Lammers (1879–1962), the head of the Reich Chancellery. These were the gate-keepers who effectively came to control Hitler's life and most of the flow of information he received.

There are other aspects of Hitler's wartime behavior that can be traced back to his service in World War I and his experiences in the turbulent years that followed. Hitler felt that Jews and socialists were to blame for many of the misfortunes that befell Germany in World War I and the post-war period. He felt it essential that they be removed from German society so as to avoid any possible interference with the gargantuan tasks that he saw ahead in what we now refer to as World War II.

Hitler's increasing turn to the more brutal type of officers for high positions, such as Generals Ferdinand Schörner (1892–1973) and Lothar Rendulic (1887–1971) was also shaped by his personal experience of conflict. These officers were not only ideologically attuned to Hitler's views, and therefore of unquestioned loyalty, but Hitler accorded high blame for the loss of World War I to the lack of effective propaganda and to the leniency of the military justice system. He noted that lax discipline in the List Regiment and in the armed forces in general had undermined the German war effort. Brutal disciplinarians such as Schörner and Rendulic therefore appealed to him. Manfred Messerschmidt and Fritz Wüllner remark that the subsequent harsh disciplinary measures in the German armed forces in World War II resulted in 20,000 to 22,000 executions.[16]

The harsh treatment that Hitler demanded be dished out to civilians in occupied territories also has roots in his experience in World War I. He thought that the German military in World War I was feeble in dealing with "unfriendly" civilians and he wanted to make sure this was not repeated in the war he was now directing. In a speech on September 19, 1933, Hitler stated: "Brutality is respected. Brutality and physical strength! The plain man in the streets respects nothing but brutal strength and restlessness—women, too, for that matter, women and children."[17] On December 12, 1941, he had Field Marshal Keitel promulgate the notorious *Nacht und Nebel* (Night and Fog) decree, which read in part:

> After lengthy consideration the Führer has decided that measures taken against those guilty of offenses against the Reich or against the occupation forces in the occupied areas must be changed. The Führer is of the opinion that in such cases penal servitude or a sentence of hard labor for life will be regarded as a sign of weakness. A more effective and lasting deterrent can be achieved only by the death penalty or by taking measures that will leave the family and population uncertain as to the fate of the offender. Deportations to Germany will serve this purpose.
>
> The attached directive for the prosecution of offenses corresponds to the Führer's conception. They have been examined and approved by him . . .[18]

Napoleon, the great practitioner of maneuver warfare, sounded a strong cautionary note with respect to withdrawals. Hitler may have had maxim number six in mind in his determined refusal to conduct voluntary withdraws. It reads:

> At the commencement of a campaign, the question of whether to advance or not requires careful deliberation; but when you have once undertaken the offensive, it should be maintained to the last extremity. A retreat, however skillful the maneuvers may be, will always produce an injurious moral effect on the army, since by losing the chances of success yourself you throw them into the hands

> of the enemy. Besides, retreats cost far more, both in men and materiel, than the most bloody engagements; with this difference, that in a battle the enemy loses nearly as much as you, while in a retreat the loss is all on your side.[19]

A statement by Hitler in December 1942 sounds eerily similar. He stated the obvious after a series of setbacks: "It is a thousand times easier to storm forward with an army and gain victories, than to bring an army back in an orderly condition after a reverse or a defeat."[20] Another analogous statement attributed to Hitler is found in *The Hitler Book*: "Anyone can deal with victory; only the mighty can bear defeat."[21]

Hitler's selective use or misunderstanding of what he had read is well illustrated. At one of his "Table Talk" sessions with industrialists in August 1942, he expounded on his grandiose plans for the future and assured his listeners that he would not repeat the mistakes made by Napoleon after his victories in Egypt by not continuing into the Middle East.[22] He failed to understand or admit that he had made the same mistakes by discarding the navy and army recommendation to adopt a Mediterranean strategy (discussed in Chapter 2) as opposed to a direct attack on the Soviet Union. He also forgot that he had repeated Napoleon's mistake by going for Moscow under winter conditions.

Hitler's Early Successes

Germany enjoyed an unbelievable string of successes before the operation against the Soviet Union was launched. These included the occupation of the Rhineland, the incorporation of Austria, and the dismemberment and occupation of Czechoslovakia. All were successfully carried out by Hitler against the advice of most of his military commanders. Hitler admitted that the start of his amazing success—the abrogation of the Versailles Treaty and the occupation of the Rhineland—was a bluff and that if France had moved to stop him, he would have been forced to withdraw.[23] Perhaps the best explanation for this string of bloodless successes is that offered by B. H. Liddell Hart:

> He [Hitler] had a deeply subtle sense of surprise,[24] and was a master of the psychological side of strategy, which he raised to a new

> pitch. Long before the war he had described to his associates how the daring coup that captured Norway might be carried out, and how the French could be maneuvered out of the Maginot Line. He had also seen, better than any general, how the bloodless conquests that preceded the war might be achieved by undermining resistance beforehand. No strategist in history has been more clever in playing on the minds of his opponents—which is the supreme art of strategy.[25]

In 1940, Hitler's spectacular successes in Scandinavia, France and the Low Countries—achieved against the advice of many in the military—solidified his standing as a "military genius," a status enhanced by his acceptance of a plan for his western offensive from a relatively young general, Fritz Erich von Manstein (1887–1973). These stunning successes were continued in the spring of 1941 in the Balkans. By now, Hitler had become, in the words of Liddell Hart, a "gigantic figure, combining the strategy of a Napoleon with the cunning of a Machiavelli and the fanatical fervour of a Mahomet."[26]

These early events led to the virtual creation of a second general staff in the form of Oberkommando der Wehrmacht (OKW; Supreme Command of the Armed Forces) under Generals Keitel and Alfred Jodl (1890–1946).[27] OKW was the 1938 successor to the powerful War Office, but now it became Hitler's personal staff. General Keitel was recommended to Hitler by Generalfeldmarschall Werner von Blomberg (1878–1946), former Minister of War, who also commented that he had only used Keitel as an office manager. This being exactly the type of man Hitler was looking for, he quickly accepted Blomberg's recommendation and continued to use Keitel as an office manager, a decision that would prove to be the seed of future troubles.[28] It was a step in the process of placing the German military under the same dictatorial powers as the rest of German society. This process was completed in early 1942 when Hitler assumed personal command of the German Army. Furthermore, Hitler was not inclined to put an end to the antagonism between the Oberkommando des Heeres (OKH; Supreme Command of the Army) and OKW.[29] It was in line with Hitler's "divide and conquer" philosophy.

Fascinations with Scandinavia

Hitler, like Winston Churchill, had a strong obsession with Scandinavia. This obsession by both men was based on sound military strategy and economic considerations. Churchill, who was absorbed in a search for a flanking strategy, argued strongly for an Allied attack against the German northern flank in 1939–40. He felt that this would not only cut Germany off from Swedish iron ore, but would present the Germans with a geo-strategic dilemma. Allied plans and actions in Norway must be viewed in this light. Churchill's fascination with flanking strategies continued even after Germany had gained control of most of Europe. He pressed for action both in the Balkans and in Scandinavia, but was dissuaded from these approaches by some of his own military advisors and by the United States.

Hitler's preoccupation with Scandinavia began in 1939–40 when intelligence was received that the Allies were preparing for military action in that region. Hitler wanted to thwart their goals of cutting off iron imports and threatening German control of the Baltic Sea and its approaches. The German Navy added its own goals of extending its base of operations against Great Britain and complicating Allied blockade measures. Denmark was included in the Scandinavian invasion to provide a stepping-stone to Norway and to secure the Baltic approaches. Action was also contemplated against northern Sweden, but this part of the plan was dropped. The reason was that German operations in the Gulf of Bothnia would upset their new ally, the Soviet Union. There was also concern on the part of the German planners that the Swedes would destroy the iron mines that were located at a considerable distance from the sea.[30]

The German invasion of Norway (Operation *Weserübung*) was considered by OKH a "lunatic" idea in that it violated all principles of war, save surprise. OKH wanted nothing to do with an operation having so many inherent flaws and dangers that it was fully expected to fail.[31] Hitler was immensely proud of and took full credit for the successful invasion of Norway, and it is referred to in his wartime magazine under the chapter headline, "The boldest deed in history"—a phrase borrowed from the British.[32] He failed to recognize that it would probably have been a disaster except for Norwegian and Allied bungling and the exceedingly professional German performance at the operational level that compensated for a very faulty command structure.

In the course of the Norwegian operation we find the first inklings of a leadership flaw in Hitler—that he could lose his nerve under pressure. It was referred to as the "first crisis in the OKW" and came about as a result of things looking bad for General Eduard Dietl (1890–1944) in Narvik. There were discussions about giving up Narvik voluntarily, air evacuation of the troops, or their internment in Sweden. General Walter Warlimont (1894–1976) writes that Hitler displayed "a spectacle of pitiable weakness lasting more than a week."[33] Another crisis about ten days later was brought about by the isolation of German troops in Trondheim. Hitler wanted to send a division to that city using the two ocean liners *Bremen* and *Europa*. Admiral Erich Raeder (1876–1960), the Commander-in-Chief of the navy, regarded this as an impossible undertaking but was only able to persuade Hitler after he pointed out that the whole fleet would be required to escort the two ships and that the likely outcome would be the loss of the ocean liners, the fleet, and the division.[34]

Hitler's interest in Scandinavia increased after his successful conquests of Denmark and Norway. His reasons were primarily strategic and economic, but he was also influenced by ideology. There were a number of high ranking Nazis—like Heinrich Himmler (1900–45) and Alfred Rosenberg (1893–1946)—who pointed to the fact that the Scandinavians were a kindred Aryan people and natural allies of Germany. Hitler wanted these countries as part of his empire, but without infringing their individuality.[35] Hitler's views on Scandinavia were decisive in opting for a third main drive into the Soviet Union in 1941 by adding a full-fledged offensive through the Baltic States towards Leningrad, and they were equally decisive in the withdrawal through those areas.

The importance of Scandinavia had also increased in other ways. Naval and air bases in northern Norway would present a constant threat to the Murmansk convoys bringing badly needed aid to the Soviet Union, starting in 1941. While the German Navy had maintained a strong presence in Norway since the invasion in 1940, using it as departure point for entry into the North Atlantic (e.g., the battleship *Bismarck*), a major build-up of German naval strength in Norway began with the February 1942 channel dash by the battleships *Scharnhorst, Gneisenau*, and the heavy cruiser *Prinz Eugen*. These ships were sent to Norway because of Hitler's concern about the possibility of an Allied invasion of Norway, and their possible exposure to bombardment while in French ports. Thereafter, for most of the war, the bulk of the German surface fleet was stationed in Norway.

A large number of German U-boats were also harbored in Norway, with their main bases in Bergen and Trondheim. After Allied anti-submarine measures caused huge losses to the U-boat fleet in 1942–43, most were withdrawn from the Atlantic and stationed in Norway since the bases on the French coast became vulnerable and were eventually lost. The Germans were waiting for the appearance of new types of submarines "that would turn the tide of the war at sea."

Failures of Strategies

It is rather well understood that strategies can fail and that it is much easier to find the reasons in retrospect than at the time of adoption. While strategies should be logical and based on sound principles, they often are not. Strategies fail for a variety of reasons:

- Objectives are not specific or well explained.
- Objectives are not adjusted according to changes in the strategic military and battlefield environments.
- Concepts are illogical.
- Resources are inadequate for the prosecution of a campaign.
- Unanticipated outside influences.
- Faulty strategic intelligence.

History is replete with examples of strategies that failed or had to be altered. Finland changed its strategy twice during its war with the Soviet Union at the side of Germany. The first change came in October 1941 due to an unanticipated outside influence—a virtual ultimatum from the United States not to attack the Murmansk railroad. The second change came in January 1943 when the Finns concluded that Germany could not win the war. The Finns realized that they had to try to attempt accommodation with the Soviets in order to ensure the survival of their country. In this case the strategy changed because the strategic military environment had changed. US strategy in Vietnam failed, to a large extent, because the United States failed to have a clear understanding of the nature of the opponent, as well as well-defined and unambiguous objectives. Twenty-five centuries ago, Sun Tzu, in *The Art of War*, put his finger on a problem that often plagues democracies more than autocratic regimes, including the US involvement in Vietnam, when he wrote "There is no instance of a country having benefited from prolonged warfare."[36]

The failure of Operation *Barbarossa* in 1941 can also, to a large extent, be blamed on a lack of accurate knowledge about the nature of the opponent. This lack of good intelligence or the refusal to believe it resulted in excessive optimism and a catastrophic underestimation of the enemy and the difficulties of the climate and terrain. When the conditions of opposing forces change to the extent they did on the Eastern Front from 1941 to 1945, it follows that tactics and even strategy must also change. It made some military sense to hold lines of communication bottlenecks when the Soviets were tied solely to roads and railroads to supply their immense military machine, but as that machine became more and more motorized and mechanized, thereby gaining cross-country mobility, these communication bottlenecks lost much of their former importance.

As the war dragged on and the Germans lost their advantage in mobility and air superiority, the "hold" strategy continued to make some sense. It was better to meet the enemy in prepared defenses than for German forces to subject themselves to superior mobility and firepower while trying to withdraw under unrelenting pressure. This situation became a real quandary for the Germans in the last two years of the war. By April 1944 Field Marshal Erwin Rommel (1891–1944) concluded that mobile defense was no longer possible in view of Allied air superiority.[37] Elastic defense—controlled and planned withdrawal after the enemy was committed to battle, but before German forces became decisively engaged—was often advocated by German military commanders. Most of these requests were habitually refused by Hitler, with the result that when a withdrawal had to be made it was made under the worst of circumstances. A defensive strategy over a front as long as that in the East was very difficult against a mobile enemy who could choose the location and muster overwhelming strength at the point of main attack (*Schwerpunkt*). To counter this disadvantage, an army needed excellent strategic and tactical intelligence, and the Germans were not strong in this area in the 1943–45 period, mainly because aerial reconnaissance was made difficult by Soviet air superiority and eventual supremacy and the fact that the Soviets were masters at deception.

As the German armies in the East were bled white from 1941 to 1944, the space/force ratio—a well-known but often neglected element in war—increasingly swung to the advantage of the Soviets, a fact that could only be remedied by a significant increase in German forces or a withdrawal to shorter defensive lines. Hitler repeatedly refused to make voluntary withdrawals to shorter lines, or when he did it was too late. Starting in 1942 Hitler ceased to listen to the advice of his field commanders and the OKH. He ridiculed and refused to believe accurate intelligence reporting large increases in the size of the Soviet Army and their rearmament with weapons and equipment that were often better than those of the Wehrmacht. Consequently, there were no efforts to put Germany on a total war footing. The primary increases in forces on the Eastern Front in 1942 came in the form of 50 divisions from nations allied with Germany—Hungary, Romania, and Italy.

The manpower situation was gloomy at this stage of the war. It was not until late July 1944 that "total war" measures were agreed to by Hitler on the urgings of Heinrich Himmler, Albert Speer, and Joseph Goebbels (1897–1945).[38] By then it was too late. The additional units raised needed equipment and training but in the dire circumstances Germany found itself, most were sent off to fight untrained and ill-equipped.

The Wellenbrecher (Wave-Breaker) Concept

This book focuses on Hitler's operational concept in the Baltic after the Soviets levered the Germans away from Leningrad during the winter of 1943—referred to by many as the "wave-breaker strategy." While several books deal with the actual withdrawal and the many hard-fought battles, this work covers these in summary fashion and instead deals primarily with Hitler's controversial—then and now—wave-breaker concept—including its validity and the reasoning put forward by Hitler at the time. The scheme Hitler adopted in the withdrawal has been ascribed by many writers as simply his absolute refusal to make any withdrawals.

However, Hitler did sanction withdrawals, as pointed out by Grier.[39] He lists a number of these but most appear to be strategic, not tactical. The withdrawals from Finland, the Balkans, and northern Italy fall into that category. These withdrawals were not made based primarily on recommendations by field commanders. For example, the August 1944 proposal by General Alfred Jodl and Albert Speer may have been convincing. Likewise, it was not primarily the advice of the OKW that led Hitler to make the decision to withdraw from Finland, but the urgings of General Lothar Rendulic, one of his favorites, and again Albert Speer. Even Hitler could see that it was necessary to withdraw Army Group G from southern France on August 16. The Falaise Pocket had formed and the Allied drive on Paris (captured on August 25) would soon isolate Army Group G.

The withdrawal from the Demyansk salient in 1943 had been argued for unsuccessfully by his generals for a year, and the arguments by Field Marshal Ritter von Leeb (1876–1956) cost him his job. It was only when Hitler realized that the divisions in this salient were desperately needed at the Leningrad Front in order to keep Finland in the war that he relented. There are not many examples of Hitler allowing tactical withdrawals of forces in contact prior to their becoming so decisively engaged that an orderly withdrawal was impossible. Such withdrawals invariably resulted in extremely heavy losses.

Hitler was convinced that his refusal to withdraw saved the German armies in Russia in the winter of 1941–42. He firmly believed that a voluntary withdrawal would have led to an uncontrolled rout and the destruction of his armies. He was not alone in this view.[40] Both German troops and equipment were worn down in November 1941 after the long drive from Germany to the gates of Moscow. Because of the short-war scenario they were not clothed and equipped for a winter campaign and the fate of Napoleon was well known to Hitler and his generals. However, in the years that followed, the Germans were properly equipped for winter warfare.

"Fortified places," many of which fell quickly to the enemy, aggravated the problem of stemming Soviet drives. The Soviets always had the choice of eliminating pockets or simply bypassing them, but for Germany the decision to leave troops in a pocket was invariably final. These pockets came into existence by a failure to execute a withdrawal when the situation so dictated. Three examples from Operation *Bagration* will suffice as illustrations. The Germans lost more than 100,000 soldiers in the pocket east of Minsk in the summer of 1944 and another 70,000 in the nearby Bobruysk Pocket at the same time. Five German divisions were cornered in Vitebsk and Hitler's failure to give timely permission for them to withdraw resulted in their loss. These pockets in so-called "fortresses" were overwhelmed after relatively short fights and did little to slow the Soviet push. The important result was that there were about 200,000 fewer German soldiers for the Soviets to worry about. Liddell Hart notes that each time the Germans were tied down by Hitler's order to defend a fixed point, a collapse was the eventual outcome. He points out that the weaker the defending side, the more essential it is to adopt a mobile or elastic defense, otherwise the stronger side can win a decisive advantage through maneuver.[41]

The "wave-breaker" concept was simply the "fortress" concept, but on a much grander scale. It was practiced both in the West and the East. A whole series of "fortresses" were designated in the West, particularly along the coast. Most of these self-styled "fortified places" were not fortified at all. These were propaganda terms that conveyed a false impression of strength when in actuality they were voluntary encirclements. The concept was based on Hitler's assumption that the enemy required more forces to take or contain these "fortresses" than were necessary for their defense.[42] This concept was more successful in the West than in the East because the Allies needed ports for logistical reasons.[43] The Soviets could care less about the ports in the Baltic; they did not need them.

Antony Beevor, who studied history under John Keegan and became an excellent military historian in his own right, wrote this about Hitler's keenness for declaring a town or locality a "fortress." By extension, it is equally applicable to the wave-breaker concept:

> Hitler's attempts to designate "fortress" towns and to refuse to allow the evacuation of encircled troops, were part of a suicidal pattern of enforced sacrifice and useless suffering. He knew that they were doomed because the Luftwaffe lacked the fuel and aircraft to supply them, and yet his policy deprived Army Group Vistula of experienced troops.[44]

Most of the "fortresses" fell after relatively short periods, but there were exceptions, such as Poznan and Breslau. However, what they all had in common was that they represented a needless sacrifice of troops, contributed little to slowing Soviet advances, and worsened the German manpower situation.

The problem was that Hitler's assumptions governing the establishment of "fortresses" were fallacious. As forces became more mobile and mechanized, even the holding of communications hubs lost some of its former importance since they could be bypassed without jeopardizing the flow of supplies. Even if the enemy decided to take a "fortified place," the assumption that it would require more forces to do so than would be required for the defense seldom proved true. In those instances where the enemy required more forces to invest a city than had been cut off, the task was usually relegated to inferior follow-on units while the crack frontline units continued their advances. Schramm agrees and points out that on the Eastern Front in particular, "Hitler made a serious miscalculation, for the German forces in the East were actually outnumbered all along." He also notes that the benefit of holding "fortresses" was more than outweighed by the disadvantage resulting from the loss of the units defending the "fortresses," which brought about still greater operational inferiority in numbers.[45]

The practice of encirclement was designed to reduce successively the opposing force and was effective since the encircled force could not easily be relieved or supplied. Since Germany had lost air superiority, or even air parity, by mid-1944, by-passed pockets could no longer be supplied except by sea in areas where Germany had naval control. Furthermore, as the German forces in the East were nearly always seriously outnumbered, leaving forces to be invested only exacerbated this fact and further damaged the space/force ratio which the Germans could have turned to their advantage as they were forced back to shorter defensive lines.

Henrik Eberle and Matthias Uhl write in their commentary on *The Hitler Book* that Hitler's frequent change of mood following victory and defeat on the Eastern Front "show that he was no longer in condition to provide the leadership which the national predicament required." They go on to note that "he lost his objective view of the strategic problem and placed tactical success in the foreground."[46]

While the issue of static defense and "fortified places" is addressed as appropriate in subsequent chapters, it is worthwhile to see what two German generals had to say about Hitler's policy. General Kurt Dittmar (1891–1959) was a divisional commander and later the Official Military Commentator of the German Armed Forces. He concluded that "The policy of clinging on at all costs in particular places repeatedly changed the campaign for the worse. . . . In the end it proved fatal." When asked if an elastic defense was possible and if such a defense might have worn down the Russians, he answered that he believed it could have, but the military leaders at the highest level were categorically forbidden to do so by Hitler. General Kurt von Tippelskirch (1891–1957), an army commander who faced Operation *Bagration*, noted that "The root cause of Germany's defeat was the way that her forces were wasted in fruitless efforts, and above all in fruitless resistance at the wrong time and place. That was due to Hitler. There was no strategy in our campaign."[47]

Many historians and military writers maintain that Hitler had no strategy to achieve his goals after 1943. While it is often difficult to discern the strategy of a losing side when the war approaches an end, I agree with those writers, since after the issuance of Directive 51 (discussed in Chapter 4) there is no expressed cohesive strategy or any evidence of one. German strategy had reached a point of bankruptcy. Professor Grier maintains that Hitler had a strategy to win the war until the very end.[48] I agree with Grier that Hitler continued to hope to win the war or create a stalemate and that he had a somewhat feasible strategy, at least until shortly after he issued Directive 51 in November 1943. Military and national strategies based solely on "hopes and prayers" are sure recipes for failure and should not even be dignified by the term strategy. Grier likens Germany's situation in 1944–45 to that of Great Britain's in the dark days of 1940 and 1941, alone and isolated. This is a false analogy. Hitler recognized when he cancelled Operation *Sea Lion* that there were serious and dangerous obstacles to success. As he stated at the time, the Channel presented a much greater obstacle than a wide river. The invasion would have to be carried out in the face of overwhelming British naval superiority because of crippling German naval losses in Norway, and with the Royal Air Force still intact. The British were not alone—they had the Dominions—and realistic hopes of aid from the United States and possibly Russia. Hitler gave as the primary reason for turning against Russia the elimination of one of the British hopes.

Strategy must have a coherent concept under which it can be achieved as well as the resources at hand to carry it out successfully. Germany was alone or rapidly losing its allies. The concept appears to have been one of hanging on in hope for the so-called miracle weapons to become operational in sufficient quantities to turn the tide of the war. This required time, a commodity that Germany was quickly losing.

Hitler's Hopes

In the closing years of the war Hitler and his cohorts were hoping for a "miracle" in line with the death of Elisabeth, the Empress of Russia, which crippled the coalition against Frederick the Great and Prussia in the Seven Years' War (1756–63). Some Nazi leaders were hoping for a similar crippling of the coalition against them brought on by Western fears of the Soviet Union.

The hopes for a turn in the fortunes of war by new "miracle" weapons such as the atomic bomb, the V-2 rocket program, jet aircraft, and revolutionary new submarines can essentially be placed in the same category—wishful thinking. A strategy not based on cold realities is in effect no strategy at all. Acquiring atomic weapons was not at the top of Hitler's agenda, to the dismay of his nuclear scientists. Germany had lost some of its best physicists in the emigrations of the 1930s; some of these were Jewish. Ronald Lewin notes that Hitler showed little interest in atomic technology even though the significance of developing an atomic bomb was explained to him. Ronald Lewin writes that "the abstruse nature of the concepts involved smelled too much like 'Jewish science' and in any case he was concerned only with quick results: nothing that would fail to bear fruit before the end of the war was acceptable."[49]

What Albert Speer had to say on this subject conforms in the main to what Lewin writes. The German nuclear program was run by nuclear physicists at the Kaiser Wilhelm Institute and it came under the auspices of the Ministry of Education. These physicists included the Nobel Prize winners Otto Hahn (1879–1968) and Werner Karl Heisenberg (1901–76). The program was brought to the attention of Speer by General Friedrich Fromm (1888–1945), the commander of the Home Army. After being appraised of the program and meeting with the scientists he promised to give the program monetary support, something that had been lacking up to then.[50]

Heisenberg told Speer that his group had been in the forefront of nuclear research after Hahn's discovery of nuclear fission in 1938. Since they had not received the money to undertake fully the costly research, Heisenberg assumed they were far behind the United States, where enormous resources were being devoted to nuclear research. The scientists told Speer frankly that the United States was benefitting from the departure from Germany of some of the greatest scientific brains.

Hitler, according to Speer, disapproved of anything that was remotely connected to Albert Einstein (1879–1955), for whom he had an irrational hatred. It was his rejection of what he referred to as "Jewish physics" that had caused the Ministry of Education not to support the nuclear program. Speer carefully avoided telling Hitler about the possibilities of nuclear weapons. According to Speer, a weapon that could decisively alter the course of the war would only lead to his enthusiastic support and, since he understood little about science, he would demand immediate results. However, there is no doubt that Speer was fully aware of this potentially devastating weapon and that he was eager to support the research.[51]

Germany needed heavy water to build a nuclear reactor. Consequently, the British and Americans became very alarmed when the Germans, after the 1940 invasion, took over Norsk Hydro, a large complex of hydroelectric and electrochemical plants in southern Norway and began turning out increasing quantities of heavy water. Allied scientists were alarmed that Germany was in the process of building an atomic bomb since heavy water was useful only for the generation of nuclear power. Norsk Hydro at Rjukan was the only commercial producer of the substance in the world.[52] This realization led to two results:

1. It helped kindle a massive effort by the United States and Great Britain in 1942 to build a bomb.
2. It initiated an Allied campaign to destroy the heavy water production facilities in 1942.

After several earlier attempts, the German atomic weapons program came to a virtual end in February 1944 after joint Norwegian–British action against the Rjukan facilities. The facilities were heavily damaged by British bombing and Norwegian commando attacks. The Germans decided to move the heavy water already produced to safety in Germany. The final blow was delivered by Norwegian commandos when they sank the ferry carrying the heavy water canisters in deep water when on the way to Germany.[53]

Hitler opted not to use weapons that the Allies could retaliate with, such as chemical munitions, but he showed no hesitation in using weapons that only Germany possessed, such as ballistic missiles. We can therefore safely conclude that he would have used nuclear weapons as long as he was the sole possessor. Possibly his own experience in World War I may have had a negative effect on his willingness to use chemical weapons.

Of the other three technological breakthroughs, the new submarines figure very prominently in Professor Grier's book. He claims that rockets and jet aircraft were not strategic offensive weapons—the inaccurate rockets were instruments of terror, and the jet aircraft were defensive weapons for the protection of German cities against Allied air attacks.[54] Yet if the lengthy and complicated disarmament and arms control negotiations between the two world wars and during the Cold War taught us anything it is that it is very problematic and hazardous to classify weapon systems as either offensive or defensive. Most modern weapon systems serve a dual purpose. The German jet aircraft program, if given a higher priority and brought into service earlier, could not only have been used defensively to protect cities and facilities, but offensively to wrest air superiority away from the Russians and Western Allies. The new submarine program is addressed later in Chapter 8.

What is written about the "fortress" concept is also true for the wave-breaker concept, since the latter was an outgrowth of the former. The conclusions reached must be weighed against the loss of the better part of three army groups, forces that could have mounted a credible defense along the shorter lines of Germany's eastern border. Professor Grier writes that "German generals (and admirals) blame Hitler for everything that went wrong and credit themselves with every success."[55] This is a damaging generalization. There are numerous examples, particularly in the early part of the war, where German officers credited Hitler with successes and there are even more examples of them having criticized fellow officers.[56] Schramm also gives three examples where General Jodl credited Hitler with successes in the military field.[57] Eberle and Uhl write that Hitler attributed his failures to the incompetence of commanders and staff officers. He frequently "accused them of inaction or cowardice, occasionally even of sabotage."[58]

Grier also overlooks the fact that many generals were relieved or retired because of their opposition to Hitler's conduct of the war and—especially during the last year of the war—paid the ultimate price for that opposition. If one reads the OKW and OKH diaries for the last three years of the war, plus statements of participants, *Hitler's Secret Conversations*, and *The Hitler Book*, it is he who blames all failures on the military services while taking all credits for success. Hitler always maintained that his generals were alone responsible for his defeats.[59] Kershaw writes, "Incapable of finding fault in himself—in his judgment, his strategy, his leadership, Hitler turned the blame for what had gone wrong more and more on the military professionals."[60]

Nothing illustrates this better than Hitler's wholesale relief of some of the best officers in the German Army in December 1941. Three field marshals were sacked. Three army commanders and four corps commanders were among the 40 high-ranking officers relieved in Army Group Center. Some of these officers had argued strenuously against Hitler's autumn gamble to resume the offensive against Moscow. In this, I see no profile in courage on the part of Hitler. The practice of relieving high-ranking officers grew in frequency as the war progressed.

Finally, with respect to the German generals who often argued for or against a particular action, Hitler used a clever ploy. The German officer corps was truly professional. Unlike their Western counterparts, the background and education of senior German officers had focused almost entirely on their profession. They had studied their vocation from youth with great thoroughness and were extremely competent. However, their background and education lacked an adequate foundation in other aspects of national power, such as economic or political understanding. When Hitler used political, economic, and scientific arguments to bolster his decisions they were very much—both by training and tradition—at a loss to counter his arguments effectively (although they surely had lingering suspicions that those arguments were contrived). Hitler used this approach again and again in 1944 and 1945.

Doctor Jörg Muth has written a comprehensive and well documented book on the differences in education and training of German and American officers.[61] This ground-breaking work deals with the period from 1901 to 1940 and the consequences that differences in training and education had on the outcome of World War II. This book ought to be a reference for anyone studying or writing about German operations in both World War I and II. Grier notes that many former generals maintain that Hitler did not have a strategy in the final phase of the war and that he was merely trying to avoid defeat by clinging to every piece of ground. If Grier includes in his interpretation of strategy any action based on conglomerations of faith and hope, and Hitler's refusal to accept or understand the overwhelming power assembled against him, then he has a point.

Grier has done a great service in laying out possible alternative reasons for Hitler's actions, and by doing this has systematically addressed subjects that other authors have merely mentioned in passing. Each of these subjects is examined in this work.

Hitler's State of Mind

In this section I've given a basic analysis of Hitler as a military strategist in a changing military environment. A fully comprehensive analysis of Hitler's decision-making capability is impossible when dealing with the actions of such a personality. The effects of the burden that came with leading a nation in war, not only as head of state but as commander of the armed forces and the army, are not explored. Neither is the state of Hitler's health, which appears to have deteriorated rapidly after the coup attempt in July 1944, and the effects of the many medications he was administered. A few of the writers cited in this work have attempted to address this issue.[62] Some believe that Hitler was suffering at the end from a form of Parkinson Disease. In September 1944, during the planning for the Ardennes Offensive, Hitler was bedridden with stomach, blood pressure, and throat problems (in January 1945 he had an operation on his throat). Hitler's health problems are still an open question.

Even Percy Ernst Schramm (1894–1970), one of Germany's most distinguished historians, who had exceptional access to Hitler (he was the official war diarist from 1943 until he was sent away from Berlin in early April 1945), admits that it is difficult to analyze Hitler's psychology. Despite these shortcomings he writes:

> But Hitler continued, in the every-day sense of the word, to be more or less "normal" to the very end. His basic approach and the overall pattern of his military orders and instructions, despite their

objective flaws, remained entirely consistent from the beginning of the war to the final catastrophe.[63]

It is very difficult to agree with the assessment that Hitler continued to be "normal" in the everyday sense of that word. In fact, as we shall see, his actions became increasingly erratic and irrational.

Hitler did mention to a number of people that the war was lost. General Warlimont writes that Hitler had concluded as early as January 1944 that if an attack in the West (Allied landing in France) was not repulsed, the war was lost.[64] Albert Speer, referring to September 1944, writes "For it had finally been borne upon him [Hitler] that even if we succeeded in stabilizing the front, the war would be lost within a few months because of lack of matériel."[65] These incidents were apparently not the first times Hitler recognized the possibility that he would lose the war. General Jodl stated after the war that it was clear to Hitler and himself that the war could not be won after Stalingrad and the subsequent Soviet winter offensive. This conclusion was reinforced by Rommel's failure at the Egyptian border in 1942 and the Allied landing in North Africa that same year.[66]

Schramm notes that if Hitler's only purpose was to postpone the inevitable, "one can no longer seriously speak of his actions as a "strategy."[67] Hitler undoubtedly wanted to drag out the war until promised new weapon systems became available that could change the fortunes of war. But his "fortress" and wave-breaker concepts may have accomplished the opposite.

Hitler's increasing meddling in tactical matters at the operational level also worked against his objectives. Most leaders who have commanded in war have experienced the phenomena of over-centralization in combat and its destructive effects on military operations. Hitler's day-to-day involvement in the tactical realm, while far removed from the battlefield, contributed appreciably to the magnitude and speed of the enemy successes in both the East and West. We also find the same involvement in the details of ground operations on the part of the loyalists that Hitler increasingly turned to toward the end of the war, such as Lothar Rendulic and Ferdinand Schörner. There is something seriously wrong when Army Group commanders get involved in ordering the relief or execution of company and battalion commanders. That is not leadership but a lack of leadership.

Hitler violated important military principles by making no effort to concentrate his forces for the defense of Germany. There were no withdrawals from northern Italy and the northern areas of the Balkans. The German forces in Norway, after the successful withdrawal of the Twentieth Mountain Army from Finland, numbered over 500,000 for a short time. Some of these divisions were brought to Germany, but not until late winter or early spring 1945, after Germany's borders had been pierced both in the east and west. According to Speer, General Jodl argued for a much earlier withdrawal (1944) from these areas.[68] While this is not mentioned by General Warlimont, such an approach is consistent with Jodl's thinking. Some withdrawals were made, but they did not result in any meaningful reinforcement of the Eastern Front.

Hitler's insistence on holding pockets and enclaves on the Baltic coast caused a further deterioration in the space/force ratio. German military leaders had hoped that as the Soviets advanced west they would be confronted by stronger German defenses because the remaining forces would be manning shorter lines. Instead, the enclaves along the coast virtually doubled the expected length of the lines that would have to be manned to defend the Oder and Neisse fronts. Not only were the forces inadequate in numbers, but parts of the Oder/Neisse line were left to be defended by ad hoc units sent into combat without adequate training and equipment and placed under the command of a rank amateur. Hitler's refusal to withdraw the forces in Latvia, East Prussia, and Pomerania behind the Oder and Neisse rivers left the best troops cornered along the coast. Schramm notes that "the most harrowing consequences of the wave-breaker doctrine were suffered by Army Group Courland (formerly Army Group North)"[69] and that it was the worst example of the many failures of the wave-breaker doctrine.

NOTES

1. Walter Görlitz, *History of the German General Staff 1657–1945*, trans. by Brian Battershaw with an introduction by Walter Millis (New York: Praeger, 1957) pp.50–68.
2. Karl von Clausewitz, *War, Politics & Power: Selections from On War, and I Believe and Profess*, trans. and edited with an introduction by Colonel Edward M. Collins (Chicago: Henry Regnery Company, 1970) pp.301–02.

3. Ian Kershaw, *Hitler 1889–1936: Hubris* (New York: W. W. Norton & Company, 1999) p.158.
4. Ernst Hanfstaengl, *Hitler: The Memoir of a Nazi Insider Who Turned Against the Führer* (New York: Arcade Publishing, 2011) pp.47–48.
5. Keegan, *The Mask of Command*, p.286.
6. Robert Payne, *The Life & Death of Adolf Hitler* (New York: Barnes & Noble Books, 1995) p.572.
7. *Ibid*, pp.66–67, 171 and 189.
8. For further details see Trevor-Roper's introduction to Adolf Hitler, *Hitler's Secret Conversations* (New York: Farrar, Straus & Young, 1953); Payne, *op. cit.*; and Kershaw, *op. cit.*
9. Kershaw, *Hubris*, p.87.
10. *Ibid*, p.68.
11. *Ibid*, p. 90.
12. Keegan, *The Mask of Command*, p. 236.
13. Ian Kershaw, *Hitler 1936–1945: Nemesis* (New York: W. W. Norton, 1999) p.454.
14. Thomas Weber, *Hitler's First War: Adolf Hitler, the Men of the List Regiment, and the First World War* (New York: Oxford University Press, Inc., 2011) p.329.
15. Gitta Sereny, *Albert Seer: His Battle with Truth* (New York: Alfred A. Knopf, 1995) p.433.
16. Weber, *op. cit.*, p.328, quoting Manfred Messerschmidt and Fritz Wüllner, *Die Wehrmachtjustiz im Dienste des Nationalsozialismus: Zerstörung einer Legende* (Baden-Baden: Nomos, 1987) pp.63–91.
17. Lynn Montross, *War Through the Ages* (New York: Harper & Row Publishers, 1960) p.769.
18. Payne, *op. cit.*, pp.438–39.
19. Phillips, *op. cit.*, pp.408–09.
20. John Strawson, *Hitler as Military Commander* (New York: Barnes & Noble Books, 1995) p.151.
21. Henrik Eberle and Matthias Uhl (eds), *The Hitler Book: The Secret Dossier Prepared for Stalin from the Interrogations of Hitler's Personal Aides*, translated from German by Giles MacDonogh (New York: Public Affairs of the Perseus Book Group, 2005) p.78.
22. Albert Speer, *Spandau: The Secret Diaries* (New York: Pocket Books, 1977) p.50.
23. Payne, *op. cit.*, p.289.
24. Hitler's zeal for surprise may have originated early in his career based on his readings, but he may also have been influenced by the writings of one of his generals, Waldemar Erfurth. Erfurth headed the German Liaison Section at the Finnish General Headquarters from 1941 to the end of the Finnish involvement in the War. Erfurth was also a doctor of philosophy, was the Wehrmacht historian, and wrote several books on military history and strategy. One of these books was published in 1938 and is titled *Die Überraschung im Krieg*. It was translated into English in 1943:

Waldemar Erfurth, *Surprise*, translated from the German by Dr. Stefan T. Possony and Daniel Vilfroy. (Harrisburg, Pennsylvania: Military Service Publishing Company, 1943).

25. Liddell Hart, *Strategy*, pp. 3–4.
26. *Ibid*, p.3.
27. Görlitz, *The German General Staff*, pp. 370–73.
28. Keegan, *The Mask of Command*, p.270.
29. Schramm, *op. cit.*, p.139.
30. See Geirr H. Haarr, *The German Invasion of Norway, April 1940* (Annapolis, Maryland: Naval Institute Press, 2009) pp.3-15; and Henrik O. Lunde, *Hitler's Pre-Emptive War: The Battle for Norway, 1940* (Philadelphia: Casemate Publishers, 2008) pp.44–84.
31. Lunde, *Hitler's Pre-Emptive War*, p. 67.
32. S.L. Mayer (ed.), *Signal: Years of Triumph 1940–42* (Englewood Cliffs, NJ: Prentice Hall, Inc., 1978). This publication has no pagination but the citation is from page 5 of the chapter titled "Successful Strategy" by Colonel Max Baron von Pitreich.
33. Walter Warlimont, *Inside Hitler's Headquarters 1939–45* (Novato, CA: Presidio Press, 1965) p.76.
34. Lunde, *Hitler's Pre-Emptive War*, p.320.
35. Speer, *Spandau*, p.50. See also Wilhelm M. Carlgren, *Swedish Foreign Policy during the Second World War*, translated from the Swedish by Arthur Spencer (New York: St. Martin's Press, 1977) p.82.
36. Phillips, *op. cit.*, p.9.
37. Heinz Guderian, *Panzer Leader* (Cambridge, MA: Da Capo Press, 2002) p.334.
38. Ian Kershaw, *The End: The Defiance and Destruction of Hitler's Germany, 1944–1945* (New York: The Penguin Press, 2011) pp.22–26.
39. Grier, *op. cit.*, pp.145–46.
40. See, for example, Schramm, *op. cit.*, p.148.
41. Liddell Hart, *Strategy*, p.297.
42. Schramm, *op. cit.*, p.158.
43. The Allies knew that they could not rely on the quick capture of ports in France and therefore developed portable temporary harbors called Mulberries to provide the port facilities required to offload the thousands of tons of supplies, men, and vehicles necessary to support Operation *Overlord* and the battle for Normandy. These enormous structures, towed across the Channel and assembled offshore, had all the elements that one would expect of any harbor—breakwater, piers, lift equipment, and roadways, to mention a few.
44. Antony Beevor, *The Fall of Berlin 1945* (New York: Penguin Books, 2003) p.91.
45. Schramm, *op. cit.*, pp.158–59.
46. Eberle and Uhl, *op. cit.*, p.299.
47. Liddell Hart, *The German Generals Talk* (New York: Quill, 1979), pp.218–19. Tippelskirch also wrote a number of military history books before he died in 1957.

48. Grier, *op. cit.*, pp.XVII–XIX.
49. Ronald Lewin, *Hitler's Mistakes* (New York: William Morrow and Company, Inc., 1986) p.87.
50. Sereny, *op. cit.*, p.317.
51. *Ibid*, p.319.
52. For a shorter summary of the story of the heavy water production in Norway and its eventual demise than that given by Dan Kurzman (next note) see Richard Petrow, *The Bitter Years: The Invasion and Occupation of Denmark and Norway April 1940–May 1945* (New York: Morrow Quill Paperbacks, 1979) pp.138–58.
53. Dan Kurzman, *Blood and Water: Sabotaging Hitler's Bomb* (New York: Henry Holt and Company, 1997) pp.ix–x and 224–41.
54. Grier, *op. cit.*, p.xviii.
55. *Ibid*, p.131.
56. See, for example, Earl F. Ziemke, *Stalingrad to Berlin: The German Defeat in the East* (New York: Barnes & Noble Books, 1996) p.502.
57. Schramm, *op. cit.*, pp. 147–48.
58. Eberle and Uhl, *op. cit.*, p.299.
59. *Ibid*, p.111.
60. Kershaw, *Nemesis*, p.754.
61. Jörg Muth, *Command Culture: Officer Education in the U.S. Army and the German Armed Forces, 1901-1940, and the Consequences for World War II* (Denton, Texas: University of North Texas Press, 2011).
62. See for example Guderian, *Panzer Leader*, pp.442–43; Kershaw, *Nemesis*, pp.736–38; John Toland, *The Last 100 Days* (New York: Bantam Books, 1967) pp.767–75. Both Payne, *op. cit.*, and Speer, *Inside the Third Reich*, address this issue at various points in their books.
63. Schramm, *op. cit.*, p.135.
64. Warlimont, *op. cit.*, p.403.
65. Albert Speer, *Inside the Third Reich*, translated from the German by Richard and Clara Winston with an introduction by Eugene Davidson (New York: The Macmillan Company, 1970), p.405.
66. Schramm, *op. cit.*, p.161 and Appendix II, pp.192–205.
67. *Ibid*, p.160.
68. Speer, *Inside the Third Reich*, p.405.
69. Schramm, *op. cit.*, p.160.

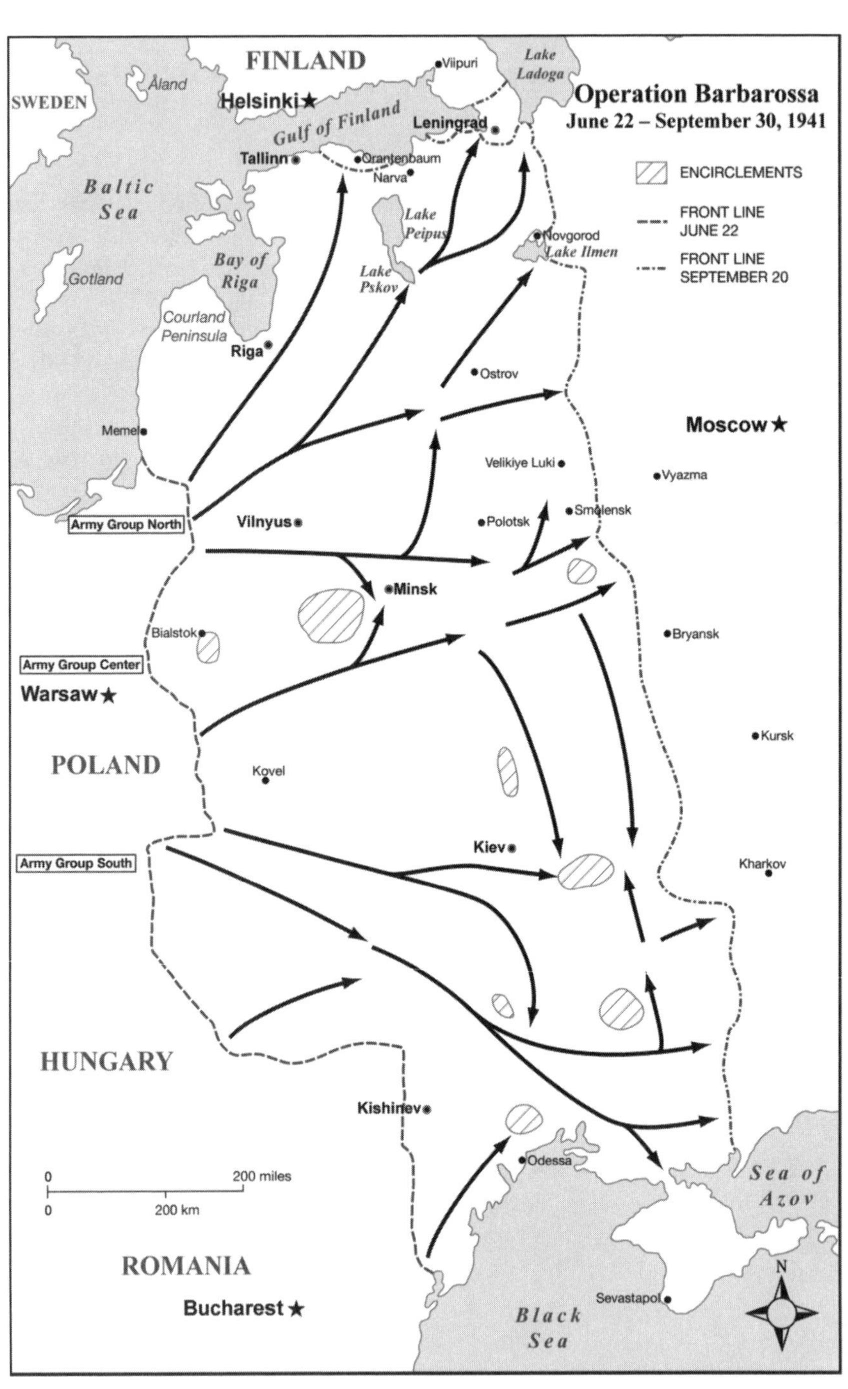
Operation Barbarossa
June 22 – September 30, 1941
ENCIRCLEMENTS
FRONT LINE
JUNE 22
FRONT LINE
SEPTEMBER 20
FINLAND
SWEDEN
Åland
Helsinki
Viipuri
Lake
Ladoga
Gulf of Finland
Leningrad
Tallinn
Orantenbaum
Narva
Baltic
Sea
Lake
Peipus
Novgorod
Lake Ilmen
Lake
Pskov
Gotland
Bay of
Riga
Courland
Peninsula
Riga
Ostrov
Memel
Moscow
Velikiye Luki
Vyazma
Smolensk
Polotsk
Vilnyus
Army Group North
Minsk
Bialstok
Bryansk
Army Group Center
Warsaw
Kursk
POLAND
Kovel
Kiev
Kharkov
Army Group South
HUNGARY
Kishinev
Odessa
Sea of
Azov
0
200 miles
0
200 km
ROMANIA
Bucharest
Sevastapol
Black
Sea
N

2

Barbarossa's Planning and Execution— Signs of Trouble

Summer of 1940—Hitler's Strategic Dilemma

Hitler's attack on the Soviet Union in 1941 had deep roots in a personal ideology that went back to the early 1920s. His entry into a closer relationship with the Soviet Union in 1939 was only a temporary adjustment to his long-range policy.

The timing of his attack was based on strategic considerations. After his "peace offering" to Great Britain in the summer of 1940, Hitler had concluded that Britain's intransigence was based on their hope of Soviet support and an eventual US entry into the war. He viewed a cross-Channel invasion as too hazardous without having a secure "backyard," and believed that the British might be more reasonable and come to terms if the Soviet Union could be eliminated from their calculations. Hermann Göring's (1893–1946) air offensive against Great Britain failed to secure the needed air superiority required for an invasion. However, it should be noted that the air battle over Great Britain had been underway for only three weeks when Hitler made his decision to invade the Soviet Union, and Operation *Sea Lion* was not cancelled until September 1940.[1]

Hitler had already decided in July 1940 that he needed to deal with the Soviet Union. His decision may have been influenced by the quick British rejection of the peace feelers floated in his speech to the Reichstag on July 19, 1940, or he used that event as a justification for his decision.

General Franz Halder (1884–1972), chief of the OKH, noted that Hitler appeared puzzled by Great Britain's stubbornness. Halder writes that Hitler believed that the British refusal to negotiate must be based on their hope for Soviet assistance and notes that he agreed with Hitler's conclusion that the Soviet Union had to be dealt with before Britain would become reasonable. However, it is equally likely that Hitler had already concluded that the British would reject a negotiated settlement and that his puzzlement was not genuine.

It is with these facts in mind that we must view Hitler's announcement to his military commanders on July 21, 1940 that he planned to attack the Soviet Union that fall. He claimed that Great Britain was inciting the Soviets to take action against Germany by cutting it off from resources such as oil. He anticipated that the forces required to crush the Soviet Army could be assembled in four to six weeks.[2]

Hitler's decision raised the specter of a two-front war. Major General Alfred Jodl, Chief of Operations at OKW, briefed his subordinates on July 29, 1940, on the intention to attack the Soviet Union. The prospect of a two-front war led to a protracted discussion. Jodl reasoned that a settlement with the Soviet Union was inevitable and it was better to make it while Germany's military prestige and power were as high as they were after the string of spectacular military successes.[3] It is difficult to tell if these were Jodl's own thoughts or whether he was merely conveying Hitler's views.

Hitler, despite his earlier views that the two-front war in World War I had contributed to Germany's defeat, and that a similar situation should be avoided in the future, now appeared to have changed his mind or overestimated British helplessness. In the wake of the French capitulation he is reported to have told his military advisers that a campaign against the Soviet Union would be child's play.[4] Most of the senior commanders present at Hitler's briefing on July 21, 1940, were uneasy when they found that he was intending to plunge into Russia. As of July 30 the Commander-in-Chief of the Army, Field Marshal Walther von Brauchitsch (1881–1948), and the Chief of the General Staff, General Franz Halder, favored remaining on friendly terms with the Soviet Union.[5] These two senior officers preferred concentrating on attacking the British in the Mediterranean and at Gibraltar.[6] Grand Admiral Erich Raeder, the Commander-in-Chief of the Kriegsmarine, was strongly opposed to the adventure in the East. He also saw a Mediterranean strategy as a viable option to further isolate Great Britain[7]—he argued this was the most vulnerable place in the British Empire. It was the quickest sea route to large portions of that empire and to the oil-rich Middle East.

The Mediterranean strategy involved closing that sea to British access by capturing or neutralizing Gibraltar, Malta, and the Suez Canal.[8] It was possible that the option argued by Raeder and the OKH could have allowed German/Italian forces to reach as far as the border of Turkey and the oil-producing countries of the region. The Mediterranean strategy would have involved considerably fewer forces and risks than a direct attack on the Soviet Union. While Hitler had listened to Raeder's proposal, he apparently shared Jodl's views or maybe Jodl was only expressing Hitler's views. General Jodl favored a "periphery strategy" involving the Mediterranean.[9] However, unlike Raeder, who saw the proposed operations in the Mediterranean as an alternative to an invasion of the Soviet Union, Jodl appears to have viewed his periphery strategy as an adjunct to that invasion. Jodl's was only a temporary solution to British intransigence by challenging them in the Mediterranean and keeping them from interfering with the German operations against the Soviet Union.[10]

Hitler's solution to the strategic dilemma he faced was not to opt for the indirect approach, but to go directly against enemy strength. In so doing a two-front war was guaranteed unless Germany could quickly dispose of the Soviet Union. The timing of the attack on the Soviet Union was also influenced by Hitler's views on a possible US intervention. He had concluded that the United States would not be ready to enter the war until 1942. A short war against the Soviet Union would present the United States and UK with an impregnable German position in Europe.[11] Hitler's decision to strike east was one of the most fateful and consequential decisions of the 20th century, ranking with the Japanese attack on Pearl Harbor and the first use of an atomic weapon in war.

Despite their misgivings, the German military leaders did not overtly oppose Hitler's decision. The General Staff had, in fact, started preparing feasibility studies for a war against the Soviet Union several weeks earlier. As specialists, their shortcomings in political matters and Hitler's earlier success kept them from objecting. Whatever doubts they had were overcome by Hitler's argument based on "political" information to which the generals were not privy, which indicated that Russia was about to take the offensive against Germany. He also had "information" that Russia's internal weaknesses would cause its rapid collapse.

The Strategic Plan

The strategic planning for the German attack on the Soviet Union in 1941 began shortly after Hitler made his announcement to his military commanders in July 1940. In the wake of the spectacular successes in the West, the now overconfident Hitler viewed the invasion of the Soviet Union as an easy task.[12] He believed the forces required for the task could be assembled within four to six weeks. This rosy scenario was quickly ruled out by the German military as impractical.[13] In a meeting with Jodl on July 29, Hitler set May 1941 as the time for the attack and this was communicated to the other military leaders two days later.[14]

The primary planning for the invasion of the Soviet Union—later code-named *Barbarossa*—was conducted by the OKH, initially under the leadership of Major General Erich Marcks (1891–1944), Assistant Chief of Staff for Operations. Marcks was an officer who is best known in the West—from his depiction in the movie *The Longest Day*—as the commander of the German LXXXIV Corps during the Normandy invasion. This was not Marcks' first involvement with eastern planning. He and his superior at the time—General Georg von Küchler (1881–1968)—were told by Halder on July 4, 1940, to work out a plan of operations against Russia. Marcks was at the time the Chief of Staff to General Küchler, who commanded the Eighteenth Army, located in East Prussia. The first version of the plan, a counter against a Russian attack, was submitted on July 9.[15]

Marcks and his officers developed the first draft study for the invasion of the Soviet Union and presented it to OKH on August 5, 1940. The general concept was in tune with the overall thinking at OKH and was no doubt based on guidance from Halder. The view at OKH was that the early capture of Moscow was the key to a decisive victory over the Soviet Union. However, Marcks saw the Pripet Marshes in Belorussia as a considerable obstacle for the center drive. For that reason, he perceived the need for a strong second drive in the south aimed at Kiev. The central and southern drives would then link up east of the Pripet Marshes for a joint offensive against Moscow. It was believed that the enemy would concentrate his defense around this economic and political epicenter, thereby giving the Germans the opportunity to deal a death blow to the Soviet Army. Although Hitler agreed in principle, he emphasized the economic and strategic importance of capturing the Baltic States early.[16]

General Marcks undoubtedly recognized the importance of Leningrad and the Murmansk railroad in providing links between the Soviet Union and the outside world. He also recognized the need for neutralizing the Soviet Baltic Fleet in order to maintain control of the Baltic Sea. However, the severing of these links and the neutralization of the Baltic Fleet apparently did not figure prominently in Marcks' scheme of things. His draft plan envisioned the main assault on the Soviet Union taking place in the south and center, primarily in the center. A major simultaneous German drive through the Baltic States to Leningrad was not part of his plan. He visualized the assault in the north taking place at a later date.

Hitler also wanted OKW involved in the planning and told Jodl, Chief of Operations at OKW, to prepare a study. This task was given to Lieutenant Colonel Bernhard von Lossberg (1899–1965) in the National Defense Section (Section L) on August 7, 1940. It would be helpful to know, in view of the rather turbulent planning effort that followed, which of his superiors gave Lossberg his planning guidance. The most likely candidates are Warlimont and Jodl, but this is questionable since these officers later showed that they were more or less in favor of the OKH position. Since Lossberg was already on Hitler's blacklist, that leaves only General Keitel. The first document Lossberg produced was an estimate called *Aufbau Ost* (Build-up East). This was followed by *Operationsstudie Ost* (Operational Study East) which was ready on September 15.[17]

Bernhard von Lossberg is at times confused with his father, General Friedrich (Fritz) Karl von Lossberg (1868–1942), who served in World War I. Bernhard also served in that war and was so seriously wounded that he was handicapped for life. As a fearless young officer, Bernhard ran afoul of Hitler on several occasions. In a virtual state of panic over the isolation of General Eduard Dietl's forces in Narvik, Hitler insisted that those forces be evacuated by air or withdraw into internment in Sweden. A written discretionary order was prepared, but Lossberg, on his own initiative, delayed its dispatch while Jodl tried to dissuade Hitler.[18] Later that same month, Lossberg was sent to Norway by Hitler who worried about the German commander in Norway, General Nikolaus von Falkenhorst (1885–1968), on account of his slow northward progress and Allied landings in central Norway. Lossberg returned and reported to Hitler that the Allies had only landed about 5,000 troops, that Falkenhorst had things well in hand, and that the conduct of operations should be left to him.[19] Hitler was not used to being spoken to in this manner and soon afterwards he banned Lossberg from his presence.

When the OKW operations staff was reorganized on January 1, 1942, Hitler's only demand was that Lossberg be replaced by another officer. Warlimont writes that Hitler had "never forgotten Lossberg's critical attitude during his own pitiful manifestations of weakness at the time of the Norwegian campaign."[20] Geoffrey Megargee and Samuel Mitcham indicate that Lossberg was involved in the planning before he was officially tasked by Jodl on August 7, 1940. Both authors indicate that Lossberg's initial involvement took place in July. Mitcham refers to a 30-page feasibility study that Lossberg produced in that month, code-named *Fritz* after his oldest son. In this study, Lossberg is reported to have argued that the main effort should be in the north, since this would lead to the encirclement of large Soviet forces in the Baltic States that had been seized earlier in the year.[21]

I have not seen the *Fritz* document unless it was an internal code-name given to *Aufbau Ost* or *Operationsstudie Ost*, mentioned above. However, the timeline does not fit. John Keegan also mentions *Fritz* and states that the OKW and OKH plans were thrashed out at a staff conference at the Chancellery on December 5, 1940.[22] It is obvious that Lossberg's plan as reported by Mitcham, above, was not fully accepted, or more likely it was never briefed to Hitler. Vestiges of Lossberg's views, however, are shown in what was presented to Jodl.

It is interesting to note that what Mitcham reports as Lossberg's position in the study was nearly identical to what Field Marshal Gerd von Rundstedt (1875–1953) stated after the war as his preferred approach:

> The 1941 operations in Russia should, in my opinion, have had their main effort directed, not at first towards Moscow, but towards Leningrad. That would have linked up with the Finns. Then, in the next stage, should have come an attack on Moscow from the

> north, in co-operation with the advance of Field-Marshal von Bock's Army Group from the west.[23]

The planning for the attack on the Soviet Union continued at both OKH and OKW. General Marcks was replaced by Major General Friedrich von Paulus (1890–1957) in September 1940. Paulus is the same officer who later commanded the Sixth Army at Stalingrad. Lossberg was replaced as planner by Colonel Hans von Greiffenberg (1893–1951) and Lieutenant Colonel Gerhard Feyerabend (1898–1965) in September 1940.[24]

The study that the National Defense Section of OKW submitted to Jodl proposed a significant change to the plan initially worked out by Marcks at OKH. The National Defense Section recommended a substantial increase in the strength of the German Army's left wing driving northward through the Baltic States toward Leningrad. This change probably represented a compromise between the thinking of OKH and that of the OKW, more specifically Hitler since both Jodl and Warlimont appear to have favored the OKH views. What started out earlier as a two-pronged offensive with the main effort in the center and a supporting and converging drive in the south, both having Moscow as the ultimate objective, now became a compromise three-pronged attack with basically no main effort. All three drives had insufficient forces to accomplish their tasks without major shifts of units within the operational theater.[25]

John Strawson writes the following about the strategic planning:

> . . . But it is to say that between June and December 1941 in the Supreme Commander's [Hitler's] handling of his struggle for Russia, singleness of aim—a necessary end, and beginning, for concentration of forces—was absent without leave. The struggle became a gigantic encounter battle which, for all the vast distances involved, for all the unthinkable destruction or capture of Russian men and material, was marred by fatal compromises.[26]

Paulus supervised war-games from November 28 to December 3. These centered on the Baltic States and Leningrad and less on Moscow. The exercises demonstrated that clearing the Baltic States would be time-consuming and have an impact on the operations of Army Group Center against Moscow.

In the end, there were no important differences between the OKW study and the draft plan which OKH presented to Hitler on December 5, 1940. This was, as mentioned above, the results of attempts to reconcile the views of the two headquarters. However, the shift away from Marcks' plan presented to OKH on August 5, 1940, was a significant change in overall strategy.

The dissipation of effort by the three-pronged attack on the Soviet Union was primarily the result of desires by Hitler, and—despite disclaimers by Warlimont—by OKW to bring Finland into the war. While Warlimont's writings are more in tune with the first OKH draft plan submitted by Marcks on August 5, 1940, there can be little doubt that the OKW and OKH had already harmonized the plan OKH presented to Hitler on December 5, 1940.[27] It is also obvious that Hitler and, to a lesser extent, the principal officers at OKW, were primarily to blame for the shift in strategy. Keitel says as much in his memoirs. He writes:

> Hitler visualized these targets on the flanks as being of great economic value in the case of the Donets basin, and political and naval value in the case of Finland and the Baltic; from the point of view of military strategy he was not so much concerned with the city of Leningrad as such . . . as with the naval base at Kronstadt and its elimination as a key naval base; it presented a considerable threat to our communications and submarine training in the Baltic. The War Office [OKH], on the other hand, believed that in their proposal lay the key to a rapid termination of the war. The Führer remained unconvinced.[28]

This directive makes it clear that after the destruction of the Soviet forces in Belorussia through giant encirclements, the main effort would switch to Army Group North and that the resumption of the advance on Moscow would not take place until after the capture of Leningrad. It reads:

> In the theatre of operations, which is divided by the Pripet Marshes into a Southern and Northern sector, the main weight of attack

will be delivered in the Northern area. Two Army Groups [Army Group Center and Army Group North] will be employed here.

The most southern of these two Army Groups (in the center of the whole front) will have the task of advancing with powerful armoured and motorized formations from the area about and north of Warsaw, and routing the enemy forces in White Russia. This will make it possible for strong mobile forces to advance northwards and, in conjunction with the Northern Army Group operating out of East Prussia in the general direction of Leningrad, to destroy the enemy forces operating in the Baltic area. Only after the fulfillment of this first essential task, which must include the occupation of Leningrad and Kronstadt, will the attack be continued with the intention of occupying Moscow, an important centre of communications and of the armament industry.

Only a surprisingly rapid collapse of Russian resistance could justify the simultaneous pursuit of both objectives.[29]

Warlimont, quoting the War Diary of Section L on January 9, 1941, writes: "He [Hitler] had his eye on 'rapidly cutting the Russians off from the Baltic Sea area in order to keep it clear for imports of value to the war effort' and because it provided the shortest line of communication to Finland; a month later he was still saying that this was the most important task."[30]

Warlimont also writes that he was in Paris when the draft *Barbarossa* directive was presented to Hitler on December 5, 1940, and saw it for the first time on December 16. He deplores the fact that Hitler had decided to switch the main emphasis to Army Group North as soon as the Soviet armies in Belorussia had been defeated. This involved considerable transfer of forces from Army Group Center to Army Group North. The advance on Moscow was to be resumed only after Leningrad and Kronstadt (home of the Soviet Baltic Fleet) had been captured.

Warlimont may be correct in his statement that he first saw the draft *Barbarossa* directive on December 16, but he should have been intimately familiar with the study prepared by his own National Defense Section in close coordination with the planning staff at the OKH. The two planning staffs had worked in close cooperation from the very beginning and apparently arrived at a compromise. The National Defense Section conference records reveal that Jodl, Warlimont's superior, was briefed on the OKW study on September 19. Warlimont writes "this seems highly improbable" and he addressed this issue in strong terms: "Any idea that the study carried out in Section L [National Defense Section] had anything to do with this momentous decision [increasing the weight in the north and eventually shifting the main emphasis to Army Group North] is wide of the mark for the very reason that, as always, our study had been agreed beforehand with the Operations Section of OKH."[31]

Warlimont is either forgetful, less than candid, or not familiar with the plans put forward or agreed to by his own staff—as he states—in close collaboration with OKH. It appears that he shifts most of the blame to Hitler and, to a lesser extent to Jodl, Chief of Operations at OKW and his immediate superior. Jodl also favored the OKH approach so this implied criticism many not be reasonable. He may have meant that Jodl did not resist Hitler's change as strongly as he should have.

Keitel's views are even more ambivalent. Earl F. Ziemke, in his 2000 introduction to Keitel's memoirs, has this to say about how the *Barbarossa* plan was developed:

> In late July 1940, Hitler put another kink in the chain of command: he set the army General Staff to work on planning the invasion of the Soviet Union and gave the army exclusive responsibility for the Eastern Front that would ensue. But he did not change the procedure with regard to the Führer directives; consequently, when he and Jodl issued his directive for what was to be called Operation *Barbarossa*, they found that the army was too far along with an altogether different plan to change without having to delay its start (the army proposed to strike toward Moscow, Hitler toward Leningrad and Kiev). Hitler allowed the army to proceed, but—even though Jodl supported the army plan—the Führer put the army on notice to expect a switch to his plan after the operation started. Consequently, the army went into the Soviet Union with two incompatible objectives: to defeat the Soviet forces forward of Moscow or to seize Leningrad and the natural resources of the Ukraine and the Caucasus.[32]

There were apparently several drafts of the *Barbarossa* directive prepared in the two weeks following the December 5 briefing of Hitler.[33] Jodl was involved in this drafting process but it appears it was his subordinate, Lossberg, who did the actual drafting.[34] The OKH emphasis on Moscow remained until Hitler ordered a final redraft. Although Jodl had been partial to the OKH solution all along, it appears that he raised no strenuous objections and this is what may have caused Warlimont's displeasure, discussed above.

It appears that the OKH did not strenuously oppose Hitler's change to their operational concept. OKH may have hoped that the course of events would result in a return to their original concept which had the drive to Moscow as the main effort.[35] The whole adventure into the Soviet Union, on which the future and survival of Germany rested, was marred from the beginning by fatal compromise, and the principles of war—the tools of the military profession—were indeed "absent without leave."[36]

Finland and Barbarossa

The Chief of Staff of the OKH, General Franz Halder, mentioned in his diary on July 22, 1940, that Finland presented one route by which to attack the Soviet Union and the *Barbarossa* directive (Directive 21), signed on December 18, 1940, lists not only the objectives of the German army groups but also what was expected from the Finns.[37] The Germans gave the quality of the Finnish armed forces a high rating and judged them a definite asset in the forthcoming operation. Joining forces with the Finns would also serve the purpose of eliminating, not just blockading, the Soviet Baltic Fleet. Another factor that influenced German attitudes involved nickel production in northern Finland. Finnish nickel was of considerable importance to the German war industry, as was the supply of Swedish iron ore. The availability of these raw materials figured prominently in Hitler's decision-making throughout the war.

Hitler hoped that the highly rated and battle-experienced Finnish military of 600,000 would assist in the quick capture of Leningrad and Kronstadt, as well as join and assist the German forces that had been moved to Finland for the purpose of capturing Murmansk or severing the railroad from that port to the Russian interior. Hitler put great emphasis on the early link-up with the Finns and the capture of Leningrad and Kronstadt—

with grave consequences for the whole campaign. It not only diluted the main effort, but in the end it also prevented Army Group North from being turned in the direction of Moscow.

Many books have been written about the epic siege of Leningrad, some of them voluminous. Grier is right in deploring the lack of comprehensive examination of Finland's role in World War II.[38] He could have gone further. It is peculiar that the roles Army Group North and Finland played in Germany's overall plans are hardly mentioned. Excepting some brief paragraphs, even books of many hundreds of pages fail to mention this game-changing aspect of the war in the East. In fact, most plans and operations by Army Group North after it arrived in the Leningrad area were designed to get Finnish participation in operations against Leningrad and the Murmansk railroad.

The purpose of the disastrous German drive to Tikhvin in 1941, the proposed Operation *Nordlicht* (Northern Lights) in 1942, the movement of Manstein's Eleventh Army from the Crimea to Army Group North in 1942, the withdrawal from the Demyansk salient, and the proposed Operation *Parkplatz* (Parking Place) in the spring of 1943 all had one thing in common: to influence the Finns to become full participants. This fact is seldom mentioned in the literature dealing with Leningrad. It is also thoroughly astonishing to view the nonchalant nature of German–Finnish planning and coordination for their joint venture. The Germans allowed themselves to enter into a very loose co-belligerency with Finland. It is hard to find any serious contemporary opposition to this condition in either the OKW or OKH.

It was a grave mistake for the Germans not to insist on a clear understanding about Finnish participation in the achievement of the dual German objectives—capture of Leningrad and cutting of the Murmansk railroad—before placing some 250,000 troops in a war theater where they would to a large extent be dependent on the actions of their new-found brothers-in-arms. If the Finns had balked at such an understanding, it would have been wise for the Germans not to waste precious resources in this theater of war. There was no joint German–Finnish campaign plan much beyond the initial attacks. The loose and informal nature of the coalition, the lack of long-range planning, and an ineffective command structure posed increasing problems as the war dragged on. Even such fundamental issues as war aims were simply brushed aside.

It is relatively easy to determine Germany's war aims vis-à-vis the Soviet Union since they are spelled out in the *Barbarossa* directive. It is much more difficult to discern the true Finnish war aims, what was expected from their participation in the war, and what they were willing to contribute to the joint venture. Officially the Finns claimed that they were only after the territories seized by the Soviet Union in 1940. However, it is patently obvious from statements and events both before and during the war that they hoped to come out of the war with much more than the territories lost in 1940.

The Finnish objections to helping the Germans in their attack on the Murmansk railroad and Leningrad were often couched in terms that such attacks went beyond the recovery of lost territories. This was a subterfuge since they showed no such reluctance in the conquest of East Karelia, an area that had never been under Finnish control and where no valid historical claims existed. It is rather incredible that the Finns did not realize that the achievement of their own goals—whether limited to the recovery of their lost territories or the expansion of the country—was totally dependent on Germany achieving its goal of destroying the Soviet Union. It therefore made virtually no difference what the Finnish war aims were, as they were intrinsically linked to those of Germany. Nevertheless, it is extraordinary that the Germans did not press the Finns for more definitive answers regarding their participation in the two main objectives of the German operations—the capture of Leningrad and the cutting of the Murmansk railroad. The failure to do so was to become a major bone of contention, as should have been anticipated. Clausewitz wrote:

> The plan of war comprehends the whole military operation; through it the operation becomes a single act, which must have one final definitive object, in which all particular objects have been merged. No war is begun, or at least, no war should be begun, if people acted wisely, without first finding an answer to the question: what is to be attained by and in war?[39]

These massive violations of long-standing military planning principles were in large measure due to the almost universal view that the war in the

East would be short. With respect to the deficient command structure, where the OKW directed the operations of German forces in Finland while the OKH was responsible for all operations on the Eastern Front, the Germans disregarded another well-known warning of their military philosopher and theorist Clausewitz: namely that the worst situation is where two independent commanders find themselves operating in the same theater of war. The Finns soon saw the opportunity to play one German headquarters against the other and used it to their advantage. The loose relationship that resulted from faulty planning was fine with the Finns, who did not want to become too tightly bound to Germany, and in the end it served them well in extracting themselves from the war. It was a totally different matter for the Germans. Hitler's unrealized desire for a quick linkup with the Finns had a serious impact on the war in the East, and from 1942 on it isolated what was the best German army in central and northern Finland, where it became a mere bystander to the war fought in Russia.

Geoffrey P. Megargee places the blame for the command relationship problem on OKW, and Brauchitsch as the Commander-in-Chief of the German Army. He writes: "The OKW, without consulting with the OKH, ordered a division from Norway into Finland for the upcoming invasion of the Soviet Union. Brauchitsch, who was piqued at this intrusion into the OKH's sphere of authority and still angry over the creation of the original OKW theater in Norway, insisted that the OKW take over responsibility for Finland altogether."[40] Keitel had this to say about the command structure: "With the commencement of operations against Russia, the Führer had defined the operational command structure for the remaining theatres as making Finland, Norway, the west, North Africa, and the Balkans immediately responsible to him, in other words to the High Command [OKW], in order to relieve the War Office [OKH} of these burdens." Keitel goes on to explain that Hitler created this command structure because these countries were either on the Atlantic Coast or they were involved in a coalition with Germany. Hitler wanted to retain the prerogative to deal with allies, not only the heads of state but also their general staffs.[41]

The OKH was no doubt happy to be relieved of the responsibility for operations in Finland, something that headquarters considered a sideshow, at least in the beginning. General Franz Halder, as Chief of Staff, OKH, wrote, "The whole undertaking [German operations from Finland] is merely an expedition; it is not an operation of war. It is a pity to squander forces by using them in this area."[42]

To say that the deployment of one division into Finland came as a surprise to OKH is misleading. It was Group XXI (Army of Norway) that prepared a staff study based on the *Barbarossa* directive, but the OKH issued an operation order based on this study at the end of January that was approved by Hitler on February 3, 1941. This included the plans for deployment and marshaling of forces so the movement of one division was obviously not a surprise to the OKH. Furthermore, telegrams and reports to and from headquarters directly subordinate to OKW were copied to OKH.[43]

In the end the Germans in Finland—Twentieth Mountain Army—failed to achieve their objectives of either capturing Murmansk or cutting the Murmansk railroad. Army Group North failed to link up with the Finns on the Karelian Isthmus or on the Svir River. The Finns, for their part, refused to move beyond the Svir or their old border on the Karelian Isthmus to meet the Germans from the north. These are interesting subjects, but their detailed treatment is not within the scope of this book. For those who are interested, these events are covered in my earlier book *Finland's War of Choice*.[44] What is important for our discussion now is the fact that Army Group North failed to achieve its objectives. The dilution of effort caused by the departure from General Marcks' two-pronged attack caused a severe drain on the German armed forces, and the hoped-for benefit of having the Finns at their side—although they fought superbly—never materialized.

The **Barbarossa** *Operation*

It is seldom an acceptable solution to advance against an enemy on a broad front, such as the one in the Soviet Union, with no real main point of effort. It violates the very core of military strategy and a number of the military principles that serve as its underpinning—such as a single decisive objective, simplicity, and mass. While the Germans threw a formidable war machine at the Soviets, their objectives were many and the dissipation of forces made it very unlikely that they would all be achieved.

The Germans had managed to double their number of Panzer divisions since the summer of 1940, but here we find the first indications of the increasingly self-delusional habit of expanding the number of units at the expense of their striking power. The increase in the number of Panzer divisions came primarily from a one-third reduction in the number of tanks per division. The number of tanks had increased since the summer of 1940, but not significantly—from 3,420 on September 1, 1940 to 4,198 on June 1, 1941.[45]

The OKH assumption that the differences in their plan and the one signed by Hitler would be ironed out during the actual operations proved correct, but not in the way OKH had envisioned. The compromise *Barbarossa* directive did not mean that the different views of OKW and OKH had gone away. Keitel notes that the old quarrels between Hitler and OKH began to break out again after the first successes of the campaign. Hitler wanted to hold on a general line running from Odessa to Lake Peipus through Orel and Smolensk. He decided to remove units from Army Group Center to reinforce Army Group South and have that group capture the whole Donets Basin and the oil fields at Maikop and Krassnodar. He also decided to reinforce Army Group North in the same manner so it could seize Leningrad and link up with the Finns. It appears that Hitler believed he had sufficient time to switch his tank forces to the flanks, have them execute their tasks, and return them in time for the resumption of the offensive in the center. The result was that the tank formations had little time to perform the maintenance required after their long drive into the Soviet Union. In addition, these decisions led to confrontations with various frontline commanders.[46]

This redeployment of forces was to have happened after the Soviet armies in Belorussia had been thoroughly defeated. That never happened. Army Group Center was able to conduct three encirclements, but was unable to close the entrapments in time to prevent sizable Soviet forces from escaping. In the Minsk encirclement, for example, over half of the encircled forces escaped. The main reason for the partial failure of the encirclement near Minsk was that the armored forces had advanced more than 198 miles (320km) in five days, while the infantry needed to seal the pocket had not been able to keep up.[47] This was also true for the other two encirclements. The result was that the bulk of the Russian force that Hitler had hoped to obliterate before reaching the Dnieper was badly mauled, but not destroyed. German optimism, however, continued high, as illustrated by this excerpt from Halder's diary on the 12th day of the campaign (July 3, 1941): "It is probably not an overstatement when I say that the campaign against Russia was won within 14 days. Of course, it is not over. The vastness of space and the persistence of all-out resistance will still take us several weeks to overcome."[48]

Hitler was equally optimistic. On July 14, 1941 he issued a supplement to Directive 32, which spelled out actions that were to be undertaken after *Barbarossa*.[49] The supplement proposed a reduction in the army, a limitation of the navy to what was necessary to prosecute the war against Britain, and an increase in the size of the Luftwaffe.

There were several reasons for the initial failure of *Barbarossa*. First and foremost the invasion had been diluted by Hitler's insistence on three simultaneous drives. This drained force away from what was to have been the main attack by Army Group Center and seriously complicated logistical and support operations. Second, Hitler's routine source of information was the Fremde Heere Ost (FHO) or Foreign Armies East of the OKH, responsible for intelligence on the Eastern Front. Until the arrival of Colonel (later General) Reinhard Gehlen[50] (1902–79) on the scene in the spring of 1942, as Chief of Intelligence at OKH, the intelligence produced by that organization was woefully inadequate and faulty. In his typical direct style, Lewin writes that FHO "was so limited in its range and competence that all its work was scarcely worth more than a few Boy Scout patrols."[51] German intelligence misread the determination of the Russian resistance and had failed to note the improvements in the Soviet armed forces (particularly tank developments) since their dismal performance in the attack on Finland in 1939. It had also underestimated the problems posed by weather and bad roads—these were much worse than expected, and an early start of rains turned the roads and ground into mud.[52] Liddell Hart views the fact that the Germans had based their mobility on wheels rather than tracks as the most important reason for failure.[53]

The armored and mechanized forces sent into the Soviet Union were divided into four groups. One armored group was assigned to Army Group North, one to Army Group South, and two to Army Group Center.[54] The German Panzer divisions, from an organizational standpoint, were unprepared for invading a country such as Russia. The bulk of the vehicles in the Panzer divisions were unarmored and lacked cross-country mobility. The German Panzer divisions of 1941 had roughly 3,000 vehicles, but only 10 percent of these were tracked, the rest were for the most part road-bound wheeled vehicles. When rains and mud became a problem the tanks could continue but most of the other vehicles in the divisions were unable to keep up. If the road system had been up to Western standards or the Panzer divisions fully tracked there can be little doubt that a decisive victory could have been achieved in 1941.

The Western campaign was fought over an area of roughly 50,000 square miles (129,500 square kilometers) with supply lines that stretched back less than 186 miles (300km). In the Soviet Union Hitler hoped to conquer a vast region comparable in size to the United States east of the Mississippi. The resulting space/force ratio was 20 times greater in the East than in the West with a supply line stretching back 1,000 miles (1,600km).[55]

When the Germans paused their offensive to bring forward supplies and reinforcements, Hitler was not sure what to do next. The halt in the center lasted six weeks. Field Marshal Fedor von Bock (1880–1945), the commander of Army Group Center, wanted to continue towards Moscow; only about 300 more kilometers to the east, but Hitler decided to turn south where he saw an opportunity for encirclement after Rundstedt's Army Group South broke through the Russian front south of Kiev. Rundstedt's own tank forces under General Ewald von Kleist (1881–1954) were to turn northeast while General Heinz Guderian's Second Panzer Group and General Maximilian von Weichs' (1881–1954) Second Army were sent from Army Group Center to Army Group South. Guderian's Panzer group was to swing in a southeast direction to become the northern prong of the encirclement. At the same time General Hermann Hoth's (1885–1971) Third Panzer Group was also detached from Army Group Center and sent to Army Group North. The two prongs of the Kiev encirclement closed about 124 miles (200km) east of the city. The encirclement succeeded and resulted in nearly 700,000 prisoners.[56] However, it was now late September and what looked like an early winter was closing in.

The Kiev encirclement had refueled Hitler's optimism and despite Rundstedt and Brauchitsch recommending a halt along the Dnieper, the temptation of Moscow for Hitler, like Napoleon, proved too strong, particularly since this was the course favored by Bock. The order to resume the drive on Moscow was given on October 2, 1941, after Army Group Center had basically remained motionless during the best two months for operations, August and September. The six week stop proved fatal for German fortunes.

The late start of the drive for Moscow was exacerbated by a further dilution of the overall effort. At the same time as Hitler decided to resume the offensive against Moscow he insisted on exploiting the success in Army Group South's area—again splitting his effort and going for two objectives simultaneously. The drive to Moscow started out well, resulting in a nearly perfectly executed encirclement in the Vyazma area that led to the capture of 600,000 prisoners. It was the end of October, however, before the Vyazma encirclement could be cleared. The Germans had planned for a short campaign against Russia and this assumption proved lethal. It had resulted in the troops not being clothed or equipped for winter, especially a winter that proved to be the earliest and coldest in many years. Despite their enormous losses, the Russians were bringing in fresh forces from their rear areas. The combination of severe cold, snow, and the seemingly endless stream of Russian reinforcements brought an end to German hopes of taking Moscow and ending the war in 1941. Instead, they found themselves involved in a ferocious defensive battle as the Soviets launched counteroffensives from all across their front, from northern Finland to the Black Sea.

None of the objectives spelled out in the *Barbarossa* plan had yet been achieved. Moscow and Leningrad had not been captured. The Murmansk railroad had not been cut and the Caucasian oilfields had not been reached. More importantly, the Soviet military—while having been dealt deadly blows—had not been destroyed. Most important for the future was the fact that Hitler had become more radical and before long this radicalism was to become absolute.

Several writers consider the faulty *Barbarossa* plan to be one of Hitler's greatest strategic mistakes. Within that plan they focus on the failure to concentrate on a single decisive objective by going after several widely separated objectives simultaneously.[57] Liddell Hart's words on these issues are hard to improve upon:

> Their strength became split in diverging directions—due partly to

> divided minds at the top, but also, ironically, to dazzling initial success in all directions. Instead of keeping a single line of operation that threatened alternative objectives, they were led to pursue several lines of operation each too obviously aimed at a single objective, which thus became easier for the defender to cover.[58]

The impact on Operation *Barbarossa* of the German invasion of the Balkans to bail out their Italian allies has also been the subject of a long and lively debate within the historical community. Some believed that the delay caused by this sideshow fatally delayed Barbarossa. William L. Shirer writes as follows:

> The delay, as things turned out, was fatal. Defenders of Hitler's military genius have contended that the Balkan campaign did not set back the timetable for Barbarossa appreciably and that in any case the postponement was largely due to the late thaw that year which left the roads in Eastern Europe deep in mud until mid-June.[59]

To bolster his arguments Shirer refers to statements by Rundstedt and Paulus after the war. Robert Kirchubel and Charles D. Winchester maintain that those who claim that the Balkan campaign delayed *Barbarossa* are wrong and that it had little or no effect on the progress of the German invasion. Kirchubel writes that "the main causes of deferring Barbarossa's start date from 15 May to 22 June were incomplete logistical arrangements, and an unusually wet winter that kept rivers at full flood until late spring."[60] Liddell Hart also concludes that in the final analysis the delay caused by the Balkan campaign made little difference to the success or failure of Operation *Barbarossa*.[61] He notes that von Rundstedt and the commander of his armored forces, General von Kleist, complained that the forces used in the Balkans arrived late and that the vehicles were in need of maintenance and repairs. Liddell Hart explains that other generals (like Halder and Manstein) express much less concern and that the key to the operation in Russia was Army Group Center, which was much less affected by the Balkan campaign than Rundstedt's army group—this was only supposed to play a secondary role in the early phase of Operation

Barbarossa. In Halder's view the invasion could not have started earlier than it did because of the weather. Liddell Hart confirms the atrocious weather conditions. He notes that "Even in normal times movement is very restricted before mid-May, but 1941 was an exceptional year. The winter had lasted longer. As late as the beginning of June the Bug was over its banks for miles."[62] In the final analysis, it was Hitler's delay and indecision during August and September 1941, the best months for operations, and the switching of armored forces to the flanks that proved fatal to *Barbarossa*, and not the delay caused by the Balkan campaign.

One writer has asserted that Hitler's refusal to concentrate at the outset to seize Moscow was "as much due to a compulsive urge to subjugate the generals" as it was to a defective strategy.[63] This is highly questionable. At this early stage of the war Hitler had not yet resorted to his later habit of insensitive and reproachful behavior towards his generals. In fact, there are numerous times during the campaign when Hitler shied away from an open head-on confrontation with his military commanders.

Hitler made another colossal mistake in Operation *Barbarossa*—his so-called Commissar Order—issued to his generals on March 19, 1941. Key parts of this order read:

> This struggle is one of ideologies and racial differences and will have to be conducted with unprecedented, unmerciful and unrelenting harshness . . . The commissars are the bearers of ideologies directly opposed to National Socialism. Therefore the commissars will be liquidated. German soldiers guilty of breaking international law . . . will be excused. Russia has not participated in the Hague Convention and therefore has no rights under it.[64]

Hitler's order, according to Halder, caused an outrage among the German generals and it was immediately protested to Brauchitsch as Commander-in-Chief of the Army. He promised to fight against the order, but apparently nothing was done. Because of the resistance of the German officers, Keitel issued an order on May 13, 1941 removing the punishment of enemy civilians in Russia from the jurisdiction of army courts martial. By its wording this broadened the Commissar Order to include partisans and other civilians showing hostility to the Germans.[65]

Hitler stated, when he announced his intention to invade the Soviet Union, that he expected the Soviet regime to collapse quickly. This may have proven true if he had instructed his forces to act as liberators instead of ruthless conquerors. The initial welcome of German troops soon turned to hatred and resulted in partisan activity becoming one of the greatest problems for the German Army in Russia.

NOTES

1. The German surface fleet was severely battered in the invasion of Norway. Had it not been, those ships under a strong Luftwaffe umbrella could have posed a severe threat to the Dunkirk evacuation.
2. Franz Halder, *Kriegstagebuch* (Nuremberg: Office of Chief Council for War Crimes, Office of Military Government for Germany, 1946), entry for 21.7.40.
3. Warlimont, *op. cit.*, pp.112-14. Warlimont notes that Hitler had already hinted at the necessity of dealing with the Soviet Union earlier in 1940, even before the campaign in the West was concluded.
4. Albert Speer, *Erinnerungen* (Frankfurt am Main: Ulstein Verlag, 1969), p.188.
5. John Keegan, *The Second World War* (New York: Viking Penguin, 1990), p.138.
6. *Halder War Diary*, entries for 21.7.40 and 30.7.40.
7. Strawson, *op. cit.*, pp.128-29.
8. Ian Kershaw, *Fateful Choices: Ten Decisions that Changed the World, 1940-1941* (New York: The Penguin Press, 2007), pp.78–87.
9. Heinz Magenheimer, *Hitler's War: Germany's Key Strategic Decisions 1940-1945* (London: Cassell & Co., 1999), pp.30–31. See also Kenneth Macksey (ed.), *The Hitler Options* (Mechanicsburg, Pennsylvania: Stackpole Books, 1995), pp.36–38.
10. Ian Kershaw, *Fateful Choices,* p.76.
11. Macksey, *op. cit.*, p.85.
12. Others, such as the Chief of the British Imperial Staff, opined that the Germans would go through the Russians like a hot knife through butter.
13. Warlimont, *op. cit.*, pp.112–14.
14. Kershaw, *Fateful Choices*, p.68.
15. Geoffrey P. Megargee, *Inside Hitler's High Command* (Lawrence, Kansas: University Press of Kansas, 2000), p.104.
16. Stephen G. Fritz, *Ostkrieg: Hitler's War of Extermination in the East* (The University Press of Kentucky, 2011), pp.52–54.
17. Megargee, *op. cit.*, p.104. Megargee notes that Lossberg had been involved—tangentially—since late June or early July by "considering some of the operational factors involved."
18. Bernard von Lossberg, *Im Wehrmachtfürungsstab: Bericht eines Generalstabsoffiziers* (Hamburg: H. H. Nölke, 1949), pp.66–69.

19. Von Lossberg, *op. cit.*, pp.71–72.
20. Warlimont, *op. cit.*, pp.217–18.
21. Samuel W. Mitcham, Jr., *The Men of Barbarossa: Commanders of the German Invasion of Russia, 1941* (Philadelphia: Casemate Publishers, 2009), p.14.
22. Keegan, *The Second World War*, p.136.
23. Liddell Hart, *The German Generals Talk*, p.184.
24. Mitcham, *op. cit.*, p.14.
25. Barry A. Leach, *German Strategy against Russia, 1939-1941* (Oxford: Clarendon Press, 1973), pp.101–03.
26. Strawson, *op. cit.*, p.134.
27. Warlimont, *op. cit.*, pp. 137–40.
28. Walter Görlitz (ed.), *The Memoirs of Field Marshal Wilhelm Keitel* (New York: Cooper Square Press, 2000), p.146.
29. H. R. Trevor-Roper, *Hitler's War Directives 1939–1945* (London: Pan Books, 1966), pp.95–96.
30. Warlimont, *op. cit.*, p.138.
31. *Loc. cit.*
32. Görlitz, *Memoirs of Field-Marshal Wilhelm Keitel.* Ziemke's introduction is on pp. 1–8, and the passage cited is on p.4.
33. Keegan, *The Second World War*, p.137.
34. Robert Kirchubel, *Operation Barbarossa 1941 (2): Army Group North* (New York: Osprey Publishing Ltd, 2005), p.15.
35. See for example, Mitcham, *op. cit.*, pp.22–23.
36. Strawson, *op. cit.*, p.134.
37. See Trevor-Roper, *op. cit.*, pp.93–98.
38. Grier, *op. cit.*, p.xix.
39. Karl von Clausewitz, *On War*, translated from the German by O. J. Matthijs Jolles (Washington, D.C.: Combat Forces Press, 1953), p.569.
40. Megargee, *op. cit.*, p.95. He cites the German edition of General Warlimont's memoirs (p.142 in the English edition) and an entry in the OKW *Krigestagebuch*, March 18, 1941.
41. Görlitz, *The Memoirs of Field Marshal Wilhelm Keitel*, pp. 154–55.
42. *Halder Diary*, May 14, 1941.
43. Görlitz, *The Memoirs of Field Marshal Wilhelm Keitel*, p.146.
44. Henrik O. Lunde, *Finland's War of Choice: The Troubled German Finnish Coalition in World War II* (Drexel Hill: Casemate Publishing, 2011), pp.26–84.
45. Lewin, *op. cit.*, p.121.
46. Görlitz, *The Memoirs of Field Marshal Wilhelm Keitel*, pp. 148–50.
47. Archer Jones, *The Art of War in the Western World* (New York: Oxford University Press, 1989), p.553.
48. Hans-Adolf Jacobsen and Hans Dollinger, *Der Zweite Weltkrieg in Bildern und Dokumenten* (München: Verlag Kurt Desch, 1963), volume 1, p.392.

49. Trevor-Roper, *op. cit.*, pp.130–39.
50. Gehlen was an ardent anti-Nazi and had a minor role in the events leading up to the assassination attempt on Hitler in July 1944. His role was not discovered and he survived the war to become head of the Gehlen Organization, which carried out espionage activities against the Soviet Union. He eventually became head of the West German Intelligence Service. He died in 1979.
51. Lewin, *op. cit.*, p.120.
52. Keegan, *The Second World War*, p. 137.
53. Liddell Hart, *The German Generals Talk*, p. 167.
54. Jones, *op. cit.*, p. 552.
55. Bevin Alexander, *How Hitler could have won World War II: The Fatal Errors that led to Nazi Defeat* (New York: Three Rivers Press, 2000), p.83.
56. Strawson, *op. cit.*, p. 138.
57. See, for example, Alexander, *op. cit.*, p.83.
58. Liddell Hart, *Strategy*, p.262.
59. See, for example, William L. Shirer, *The Rise and Fall of the Third Reich: A History of Nazi Germany* (New York: Simon and Schuster, 1960), pp.829–30.
60. Kirchubel, *op. cit.*, p.16 and Charles D. Winchester, *Hitler's War on Russia* (Oxford: Osprey Publishing Ltd, 2007), p.24.
61. B. H. Liddell Hart, *History of the Second World War* (New York: G. P. Putnam's Sons, 1971), pp.131–32.
62. *Ibid*, p.134.
63. Macksey, *op. cit.*, p.221.
64. Shirer, *op. cit.*, p.830. The excerpts are taken from Shirer's quote of General Halder's affidavit at the Nuremberg Trial.
65. Keitel ordered all copies of the May 13 directive destroyed on July 27, 1941, but with the understanding that its validity remained in effect. However, copies of both the directive and his order for its destruction survived and showed up at the Nuremberg Trials.

3

Army Group North's Years of Hope and Frustration

The German Push to Leningrad

The OKH issued the marshaling order—*Aufmarschanweisung Ost* (Deployment Directive East)—for the invasion of the Soviet Union on January 31, 1941. With respect to Army Group North, it called for an encirclement of major portions of enemy units west of the Dvina River. The main axis of advance would be from Dünaburg via Opocka to Leningrad. The town of Dünaburg is located on the Dvina River in the southeast corner of Latvia and the village of Opocka is located about 80 miles (130km) south of Pskov. This meant that the main effort was on the right. The missions assigned to Field Marshal Wilhelm Ritter von Leeb's Army Group North were:

1. Destroy the Soviet armies in the Baltic States.
2. Neutralize Kronstadt.
3. Capture Leningrad.
4. Link up with the Finnish Army.

The distance Army Group North had to travel was 500 miles (800km). Army Group North consisted of the Sixteenth Army with ten infantry divisions under the command of General Ernst Busch (1885–1945), and the Eighteenth Army with eight infantry divisions under General Georg von

Küchler. Leeb planned to lead with the Fourth Panzer Group, under the command of General Erich Höpner (1886–1944).[1] This Panzer Group was redesignated the Fourth Panzer Army in January 1942. On June 22, 1941, it consisted of XCI and LVI motorized corps with three Panzer, three motorized infantry, two infantry, and three security divisions.[2]

When reaching Leningrad, Höpner was to continue north or northeast, depending on the situation. The Eighteenth Army's mission was to clear the Baltic area and be ready to capture the islands off Estonia. The Sixteenth Army, on the right flank, was responsible for maintaining contact with Army Group Center and thus constituted a screen for the right flank of Army Group North.

Army Group North made rapid progress through the Baltic States mainly because, contrary to German planning assumptions, the Soviets did not intend to make a stand in those areas. General Fyodor I. Kuzuetsov (1898–1961), the commander of the Northwest Front, successfully withdrew his forces virtually intact and nothing came of the great encirclement the Germans had planned west of the Dvina River. The Soviet retreat allowed the Germans to overrun Lithuania and Latvia quickly and they entered Estonia on July 4, reaching the old Russian border on July 8.[3] Soviet forces began to offer stiffer resistance when the Germans reached Russian soil, and the advance of Army Group North slowed to a crawl. Field Marshal Leeb began his final push from the area west of Lake Ilmen and Hitler reinforced him with an armored corps from Army Group Center. Such transfers were planned for in the *Barbarossa* directive, but only after the enemy in Belorussia had been routed.[4]

The primary mission of the German Navy in the Baltic was the protection of the sea route from Sweden. Support of *Barbarossa* was accorded a lower priority. Recognizing their own inferiority to the Soviet Navy, the Finns and Germans had agreed before the war began to rely primarily on mine warfare to neutralize the enemy surface fleet. This fleet was substantial—2 battleships, 2 light cruisers, 19 destroyers, and 68 submarines. In addition there were over 700 naval aircraft. Belts of mines were laid in the Baltic and Gulf of Finland beginning shortly before the commencement of hostilities. The German/Finnish tactics proved very successful and the Soviets were unable to make use of their naval superiority. The fleet remained, for the most part, bottled up in Kronstadt.

Army Group North's drive toward Leningrad resumed on August 10, 1941, and it was rapidly approaching Leningrad. The question about what to do with Leningrad now surfaced. In line with his twisted ideology, Hitler decided that Leningrad should not be occupied. Its population would be reduced through a process of starvation and bombardment. In the end, it was expected that the city would be leveled to the ground. Halder notes in his diary that the decision was announced by Hitler on July 12 and Moscow was to be destroyed in the same way when that city was reached. Halder refers to it as a "humanitarian tragedy" that would strike communists and non-communists alike.[5] The Finns had already expressed a desire to have the Neva River as their southern border and Hitler agreed that the territory north of the river should be given to them.[6]

A memorandum prepared by the German Navy clearly lays out what had been decided. It reads in part:

> The Führer is determined to raze Petersburg [Leningrad] to the ground. There is no point in the continued existence of this vast settlement after the defeat of Soviet Russia. Finland, too, has announced that it has no interest in the continued existence of a large city so close to its new frontiers.
>
> The original request by the Navy that the wharf, harbor, and other installations of naval importance should be spared . . . has to be refused in view of the basic policy in regard to Petersburg.
>
> It is intended to surround the city and then raze it to the ground by a general artillery barrage and by continuous air bombardment. Individual surrenders are unacceptable, because we cannot and do not wish to deal with the problem of quartering and feeding the population. We, for our part, have no interest in preserving any section of the population in the course of this war for Germany's survival.[7]

The Finns Go Their Own Way

Army Group North was ordered to encircle Leningrad, but not to enter the city or accept surrender. To isolate Leningrad, Army Group North planned to cross the Neva River near Schlüsselburg. It would then establish contact with the Finns on the Karelian Isthmus. It also intended to drive north to Volkhov and Tikhvin and link up with the Finnish Army of Karelia near the Svir River.

To assist in the accomplishment of its mission, Army Group North wanted the Finns to advance south on both the Karelian Isthmus and from the Svir River to meet the Germans moving north. These proposals were contained in a letter from Keitel to Marshal Carl Gustaf Emil von Mannerheim (1867–1951) on August 22, 1941.[8] Keitel's proposal elicited a refusal by Mannerheim based on gloomy and somewhat contrived reasoning. The real reason was that the Finnish leaders did not believe it was in Finland's interests to cross the Svir River or launch an offensive against Leningrad. The failure of proper pre-war planning was now coming back to haunt the Germans. In the end the Finns moved their front south on the Karelian Isthmus a short distance, not to cooperate with the Germans but for occupying better defensive terrain.

The letter from Mannerheim to Keitel created dismay at OKW and OKH. It resulted in an immediate message to Army Group North from OKH ordering it to link up with the Finns as quickly as possible, even at the cost of delaying the encirclement of Leningrad.[9] Leeb was not impressed when Keitel informed him on September 3, 1941, that the Finns were moving their front south a short distance on the Karelian Isthmus. Leeb observed that a kilometer or two of territory was of no importance. What was essential was to have the Finns undertake operations to tie down the maximum number of Soviet troops on their fronts. If they failed to do that the Soviets could create serious problems for the Germans by withdrawing substantial forces from the Finnish front for use against his army group.[10]

Leeb was correct. The Soviets quickly realized that the Finnish offensive on the Karelian Isthmus had ended. They had six divisions and several separate battalions and regiments defending Leningrad from the north. They quickly withdrew two of these divisions on September 5 and threw them against the Germans. Army Group North's arrival in the Leningrad area in September 1941 coincided with the Finns reaching the Svir River and the start of their drive into East Karelia.

Early September was a momentous period for the Germans and the course of the war. Despite signs of an early winter and the exhausted state of his troops, Hitler decided that the time was right to resume the German offensive against Moscow, notwithstanding the wording of the *Barbarossa* directive stating that the offensive against Moscow would resume only after the objectives in Army Group's North's area—the capture of Leningrad and the link-up with the Finns—had been achieved.[11] Hitler's decision to resume the offensive against Moscow involved removing Höpner's Fourth Panzer Group from Army Group North and transferring it to Army Group Center. This left only one mechanized formation in Army Group North, the XXXIX Corps. This corps had belonged to General Hermann Hoth's Third Panzer Group and had been sent north after Army Group North paused in the vicinity of Lake Ilmen.

Schlüsselburg fell to the Germans on September 8, 1941, and the Germans now had a foothold on Lake Ladoga, and the city of Leningrad was encircled.[12] This was the moment when OKW had planned that Leeb should send the XXXIX Corps on an eastward drive to Volkhov and Tikhvin. Leeb objected on the grounds that the operation would dissipate his strength at a time when he needed to make the ring around Leningrad secure. He was successful in his appeal—for the time being. Instead, the OKH ordered him to cross the Neva River and link up with the Finns on the Karelian Isthmus. However, he did not have the strength to cross the Neva.

The Soviets upset the German plans by launching heavy counterattacks against Schlüsselburg. Leeb pointed out to OKH on September 15, 1941, that the Soviets were withdrawing forces from the Finnish fronts and using them against the Germans.[13] He urged that the Finns resume their offensive on the Karelian Isthmus and predicted that if they did, the battle for Leningrad could be decided within a few days. If they did not, he could not predict when he would be able to cross the Neva River.

There can be little doubt that Leeb was correct. The handful of mauled Soviet divisions north of Leningrad could have been brushed aside easily by the Finns, particularly if they had not transferred forces to East Karelia or if those transfers had been delayed until after the requested German operations on the Karelian Isthmus. Such operations would also have closed the one opening in the German encirclement—across the southern part of Lake Ladoga. The OKH answered Leeb on September 18, 1941.[14] General Halder assured him that the Finns intended to resume their attacks both on the Karelian Isthmus and south of the Svir River. But there were conditions. The Finns told their brothers-in-arms that the offensive on the Karelian Isthmus would be undertaken as soon as the Germans had crossed the Neva River. The drive out of the Svir bridgehead would be pursued as soon as the effects of a German drive to the east became observable.

These conditions caused a conundrum for the Germans and doomed the hoped-for cooperation from the Finns, since the drive to the east had been cancelled temporarily and Leeb had just stated that he did not have the strength to cross the Neva River in force. It appears that the Finns were well informed on what was happening at OKH and used that information to their advantage.

The Tikhvin Thrust

OKW ordered Leeb to attack eastward on October 14, although there was no evidence that the Soviets had reduced their force levels in the Leningrad area to counter the offensive against Moscow.[15] The plan was to drive eastward and envelop the Soviet forces south of Lake Ladoga. It was expected that XXXIX Corps would link up with the Finns in the area between Tikhvin and Lodeynoye Pole. It appears from this intention that the Germans still harbored hopes that the Finns would undertake operations south of the Svir River.

XXXIX Corps began its advance on October 16, 1941. The advance was slow due to strong Soviet resistance and the onset of rain that turned the roads and earth into mud. The mud and soft ground was so bad that the armored divisions were forced to leave their tanks behind after a few days. The situation became bleak enough for Hitler to want to cancel the operation, but OKH and Leeb persuaded him to continue.

By the first week in November, the Germans were still 6 miles (10km) from Tikhvin. They planned one final push on November 6. The attack succeeded and Tikhvin was captured on November 9, 1941. Thereupon, one division was turned north along the railroad toward Volkhov. However, the Russians were not giving up the fight for the town and began a counteroffensive against Army Group North with new forces. Some of these forces, according to General Waldemar Erfurth (1879–1971), chief of the German liaison detachment at Mannerheim's headquarters, had been withdrawn from the Karelian Army front.[16] The Soviet forces succeeded in virtually encircling the Germans and Leeb found it necessary to commit two additional divisions to hold the flanks of the Tikhvin salient. Any plans for linking up with the Finns in the Lodeynoye Pole area or of a continued advance to Volkhov were out of the question.

On December 3, 1941, General Hans-Jürgen von Arnim (1889–1962), who commanded the German drive to Tikhvin, reported that he would not be able to hold that town. Leeb gave him a "be prepared" order to withdraw on December 7, but not to execute it until Hitler had given his permission. Hitler then issued Directive 39 on December 8, 1941, which stopped all offensive operations on the Eastern Front.[17] Tikhvin was ordered held and XXXIX Corps was fighting desperately to hold on to the town in the middle of a blizzard with temperatures well below zero. Leeb notified OKW that he intended to withdraw XXXIX Corps and Hitler grudgingly agreed, provided that the railroad between Volkhov and Leningrad was held. Tikhvin was evacuated on December 9 and Leeb decided to withdraw behind the Volkhov River, despite Hitler's insistence that he should establish his new front closer to the town of Volkhov. Hitler relented on December 15 after Leeb told him that a failure to withdraw behind the Volkhov River would lead to the destruction of XXXIX Corps. That corps was behind the river on Christmas Eve; it had sustained heavy losses in the fighting for Tikhvin and in the withdrawal.

The year 1941 had been full of disappointments for the Germans. They had not succeeded in convincing their co-belligerent to participate in the attack on Leningrad or even to take aggressive action to tie down Soviet forces north of Tikhvin and Leningrad. This doomed any hopes of capturing Leningrad. The Germans in Finland had not accomplished their objectives of severing the Murmansk railroad and/or capturing Murmansk. The support of the Finns became just a token gesture after the United States issued a virtual ultimatum with regard to the Murmansk railroad.[18]

The Leningrad Front in 1942

The southern fronts in the Soviet Union were accorded the highest priority in the 1942 summer offensive, and Army Group North had its forces spread over an extensive area in a defensive posture. It was disposed in a very irregular frontline, a legacy of the previous year and the Soviet winter offensive. On the left, the Eighteenth Army held an arch around Oranienbaum on the Gulf of Finland. The front then bent eastward south of

Leningrad, anchoring on Lake Ladoga at Schlüsselburg. From there, it bent sharply southeastward along the Volkhov River to the northern tip of Lake Ilmen.

The Sixteenth Army held a jagged line south of Lake Ilmen. The main feature of its front was a large salient jutting out from the main line in the direction of the Valday Hills, known as the Demyansk Salient, after the largest city in the area. From its easternmost point it curved sharply westward to Kholm and then southwestward to the northern boundary of Army Group Center, north of Velikiy Luki.[19]

In 1942 the Eighteenth German Army was primarily involved in preparations for an operation that Hitler hoped would bring about Finnish cooperation in the prosecution of the war. The Twentieth Mountain Army had reached agreement with the Finnish High Command to undertake a major operation against the Murmansk railroad—Operation *Lachsfang* (Salmon Catch).[20] The Finns promised to make 11 divisions available for a drive to cut the southern part of the railroad, while two corps from the Twentieth Mountain Army directed their offensive against the railroad further north, at Kandalaksha. The Finns stated that the forces needed would come from the Karelian Isthmus and Svir fronts and would be assembled as soon as the Germans captured Leningrad and moved their front eastward to give cover for the Finnish front on the Svir River. The Finns considered this pre-condition necessary in order for them to have the requisite forces available.

To accommodate the Finnish wishes, Hitler ordered the preparation of an operation—*Nordlicht*—to capture Leningrad. The German plan was rather simple. After a preliminary softening of the enemy by the Luftwaffe and massed artillery, the Germans planned to advance across the Neva River above Leningrad, link up with the Finns if that were possible, and then capture the city. The Eighteenth Army, in the Leningrad sector, estimated the Soviet Forces confronting it at 13 divisions and three armored brigades. The Eighteenth Army had five divisions and it would have four more with the arrival of Erich von Manstein's Eleventh Army which Hitler was moving from Sevastopol in southern Russia.[21] The Eighteenth Army was still eight divisions short of what it believed was necessary for Operation *Nordlicht*.

Georg von Küchler (now a field marshal), the new commander of

Army Group North after Leeb asked to be relieved in January 1942, briefed Hitler on Operation *Nordlicht* on August 8, 1942. He pointed out that the Germans were outnumbered two to one in the Leningrad area and requested additional divisions. Hitler answered that Küchler would have to do with what he had, since he could not give him divisions that he did not have. Küchler indicated that he would be ready to launch *Nordlicht* at the end of October. General Jodl objected and pointed out that it would have to be launched earlier because it was not an end in itself but a preparatory operation for *Lachsfang*.[22] Hitler set September 10, 1942 as the date of the offensive.

No one was happy with either the outcome of the conference on August 8 or Jodl's later recommendation and Hitler's acceptance that the mission of taking Leningrad be given to Manstein's Eleventh Army. Küchler protested that a switch in the command of Operation *Nordlicht* at this stage would only create confusion in view of all the plans and preparations made by Eighteenth Army. This argument did not change Hitler's mind.

The Eleventh Army headquarters arrived on the Leningrad front on August 27, 1942, and its staff began to plan for an attack on Leningrad. It was agreed that the Eleventh Army would take over that part of the Eighteenth Army's front which faced north, while the latter retained responsibility of the Eastern Front on the Volkhov River. The Eleventh Army, which was made directly subordinate to OKH, ended up holding three sectors: the Neva sector from Lake Ladoga to the southeast of Leningrad; the assault area south of Leningrad; and the sector blocking the Soviet forces in the Oranienbaum pocket.[23]

Manstein had grave misgivings about the operation and stated in his first meeting with Küchler on August 28, 1942, that he did not believe artillery bombardment would break Soviet resistance. He concluded that *Nordlicht* would be difficult and that the main attack should be made from the Karelian Isthmus or from both directions. Manstein wrote that "it would naturally have been of tremendous assistance to us if the Finns . . . had participated in the offensive."[24]

The lack of forces continued to plague the operation. Despite these difficulties, preparations for *Nordlicht* proceeded well and it held out great promise if successful. However, fate decided otherwise. The Soviets launched an offensive from the east along the south shore of Lake Ladoga on August 27, 1942, against the front of the Eighteenth Army commanded by General of Cavalry Georg Heinrich Lindemann (1884–1963). This area was referred to as the "bottleneck" and was that part of Army Group North's front which projected like a wedge from Schlüsselburg in a southwest direction. This wedge was vulnerable to attack from both the west and east and had grown very narrow, less than 6 miles (10km) across in certain locations. The objective of the Soviet offensive was to lift the siege of Leningrad by opening a land route through the wedge.

After the Soviets achieved local breakthroughs over a wide stretch of the slender Eighteenth Army's front south of Lake Ladoga, Hitler telephoned Manstein on September 4 and placed him in command of the breakthrough areas, since they threatened the German hold on Leningrad.[25] The first concern now was to restore the front. As usual, there was a scramble to find forces to restore the situation. The 3rd Mountain Division, already at sea from Norway to Finland, was diverted to Army Group North's front on August 31, 1942. Four divisions planned for use in *Nordlicht* also had to be moved to the bottleneck area.

The Eighteenth Army front was penetrated south of Lake Ladoga by strong Soviet forces; the army, however, was able to seal the penetration, which progressed some 8 miles (13km) to the vicinity of Mga. The attack against the base of the pocket was carried out by the Eleventh Army using three corps, and the German encirclement was completed on September 21. Despite desperate Soviet attacks from both within and outside this pocket, Manstein writes that the Soviets lost seven infantry divisions, six infantry brigades, and four armored brigades in ferocious fighting.[26]

The front was not restored until October 15. OKW, which had to watch helplessly as its own offensive plans evaporated, announced on October 20 that Operation *Nordlicht* was indefinitely postponed. This also doomed plans for Operation *Lachsfang*. The heavy siege artillery brought north with Manstein's army was to be used to support incremental advances in the front around Leningrad as long as that could be done without a great commitment of troops. After their experience the past winter, the Germans, including Hitler, were wary about any offensive which would extend into the winter season. Manstein and his Eleventh Army were shifted to the Velikiy Luki area between Army Group Center and Army Group North.[27]

The Demyansk Salient

The Soviets had managed to drive a huge bulge into Army Group Center's front during their 1941/42 winter offensive around Toropets in the northern part of the army group's sector. This bulge actually extended into Army Group North's sector, and the Soviets hurled nine armies against Army Group North in the same offensive. Their aims were to break the siege of Leningrad and push the front away from Moscow by levering the Germans from the strategic Valday Hills.

The Sixteenth Army tied into LIX Corps of Army Group Center in the vicinity of Velikiy Luki. It was a long front, since it incorporated the large salient extending towards the Valday Hills. This is not the place, for reasons of space, to discuss the lengthy fight for the Demyansk Pocket, or Salient, located about 100 miles (160km) south of Leningrad. It nevertheless produced some of the most ferocious fighting on the Eastern Front. Two German corps of six divisions were trapped in the pocket and these forces were later increased. Since the location of the pocket presented a German threat against the gigantic Toropets bulge, the Soviets were eager to eliminate it, as well as a pocket around Kholm that served to block a possible Soviet thrust into the rear areas of both Army Group North and Army Group Center. It was also a good jump-off position for a renewed German offensive against Moscow; this was probably the greatest worry for the Soviets, who misread German intentions in their 1942 summer offensive.

Leeb was very concerned about the situation in the Sixteenth Army area. He considered the Demyansk Salient valueless unless it was planned to move against the Toropets bulge. He called Führer headquarters on January 12, 1942, and proposed that his armies be withdrawn behind the Lovati River. Hitler immediately turned down the proposal, and Leeb thereupon flew to East Prussia to argue his case personally. Hitler again refused. Leeb then requested to be relieved of his command and Hitler agreed. Küchler was given command of the army group, and his place as commander of the Eighteenth Army was taken by General Lindemann.

While the Germans were aware of the opportunities presented by the Toropets bulge and the fact that the Soviets were overextended, they were unable to do anything about it. The German armies were bled white in the 1941 offensive and the subsequent Soviet winter offensive. The bloodletting could not be offset by replacements, which were slow in arriving, and there were virtually no reserves. Despite this situation, Hitler refused to abandon both Kholm and Demyansk. After being assured by the Luftwaffe that the reinforced First Air Fleet could deliver the required 240–65 tons of daily supplies to the two pockets, Hitler ordered them held until relieved. This air supply operation used almost all of the Luftwaffe's transport capability, as well as elements of its bomber force. The supply operations involved both airdrop and airlanding operations and were generally successful, primarily due to the weakness of the Soviet air forces in the area.

The Luftwaffe flew 33,086 sorties before the Demyansk Salient was evacuated in March 1943. The two pockets—Demyansk and Kholm—received 64,844 tons of supplies.[28] A total of 31,000 replacement troops were brought in and almost 36,000 wounded evacuated.[29] Several writers maintain that this was the first air bridge in history.[30] This is not correct. In the invasion of Norway in 1940, an air bridge was established from Germany and Denmark to Norway. Five-hundred and eighty-two transport aircraft flew 13,018 sorties and brought in 29,280 troops and 2,376 tons of supplies.[31] Yet the successful re-supply of the Demyansk and Kholm pockets had an ominous legacy. It confirmed in Hitler's mind that encircled forces could hold out until relieved, and thus contributed to a policy that was to have disastrous results for hundreds of thousands of German soldiers.[32]

Army Group North continued to worry about the Demyansk Salient. Küchler sent a personal letter to OKH on September 14, 1942, in an attempt to persuade Halder that continuing to hold the pocket was useless.[33] Küchler hoped to use the divisions freed by a withdrawal from the salient to form reserves for the army group. Halder answered on September 23 after raising the issue with Hitler. Hitler's earlier *Haltenbefehl* (hold order) remained unchanged. Halder acknowledged that Army Group North would gain 12 divisions by abandoning Demyansk, but pointed out to Küchler that such a withdrawal could also free 26 Russian infantry divisions and seven tank brigades.[34]

The spectacular success of the German Army in the southern part of the Soviet Union during the summer of 1942 had expanded the territory conquered by German arms to the greatest extent of the war. However, the Germans had not achieved their primary aim: the destruction of the Soviet Army. The Soviets, now more mobile, had learned to avoid encirclements.

The military situation that had looked so good and hopeful for the Germans in the East during the summer turned downright deplorable by the end of the year. By the middle of November, the situation at the front in southern Russia became critical for the Germans and their allies. A large-scale Russian offensive began northwest and south of Stalingrad on November 19, 1942, by vastly superior Soviet forces. The Romanian Third Army was routed and overrun. Disasters quickly followed on the neighboring fronts on the Don and Volga, and the Soviet avalanche brought Italian, Hungarian, and also German divisions into a vortex of defeat. Battles of tremendous size developed in the last third of November between the Volga and Don.

The situation on the German central front in Russia became grave when on November 25, 1942, the Soviets began their expected offensive on a wide front south of Kalinin. The fact that the Soviets retained the capability to launch so many large-scale offensives after suffering repeated defeats and enormous losses during the summer was dismaying to the Germans and a surprise to the world.

Germans on the Defensive and Finnish Loss of Confidence

A Soviet offensive to open a land bridge to Leningrad began on January 16, 1943. While they broke through the "bottleneck" and managed to open a corridor to Leningrad on January 19, the ferocious fighting lasted until the end of March and cost the Soviets 270,000 casualties. The Germans managed to restrict the Soviet corridor to a width of 6 miles (10km), which could be brought under artillery fire, thus reducing its usefulness.

By mid-January 1943 the fighting had drained off the last army group reserves. General Kurt Zeitzler (1895–1963), the new OKH Chief of Staff, told Küchler on January 19, 1943, that he intended to raise the issue of evacuating the Demyansk Salient with Hitler. Army Group North had just suffered a serious setback south of Lake Ladoga, and Zeitzler and Küchler agreed that the principal reason for the setback was the shortage of troops and that the only way to avoid similar mishaps in the future was to create reserves by giving up the Demyansk Salient. However, it was obvious to both officers that Hitler would adamantly resist such a proposal.

On the night of January 31, 1943, after a week-long debate, Hitler finally accepted Zeitzler's arguments. The earlier setback around Leningrad influenced Hitler's change of mind. He was anxious to keep Finland in the war and this involved holding around Leningrad. Küchler decided to conduct a slow withdrawal which began on February 20, 1943. He then collapsed the salient in stages, completing the last one on March 18.

On February 3, the day after Stalingrad fell, there was a high-level policy meeting at Finnish military headquarters which included Mannerheim, President Risto Ryti (1889–1956), and several influential members of the cabinet. Those assembled concluded that there had been a decisive turning point in the war and that Finland should conclude peace at the earliest opportunity. Parliament was briefed in a secret session on February 9, 1943, to the effect that Germany could no longer win the war. Mannerheim explains that the briefing "had the effect of a cold shower" on the members of Parliament.[35]

The Germans were fully aware of the importance of Leningrad for the Finns. Hitler therefore ordered Army Group North to prepare an offensive in late summer to capture the city.[36] This was wishful thinking. Army Group North, fighting defensive battles, was primarily worried about what the Soviets would do. It was especially feared that the Soviets would strike at the boundary between Army Group Center and Army Group North south of Lake Ilmen. This would split the German front and pin Army Group North against the Baltic coast. Nevertheless, Army Group North proceeded to plan for the capture of Leningrad—code-named Operation *Parkplatz*. Much of the siege artillery brought north by the Eleventh Army was still in place, but Army Group North needed eight or nine divisions in order to launch the offensive. These were promised only after Army Group South had completed its operation to pinch off the large Russian salient at Orel west of Kursk—Operation *Zitadelle* (Citadel).

Zitadelle was launched on July 5, 1943, but after initial successes, fortune turned against the Germans as the Soviets launched a strong counteroffensive, and the conflict developed into the largest tank battle in history. The Germans were forced to retreat and the much hoped for success turned into a serious German defeat.[37] As the fighting spread, the Soviets broke through the German front on the Donets River by the end of July. In August and September the German armies were driven back from the Donets River to the Dnieper River. By the end of September the Soviets had captured Kharkov and Field Marshal Günther von Kluge's (1882–

1944) Army Group Center was forced back to the edge of the Pripet Marshes.

Disastrous news for the Germans was piling up during the summer and fall of 1943. Sicily was invaded on July 9 and by August 17 the island was in Allied hands. Hitler's ally Benito Mussolini was overthrown on July 24, 1943, and an armistice was signed with Italy. With their offensives making rapid progress in the south with enormous losses, the Soviets turned their attention to Army Group North. A full-scale offensive to lift the siege of Leningrad was launched on July 22, 1943. Repeated Soviet attacks south of Lake Ladoga were repulsed by Army Group North in July and August. However, the Germans knew that this offered only a temporary respite; OKH ordered Army Group North to prepare a new defensive line along the Narva River and Lake Peipus, 124 miles (200km) southwest of Leningrad. These positions eventually became the Panther Line. This spelled the end of Operation *Parkplatz.*

OKW asked the Twentieth Mountain Army in Finland for its opinion about a possible withdrawal to the Panther Line. The answer stated that a withdrawal should not take place. The Twentieth Mountain Army argued that the Finns already felt let down by the failure of the Germans to capture Leningrad, despite repeated assurances to the contrary. Eduard Dietl, commander of the Twentieth Mountain Army, pointed out that after such a withdrawal the Finnish fronts on the Svir River and at Maaselkä would become indefensible and the Finns would be forced to withdraw. Dietl went on to caution that a likely result of a withdrawal to the Panther Line would be a Finnish approach to the Soviet Union for peace. If an acceptable peace was offered, the Twentieth Mountain Army would be cut off and a retreat to Norway over bad roads in wintertime would be extremely hazardous.[38] Dietl's warning was followed by a Finnish notice through Wipert von Blücher (1883–1963), the German Ambassador to Finland, that a withdrawal would have serious consequences for Finland.[39] This could only be interpreted by the Germans as a forewarning that Finland would be forced to leave the war if the Germans withdrew to the Panther Line. Mannerheim also expressed concerns to General Erfurth about the reports of a pending German withdrawal. OKW sent an explanatory message on October 3, 1943, which stated that there were no intentions to withdraw, but that rear positions were being constructed in case of an emergency.

An OKW planning conference on January 14, 1943, made a complete revision of its view of Finland as a co-belligerent. It amounted to writing Finland off as an ally that could be counted on to carry its weight. The revised estimate concluded that the Finns would not be able to prevent setbacks in case of a major Soviet attack because their defenses were poorly constructed and they had few reserves. Despite the serious situation for Germany on other fronts, it was decided not to remove any units from the Twentieth Mountain Army.[40]

A planning conference for the whole Scandinavian region took place at OKW in mid-March 1943. It included representatives from the OKW operations staff, the Chief of Staff of the Twentieth Mountain Army, and the operations officer of the Army of Norway. The conference recognized that the fall of Stalingrad had caused a decisive shift in Finnish opinion and that Finland's government and military leaders no longer believed in a German victory. The Chief of Staff of the Twentieth Mountain Army opined that the Finns were preparing to exit the war and could only be prevented from doing so by a convincing German military victory in the summer of 1943, or by their inability to obtain acceptable peace terms from the Soviets.[41]

Finnish leaders were fully aware that an offensive beyond the current positions would result in an immediate declaration of war by the United States, their only friend of any consequence in the Allied camp. The United States was viewed as Finland's best hope of securing an acceptable settlement with the Soviet Union. Taken together with the view that Germany could no longer prevail in the war, this conclusion dictated a policy designed to keep the United States from declaring war. Finnish military leaders exercised great care not to put themselves in a position where they could be blamed by the government and parliament for a US declaration of war.

We can safely assume that Germany, the Soviet Union, and the United States were fully aware of the Finnish dilemma. Germany's knowledge of the state of affairs is undoubtedly the reason they did not press the Finns to undertake offensive operations in 1943. The Soviet Union's knowledge allowed them to take the risk of removing great numbers of troops from the German–Finnish fronts in 1943. The United States was the trump card and Ziemke is right when he writes that an offensive by the Finns in late 1943 "would in the long run have been suicidal for the Finnish nation."[42]

The OKW operations staff informed Hitler on September 25, 1943, that there were increasing signs that Finland desired to leave the war and it was expected that they would take action in this direction if Army Group North was forced to withdraw. This warning resulted in the OKW issuing Führer Directive 50 on September 28. It dealt with a possible Finnish collapse and the preparations required by the Twentieth Mountain Army for a withdrawal to North Finland and North Norway. Parts of the directive read: "It is our duty to bear in mind the possibility that Finland may drop out of the war or collapse. . . . In that case it will be the immediate task of the 20th Mountain Army to continue to hold the Northern area, which is vital to our war industry . . ."[43]

Jodl visited Finland on October 14–15, 1943. The reason for the visit was apparently to try to bolster the confidence of the Finns in Germany and also to discuss Directive 50 with Dietl. Jodl pointed out to the Finns that Germany knew about Finnish efforts to get out of the war. Commenting on this, Jodl stated: "No nation has a higher duty than that which is dictated by concern for the existence of the Homeland. All other considerations must take second place before this concern, and no one has the right to demand that a nation go to its death for another."[44]

In his discussions with Dietl, Jodl pointed out that Hitler was adamant about holding the mining districts since the nickel was critical to Germany's war effort. He opined that communications to the nickel mines could be kept open via Norway.[45] Dietl replied that he had no confidence in the ability of the navy and air force to keep the Allies from cutting the sea supply lines around Norway, and that included the ore traffic. While agreeing with much of what Dietl had to say, Jodl did not believe it possible to withdraw the Twentieth Mountain Army by any other route than through northern Norway.[46]

The situation south of Leningrad continued to deteriorate at the end of 1943 and the beginning of 1944. The Soviets made a deep penetration southwest of Velikiy Luki at Nevel on November 5, 1943. This penetration tore open the front of the Sixteenth German Army. Only a lack of immediate exploitation by the Soviets averted the disastrous possibility of their outflanking the Panther positions, thereby causing the collapse of Army Group North's front.

NOTES

1. Höpner was relieved of command by Hitler after he pulled his troops back in the face of a massive Soviet offensive in January 1942. Hitler dismissed him from the army and stripped him of his rank, decorations, and pension. A court later restored the pension. Höpner was deeply involved in the plot against Hitler and was tried and executed in 1944 following the abortive assassination attempt.
2. Bob Carruthers and John Erickson, *The Russian Front 1941–1945* (London: Cassell & Co, 1999) p.189.
3. Jacobsen and Dollinger, *op. cit.*, volume 1, p.380.
4. Trevor-Roper, *op. cit.*, p.95.
5. Jacobsen and Dollinger, *op. cit.*, volume 1, p.392.
6. Earl F. Zimeke, *The German Northern Theater of Operations 1940–1945* (Washington, D.C.: Department of the Army Pamphlet No. 20–271, 1959) pp.195–96. For more on this issue see also Lossberg, *op. cit.*, pp. 131–34; and C. Leonard Lundin, *Finland in the Second World War* (Bloomington: Indiana University Press, 1957) p.151.
7. Payne, *op. cit.*, p.437.
8. Army Group North, *Kriegstagebuch*, letter from the Chief of the OKW to Marshal Mannerheim (No. 44 1418/41, Abteilung L) August 22, 1941.
9. Army Group North, *Kriegstagebuch*, August 28, 1941.
10. *Ibid*, September 3, 1941.
11. Trevor-Roper, *op. cit.*, pp.95–96. The directive allowed for the pursuit of both objectives only in case of a rapid collapse of Russian resistance. Such a collapse was not evident at the time of the decision.
12. The encirclement was not total. There was a 15½–25-mile (25–40km) area between the Neva River and the Finnish front on the Karelian Isthmus that allowed for communications across Lake Ladoga to areas under Soviet control outside the encirclement. This route across the lake became known as the "Ice Road"; in winter and in summer it was used by numerous boats. German attempts to stop this lake traffic were unsuccessful—they just did not have the resources required. If the Finns had moved south on the Karelian Isthmus as the Germans wanted, this route would have been severed and the outcome of the battle for Leningrad would undoubtedly have turned out differently.
13. Army Group North, *Kriegstagebuch*, September 15, 1941.
14. *Ibid*, September 18, 1941.
15. Görlitz, *The Memoirs of Field Marshal Keitel*, pp.161–62. Keitel wrote that OKH had opposed this operation, but that it was launched by Hitler over the objections of that headquarters. This may be true, but when Hitler wanted to cancel the operation on October 24, 1941, only eight days after it started, it was OKH and Leeb who convinced him not to issue a cancellation order.
16. Waldemar Erfurth, *The Last Finnish War* (Washington, D.C.: University Publica-

tions of America, Inc., 1979) p.52. Written under the auspices of the Foreign Military Studies Branch of the Historical Division, Headquarters European Command.

17. Trevor-Roper, *op. cit.*, "Führer Directive Nr. 39," dated December 8, 1941, pp.166–70.
18. The US government sent a memorandum to President Ryti on October 27, 1941, which reads in part: "In the event that attacks are made against shipments of military supplies from the United States en route to Russia via the Arctic Ocean, and such attack is presumably made or may be claimed to be made from Finish-controlled territory, it must be assumed that in view of the public opinion now prevailing in the United States such an incident must be assumed to lead to an immediate crisis in Finnish-American relations." Another memorandum on October 30, followed by a press conference by Secretary of State Cordell Hull (1871–1955) on November 3, 1941, elaborates on the October 27 memorandum by stating that action by the Finns [against the Murmansk railroad] "constituted a definite threat to the security of the United States." John H. Wuorinen (ed.), *Finland and World War II, 1939–1944* (New York: The Ronald Press Company, 1948) pp.136–37.
19. Ziemke, *Stalingrad to Berlin*, pp.200–09.
20. Trevor-Roper, *op. cit.*, "Führer Directive Nr. 45," dated July 23, 1942, pp.193–97.
21. The absence of the Eleventh Army had profound consequences for the Stalingrad operation in the winter of 1942/43.
22. Army Group North, *Kriegstagebuch*, Ia, August 8, 1942.
23. Erich von Manstein, *Lost Victories* (Minneapolis, Minnesota: Zenith Press, 2004), p.262.
24. *Ibid*, p.263.
25. *Ibid*, p.264.
26. *Ibid*, p.266.
27. The short stay near Leningrad was a period of personal sorrow for Manstein. His aide-de-camp, Leutnant Specht, had wanted to join a frontline unit and was allowed to do so, but was killed in a plane crash on his way to join his regiment. An even harder blow came a few days later (October 29), when Manstein's eldest son Gero, who served on the Leningrad Front, was killed in action.
28. Werner Haupt, *Army Group North: The Wehrmacht in Russia 1941–1945* (Atglen, PA: Schiffer Military History, 1997) pp.124-25. Since a corridor to the pocket from the west was opened by the end of April 1942, it is not clear whether this tonnage also included supplies brought in by ground.
29. The success of the Demyansk/Kholm airlift undoubtedly led Reichmarschall Hermann Göring and Hitler to think that a similar operation would work at Stalingrad. What they apparently failed to factor into their calculations was that Stalingrad was much different. It would require more than three times as much in supplies to keep the Sixth Army provisioned and over greater distances against much better organized Soviet air forces.
30. See for example Paul Carell, *Scorched Earth: The Russian-German War 1943–1944*,

translated from the German by Ewald Osers (New York: Ballantine Books, 1973), p.283 and Haupt, *op. cit.*, p.124.

31. Lunde, *Hitler's Pre-Emptive War*, pp.311 and 320.
32. Carruthers and Erickson, *op. cit.*, p.92.
33. Army Group North, *Kriegstagebuch*, Ia, September 14, 1942.
34. *Ibid*, Ia, September 23, 1942.
35. Carl Gustaf von Mannerheim, *The Memoirs of Marshal Mannerheim*, translated by Count Erich Lewenhaupt (New York: E. P. Dutton & Company, Inc., 1954) pp.460–62.
36. OKH, Operations Division, *Operational Order Nr. 5*, dated March 13, 1943.
37. According to Richard Ernest Dupuy and Trevor N. Dupuy, *The Encyclopedia of Military History* (New York: Harper & Row, 1970) p.1100, the German losses were 70,000 killed or wounded, plus 3,000 tanks, 1,000 artillery pieces, 5,000 motor vehicles, and 1,400 aircraft destroyed. The Soviet losses were probably slightly less.
38. Twentieth Mountain Army, Ia, message to OKW for General Jodl, dated September 14, 1943.
39. Wipert von Blücher, *Gestandter zwischen Diktatur und Demokratie* (Wiesbaden: Limes Verlag, 1951) pp.341–42.
40. A Twentieth Mountain Army document dated January 14, 1943, as cited by Ziemke, *The German Northern Theater of Operations*, p.243.
41. Ziemke, *The German Northern Theater of Operations*, pp.244–45, citing Twentieth Mountain Army records.
42. Ziemke, *The German Northern Theater of Operations,* p. 249.
43. Trevor-Roper, *op. cit.*, pp.216–17.General Dietl objected strenuously to Directive 50. He considered a withdrawal in winter to northern Norway over bad roads an extremely hazardous undertaking and the requirement to defend the nickel mining district in North Finland ridiculous, since they would be of no use once Finland withdrew from the war. He also felt that there was a distinct possibility that his corps on the Murmansk Front would be attacked and if such an attack should be successful the route of retreat into Norway would be severed. Dietl favored a withdrawal of his army across the Baltic where it could join Army Group North. His opinions carried considerable weight since he was one of Hitler's favorite generals. Dietl was killed in an aircraft accident when on the return flight from a visit to Hitler in June 1944.
44. Mannerheim, *Memoirs*, pp.46–-69.
45. Warlimont, *op. cit.*, p.398.
46. Twentieth Mountain Army, *Kriegstagebuch*, Ia, October 14, 1943, with an enclosure containing the discussion points of the meeting in Mikkeli between Jodl and Dietl.

4

The Retreat Begins and Finland Opts for Peace

Retreat to the Panther Line

The year 1944 opened with heavy fighting along the entire Eastern Front. The German armies, bled white in numerous battles in 1943, found themselves withdrawing from one position to the next. The German situation in the Leningrad area remained precarious, and this led Army Group North, supported by the OKH, to propose an immediate withdrawal to the Panther Line in order to avoid a disaster. Hitler failed to make a timely decision because he worried about the impact of such a withdrawal on the Finns.

Leningrad and the Baltic were for Hitler, in the words of Harrison Salisbury, "an idée fixe, and a preoccupation that never left him."[1] The reasons for this fixation are described in Chapter 1 and these had not changed by the beginning of 1944. Some, like hanging on to Finland, had become rather shaky. Any signs that the Germans were giving up in the area south of Leningrad, when viewed in the context of what was happening on other fronts, sent shivers through Helsinki. However, while keeping Finland in the war had lost much of its earlier hope of great benefits, it kept a German army of over 200,000 men from being trapped and for all practical purposes removed from the war. It also ensured that the Soviet Baltic Fleet remained bottled up, facilitated the control of the Baltic Sea, and kept nickel and iron flowing from Finland and Sweden. Statements that Hitler wanted the Eighteenth Army to hold the sector around Leningrad primarily for reasons of prestige fail to tell the whole story.[2]

The withdrawal of Army Group Center to its portion of the Panther Line in the autumn of 1943 had increased Field Marshal Küchler's difficulties. The westward move of Army Group Center forced Army Group North (Sixteenth Army) to extend its right flank in a southwesterly direction by 47 miles (75km) to cover the important rail and road hub at Nevel. The countryside around Nevel was characterized by extensive forests and many lakes and swamps. It was a favorite place for partisan activities. Since it was located on the boundary with Army Group Center it was assumed to be a likely place for the next Soviet offensive.

As 1944 began Army Group North was only a shell of its former self. It had begun the invasion with about 700,000 men in total.[3] By July 1943 its strength had dropped to about 360,000 men. Much of the drop in strength resulted from the transfer of five divisions to other areas of the Eastern Front. However, the numbers only tell part of the story. The tank strength had fallen from 1,500 in 1941 to 40 tanks and assault guns in July 1943. In the same period aircraft available to the First Air Fleet had dropped from 1,070 to seven! Mobility was likewise reduced, making it virtually impossible to conduct mobile operations—thus forcing units into prepared positions.[4]

The debilitating German manpower shortage was felt in Army Group North as it was all along the Eastern Front. Many units were replaced by Waffen-SS and Luftwaffe field units of dubious quality, and in most cases existing units were highly understrength. The quality of new recruits was such that German units were often no longer able to withstand determined enemy attacks as they had been in the past.

The anticipated Soviet offensive on the boundary between Army Group North and Army Group Center began on October 6, 1943, with the Soviets quickly penetrating the German lines and capturing Nevel. Hitler ordered the shoulders of the penetration held and counterattacks to close the gap that had developed between the two army groups. This may have been the correct decision but only because the Soviets failed to follow up on their initial success—they sustained heavy losses in unsuccessfully trying to expand the salient.

Nothing happened in Army Group North's sector during the first half of January 1944 to force Hitler's hand in regard to Küchler's request to withdraw to the Panther Line; the Soviets were still not ready to exploit their earlier success that had created the Nevel salient. In the meantime, Küchler lost two more of his best divisions to Army Group South. He no longer had any armor or mechanized units. Küchler may have himself contributed to the loss of divisions. General Lindemann, commander of the Eighteenth Army, had not objected to the loss of one division from the lines around Oranienbaum, and Küchler had foolishly mentioned this fact to Hitler at a conference on December 29, 1943—as well as noting that the lines in the Eighteenth Army area were well fortified.[5] It was not until the next day that Küchler realized what he had done when an order to transfer a second division arrived. A third division was on its way by January 4, 1944. Attempts to get Lindemann to change his earlier statements failed. He maintained that his unit commanders in the most threatened sectors had great confidence in their ability to withstand a Soviet offensive.[6]

One of the most dangerous sectors was the one around the Oranienbaum pocket, and there we find a motley array of Waffen-SS and Luftwaffe field units. In a conversation with General Warlimont, Lieutenant General Eberhard Kinzel (1897–1945),[7] the army group Chief of Staff, was more realistic by stating that the army group was marching to disaster with its eyes open.[8]

The work on the Panther Line was accelerated. In an attempt to economize on forces, this line made use of natural obstacles such as the Narva River, Lake Peipus, and Lake Pskov. However, Küchler was under no illusion about his abilities to prevent disasters either in the Leningrad or the Nevel sector. Unable to secure Hitler's permission to retire in good order behind the Panther line, Küchler could only wait uneasily for the blow to fall.

The anticipated blow came on January 14, 1944, when the Soviets started offensive operations against the Eighteenth Army. They began strong, simultaneous attacks in the Oranienbaum–Leningrad sectors and against the army's right flank at Novgorod, at the north end of Lake Ilmen. The ultimate Soviet goals were to lift the siege of Leningrad and to drive to the border of the Baltic States. There was little chance that Army Group North, with a frontline strength of only 250,000, could successfully cope with an enemy numbering 1.25 million.[9] Nevertheless, the Germans held

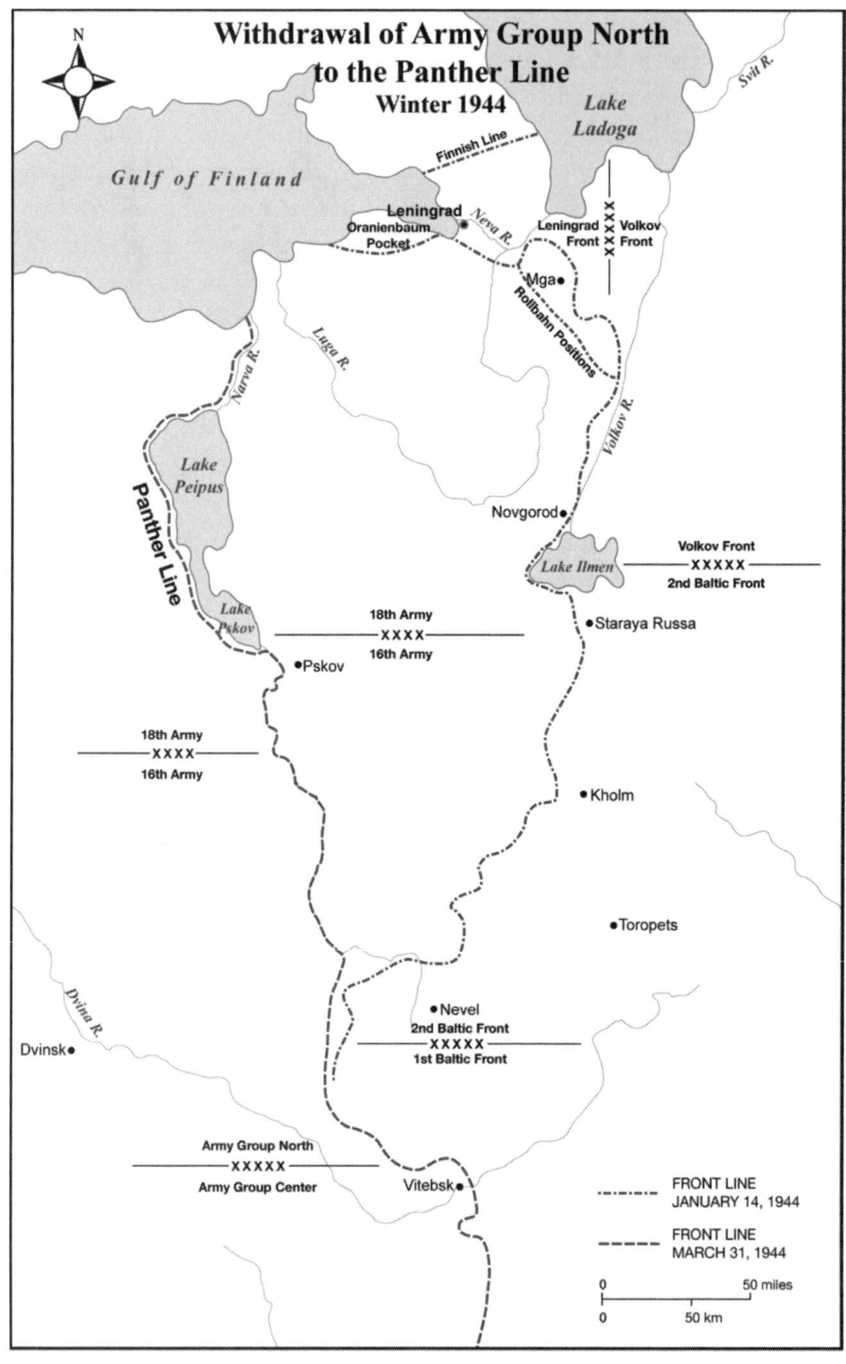
Withdrawal of Army Group North
to the Panther Line
Winter 1944
N
Gulf of Finland
Lake Ladoga
Svir R.
Finnish Line
Leningrad
Oranienbaum Pocket
Neva R.
Leningrad Front
Volkov Front
XXXXX
Mga
Rollbahn Positions
Luga R.
Narva R.
Volkov R.
Lake Peipus
Panther Line
Novgorod
Lake Ilmen
Volkov Front
XXXXX
2nd Baltic Front
Lake Pskov
18th Army
XXXX
16th Army
Pskov
Staraya Russa
18th Army
XXXX
16th Army
Kholm
Toropets
Nevel
2nd Baltic Front
XXXXX
1st Baltic Front
Dvina R.
Dvinsk
Army Group North
XXXXX
Army Group Center
Vitebsk
FRONT LINE
JANUARY 14, 1944
FRONT LINE
MARCH 31, 1944
0
50 miles
0
50 km

against the Soviet onslaught until January 17. The hopes that the Eighteenth Army might be able to contain the Soviet offensive vanished on that day when the Soviets broke out of the Oranienbaum pocket in a sector held by the 10th Luftwaffe Field Division, which crumbled the moment it was attacked. The Soviets also began to encircle Novgorod.

It became obvious on January 18, 1944, that two sectors of the Eighteenth Army's front were crumbling as the commitment of Lindemann's last reserves failed to contain the breakthrough in the area of the routed Luftwaffe field division. The Soviet forces driving out of Oranienbaum, the Second Shock Army, turned southeast to link up with the Soviet Forty-Second Army coming west. Since this threatened to trap two divisions from the Eighteenth Army on the shores of the Gulf of Finland, Küchler ordered, on his own authority, those two divisions to withdraw to avoid being encircled. The order came too late to save the two divisions, and only a few elements escaped.

On January 19 eight Soviet divisions were in the process of encircling five German divisions at Novgorod. General Zeitzler, the Chief of Staff of the Army, had tried to secure Hitler's permission for a withdrawal, but it was not until Küchler called him that permission was secured for giving up Novgorod and also to pull back the salient front south of Leningrad to an intermediary position called the *Rollbahn*, a highway embankment on the road from Leningrad to Moscow. Later that night Hitler tried to rescind the approval for the withdrawal south of Leningrad, but was told that the orders had already been issued.

Hitler also tried to get assurances from Küchler that the *Rollbahn* position would be held. However, a salient still existed even with the occupation of the *Rollbahn* position, and Küchler—who was in desperate need for reserves—maintained that three divisions would be freed up by withdrawing directly to the Panther Line. He intended to use two of these divisions southwest of Leningrad and one west of Novgorod.[10]

Küchler flew to Hitler's headquarters that night (January 21, 1944) to plead his case in the morning as the units withdrawing to the *Rollbahn* position were already under full attack. Hitler would not listen and berated his visitor: "I am against all withdrawals. We will have crises wherever we are. There is no guarantee we will not be broken through on the Panther. . . . If we go back voluntarily he [the Russians] will not get there with only half his forces. He must bleed himself white on the way. The battle must be fought as far as possible from the German border."[11] Küchler pointed out, to no avail, that not to withdraw risked the army group reaching the Panther Line too weak to fight. Hitler did have other things on his mind that day as Allied troops were landing at Anzio in Italy.

The Eighteenth Army was in the process of disintegration, and Lindemann ordered the towns of Pushkin and Slutsk evacuated. He told the OKH either to accept his action or send a replacement. By the time the withdrawal to the *Rollbahn* was completed on January 23, those positions had already been penetrated in several places. The German troops continued to fall back, with the result that, by 26 January, the Soviets were able to seize the rail line to Moscow and effectively end the siege of Leningrad.

On January 27, 1944, Küchler, like other group and army commanders, attended a National Socialist Leadership Conference at Königsberg. By now the Eighteenth Army had lost 52,000 men and its infantry strength was down to 17,000 men. Küchler again tried unsuccessfully to convince Hitler in a private meeting of the urgent need to withdraw to the Panther Line, pointing out that the Eighteenth Army was being cut to pieces and that if the Luga River line was not held the supply route for most of Lindemann's corps would be cut.

Lieutenant General Kinzel, Küchler's Chief of Staff, took matters into his own hands on January 28. He told the Chief of Staff of the Eighteenth Army that the time had come to take action. He pointed out that the army group was forbidden to issue a withdrawal order, but that he would ensure that the Eighteenth Army was covered. On January 29 Kinzel also convinced Küchler to point out to Hitler that the Eighteenth Army, now cut into three parts, would not be able to hold a front east of the Luga River, which was located about halfway to the Panther Line.[12]

The withdrawal to the Luga River was approved when Küchler met Hitler the following day. Kinzel again intervened to protest the conditions under which Hitler had approved the withdrawal. He argued that the large 31-mile (50km) gap between the Sixteenth and Eighteenth Armies could not be closed without additional resources and that the Soviets had already crossed the Luga River in the vicinity of Staritza. Küchler was ordered to report to Hitler on January 31, 1944.

In the January 31 meeting Küchler was instantly dismissed as army group commander. That position was given temporarily to General Walter Model (1891–1945), a Hitler favorite. Model had recently returned from a three-month home leave in Germany. This aggressive and energetic officer issued his first order to the army group while still at Hitler's headquarters. The operative part of the order was, "Not a single step backward without my express permission."[13] This must have been music to Hitler's ears.

For all practical purposes the Eighteenth Army line had disintegrated. The only two combat-capable divisions were two that had just joined the Eighteenth Army at the end of the month. Model forbade any mention of the Panther Line since it served as a magnet by giving the impression that it was a haven of security.

Instead he instituted a new concept called *Schild und Schwert* (Shield and Sword).[14] Under this concept it was appropriate to surrender ground as long as it was only temporary and served to further future offensive operations. Model had managed to establish a somewhat coherent front on the Luga River and was now ready to fall back on the Panther Line. Hitler and the OKW wholeheartedly approved Model's plan. It was probably not Model's intent to launch offensive operations, but this doctrine served as a means by which he could immediately fall back on the Panther Line without causing difficulties with Hitler. It amounted to nothing more than a planned controlled retreat with the vague promise of future offensive action.

In the end it was an unusual order of caution by Hitler and lack of follow-up by the Soviets that saved the day. Two corps of the Eighteenth Army had retired through the Luga position along the coast. By February 1, 1944, they were on the Narva River, which was the western anchor of the Panther Line. No further withdrawal was possible without endangering that whole line and the shale oil refineries about 19 miles (30km) to the west. The rest of the Eighteenth Army was regrouping near Luga. The greatest pressure on Army Group North's front in the first days in January had been in the Sixteenth Army's area, where the Second Baltic Front pushed back the German front south of Staraya Russa.

By February 4, the Soviet Leningrad and Volkhov Fronts had regrouped and were again ready for offensive operations. Model was talking about attacking, but Hitler issued a personal directive to the energetic general ordering him to reinforce the Narva area immediately, probably to protect the oil shale refineries. He was also concerned that the other remnants of the Eighteenth Army could be encircled or pushed to the east away from Lake Peipus. Hitler told Model to submit a request for withdrawal to the Panther Line if Model suspected that these events could happen.[15]

Model set about closing the gaps in the army group's front. The strength of the group had increased as a result of reinforcements, primarily from Army Group Center, a collection of stragglers, and by moving some of the rear-echelon personnel into frontline units. The end result was that a cohesive front was established behind the Panther Line by March 1, 1944. The Soviets made costly attacks against Narva and Pskov, but the Germans held their positions. Model, who was promoted to field marshal on March 1, 1944, was reassigned at the end of the month. Hitler had decided that he should replace Field Marshal Manstein as commander of Army Group South.[16] The senior army commander within Army Group North, General Lindemann, was appointed as its temporary commander.

A Recalcitrant and Wavering Cobelligerent

Efforts to arrange a separate peace between the Soviet Union and Finland had gone on since 1942. It may be helpful to review some of them as we approach the decisive events in the summer of 1944.

Hitler's visit to Finland to pay his respects to Mannerheim on his 75th birthday on June 4, 1942, was an unwelcome event for the Finns, since it resulted in an immediate reduced level of diplomatic relations with the United States. Only a legation secretary remained in Helsinki to keep alive the hope that the United States would still be a positive influence in Finland's negotiations with the Soviet Union. This may have been the high point in German-Finnish relations, as they deteriorated significantly in the wake of German failure to achieve a decisive victory in the summer campaign against the Soviet Union. There was also a noticeable change in public opinion, a trend that accelerated with the news of German defeats in Russia during the winter of 1943.

There was an election in Finland in the middle of February 1943. This gave President Ryti, who was re-elected, an opportunity to reshuffle his cabinet in a way that would make the government more acceptable to the Allies. The new Foreign Minister, Henrik Ramsay (1886–1951), had good connections to both the United States and the UK, and his appointment was an unmistakable signal of a change in policy. On March 20, 1943, the

United States made an offer to establish contact between Finland and the Soviet Union. Ramsay naively traveled to Berlin on March 25, 1943, to seek that country's friendly acquiescence in Finland's withdrawal from the war. His illusions were quickly dispelled. The Germans demanded that the US offer be rejected and Germany be given written assurance that Finland would not negotiate a separate peace.

The first part of the demand was satisfied before Ramsay departed Germany. The more difficult second part was not dealt with by the Finns until May, when the Finnish Prime Minister in a speech stated that the Finns would fight to the end rather than submit itself to the mercy of the Soviet Union. The Germans did not feel this was specific enough and recalled their ambassador to Helsinki for two months.

Sweden also began to exert pressure on Finland to withdraw from the war. In July 1943 Sweden forwarded an oral offer from the Soviets to discuss peace. The Finns rejected this offer but Sweden continued to be a relay station between Finland and the Soviet Union. The same month Ramsay informed the United States in a personal message to the Department of State through the Finnish Embassy in Portugal that the Finns would not join the Germans in resisting a US invasion of Norway. According to Mannerheim the message went as far as stating that the Finns would not resist even if the United States were to extend its operations into Finland.[17]

Joseph Stalin had promised Winston Churchill and Franklin Roosevelt at Teheran in December 1943 to make a peace offer to the Finns that would preserve their national independence. That peace offer was now made through the Soviet ambassador in Stockholm, Alexandra Kollontai (1872–1952). Finland did not dare jeopardize its relationship with the United States, and dispatched a former Prime Minister, Dr. Juho K. Paasikivi (1870–1956), to Stockholm to receive the Soviet offer. Paasikivi returned from Stockholm on February 24, 1944, with the Soviet terms. They involved the restoration of the 1940 borders, Finnish internment of the German troops in Finland, large war reparations, and the demobilization of the Finnish armed forces. The Soviet offer was more stringent than expected and it was rejected by the Finns, particularly the part dealing with the internment of German troops which they considered impossible. However, both the Finns and Soviets indicated willingness for further negotiations, and this led to an invitation for a Finnish delegation to come to

Moscow. The invitation was accepted and Paasikivi and former Foreign Minister Carl Enckell (1876–1959) flew to Moscow on March 26, 1944. Since the terms offered to the Finns were the same as those in the previous year, they were again rejected but with the understanding that it was not an end to negotiations.

The alarm in Finland that had resulted in Paasikivi's visit to Stockholm had subsided by the beginning of March 1944. Model had brought Army Group North back to the Panther Line and managed to establish a somewhat stable front. This stabilization had a calming effect on the charged political atmosphere in Finland. The German occupation of Hungary in March 1944 also demonstrated the fate that could befall a defector from the German cause.

The Finnish attempts to find a way out of the war came as no surprise to the Germans. The free Finnish press, which had been very supportive of the war in 1941, had now turned hostile towards Germany. Most Germans viewed these events as a betrayal of the brothers-in-arms concept, but initially adopted a wait-and-see attitude. They did not think the Finns were ready for the expected harsh Soviet terms.

Hitler, with his distrustful nature, had become increasingly annoyed and deeply offended by the Finns going their own way. He began taking steps to ensure that their peace offensive would come to a final end, thus binding Finland irrevocably to the fortunes of Germany, as soon as Model managed to stabilize the military situation on the Narva front. Hitler directed General Dietl to inform Mannerheim that further German weapons needed by the Finns to increase and modernize their forces would not be provided until the possibility of their falling into Soviet hands was removed. To increase the pressure on the Finns, Hitler ordered grain shipments to Finland stopped on April 13, 1944. This was followed by an embargo on war materials on April 18. Only such equipment as was absolutely necessary for the fighting ability of the Finnish Army would be provided in the future. This meant an end to Finnish hopes for modernizing and expanding their army.

A Change in German Strategy—on Paper

Hitler had always held the view that the two-front war in World War I had contributed to Germany's defeat and that a similar situation had to be avoided in the future. The westward advance by the Soviets, the United States' entry into the war, and obvious preparations by the Allies for an invasion brought back the specter of a two-front conflict. Führer Directive 51, dated November 3, 1943 tried to deal with this dilemma and laid out priorities, after considerable wrangling by the various headquarters.[18] In his introduction to this strategic document Hitler writes:

> The hard and costly struggle against Bolshevism during the last two and a half years, which has involved the bulk of our military strength in the East, has demanded extreme exertions. The greatness of the danger and the general situation demanded it. But the situation has since changed. The danger in the East remains, but a greater danger now appears in the West: an Anglo-Saxon landing! In the East, the vast extent of the territory makes it possible for us to lose ground, even on a large scale, without a fatal blow being dealt to the nervous system of Germany.
>
> It is very different in the West! Should the enemy succeed in breaching our defences on a wide front here, the immediate consequences would be unpredictable. Everything indicates that the enemy will launch an offensive against the Western front of Europe, at the latest in the spring, perhaps even earlier.
>
> I can therefore no longer take responsibility for further weakening the West, in favour of other theatres of war.

The directive goes on to describe in detail the measures that were necessary to strengthen the defenses in the West. The OKH was ordered not to withdraw any units from Western Europe without Hitler's approval.

Directive 51 must be considered an incomplete grand military strategy directive, since there is no mention of the situation in the East or actions to be taken there, except for alluding to trading space for time, something that was alien to Hitler's nature. With German troops still on Russian soil from Leningrad in the north to the Black Sea in the south, Hitler obviously did not consider the situation there overly threatening at the time Directive 51 was issued.

If Hitler ever entertained the notion of an elastic defense in the East, his actions over the next 18 months show the exact opposite. He became more determined than ever not to allow withdrawals, and designated cities in the path of the Russian advance as "fortified places," never mind the fact that most were completely lacking in fortifications. It appears that he considered this approach as an "economy of force" measure that would tie down a disproportionate number of enemy units.[19]

Warlimont writes that on December 20, 1943, Hitler stated for the first time: "if they attack in the West that attack will decide the war." Warlimont writes that this meant that if the attack was not repulsed the war was lost, but if the attack was defeated, there might be a more favorable outcome.[20] Directive 51 gave clear priority to the West but, as so often is the case, the follow-through was not in accordance with the plan. Contrary to what appeared to be his evident convictions both in the directive and his subsequent statement reported by Warlimont, Hitler and his subordinates continued to jeopardize the defense in the West until the invasion. They continued to send forces to other theaters. When this was brought to Hitler's attention in the form of complaints, he would invariably brush them aside or blame others.

The first of many deviations from the directive came at the time of the Anzio landing on January 22, 1944. Warlimont writes that Hitler said, "If we succeed in dealing with this business down there [Anzio] there will be no further landing anywhere."[21] While Hitler had given priority to the west his actions spoke to a rigid defense in the east, and this resulted in the steady flow of forces in that direction. A total of 43 divisions were shuffled around after the priority was given to the west. It was always tempting and easy to send units sitting idle in France or the Low Countries to the east or to other active fronts clamoring for reinforcements. It is in the context of this disconnect between a partial grand military strategy and the resulting vacillations that we need to look at the situation in the east in the summer of 1944.

The Soviets and the West Orchestrate Their Strategy

While the Germans developed an ineffective military strategy to cope with the situation in 1944, a complete grand military strategy was developed within a month by the leaders of the three great powers confronting Germany. The meeting between Roosevelt, Churchill, and Stalin at Teheran at the end of November and beginning of December set the agenda for

1944. While many subjects of great importance were covered at this conference, the most important for our purpose was their agreement to orchestrate operations against Germany in 1944 and what to do about Finland. Churchill and Roosevelt informed Stalin that they intended to open the long-awaited second front by landing in France in May 1944. In turn, Stalin promised to support this operation by launching a massive strategic offensive of his own (Operation *Bagration*).

No action was contemplated against Finland unless that country refused to withdraw from the war prior to the offensive in Belorussia and accept a list of Soviet conditions for peace. The Western Allies had insisted on a peace offer by the Soviet Union that would guarantee the independence of Finland. The Finnish rejection of the Soviet demands accompanying the peace offer in April 1944 was viewed by Stalin as a fulfillment of this promise.

The Soviets and Finns had basically left each other alone on the Finnish Front since the completion of the Finnish offensives at the end of 1941 and a Soviet counteroffensive in early 1942, but that was about to change. The Finns had resisted all German requests that they cross the Svir River in force, participate in the attack on Leningrad, or make serious attempts to cut the Murmansk railroad. This soon became apparent to the Soviets and it was therefore not in their interest to undertake offensive operations on the Finnish front until the danger to Leningrad was removed and until alternate routes for Western aid had been fully developed.

There were at least two reasons for the Soviet decision on the timing of the offensive against Finland. Stalin was still skeptical about the planned US and British landings in France. Spending some time after that landing attending to Finland would give him a chance to see how that operation developed before beginning Operation *Bagration* in Belorussia. Probably more important was his strong desire to have the Finnish question decided early. He was aware that Finland still enjoyed considerable sympathy in the West and that the US had not declared war on that country. Stalin wanted to settle things with Finland so that its fate rested in the hands of the Soviets alone and did not become part of the wider settlement of issues after the war against Germany ended.

While the above political objectives were overriding, the Soviets also saw some military advantages in now dealing with Finland. First, an attack against Finland would draw German attention away from the planned operation in Belorussia. Second, knocking Finland out of the war would free about 450,000 troops for other missions. Finally, forcing a Finnish withdrawal from the war would isolate and neutralize the German Twentieth Mountain Army in central and northern Finland.

Soviet Offensive Against Finland in 1944

In accordance with Stalin's wishes, the initial Soviet plans for a campaign in Finland were based on an offensive against the Twentieth Mountain Army. Every effort was to be made to trap the Germans and keep them from withdrawing into Norway. It was assumed that the defeat of the German forces in Finland would finally convince the Finns to withdraw from the war.[22]

The Soviets disbanded the Volkhov Front on February 3, 1944, and its commander, General Kiril A. Meretskov (1897–1968), was summoned to Moscow, where Stalin gave him the Karelian Front. Its area of responsibility ran from the Arctic to East Karelia and included seven armies as of September 1944. Stalin tasked him to assess the situation in his new command and the chances that an offensive against the Germans would succeed. Meretskov's conclusions were that the Germans were expecting an attack and were well prepared. It would be a tough mission to defeat the Twentieth Mountain Army. Meretskov's report and the Finnish rejection, on April 19, 1944, of the terms offered them caused the Soviets to reconsider their earlier plan to attack the Germans first. The Finnish forces were considered weaker and it was decided by Stalin that they be dealt the first blow.[23] General Leonid Aleksandrovich Govorov (1897–1955) had command on the Karelian Isthmus and was given two armies—the Twenty-First and Twenty-Third (later also the Fifty-Ninth)—consisting of seven corps. Meretskov was responsible for operations in East Karelia and he also had two armies at his disposal—the Thirty-Second and Seventh.

The massive Soviet offensive began on June 10 using 455,000 troops, 3,800 pieces of artillery, about 1,000 tanks, and 2,200 aircraft. Göran Westerlund calculates that the quantitative advantages enjoyed by the Soviets on the Karelian Isthmus alone were as follows: troops 1:4, armor 1:5, artillery 1:6, and aircraft 1:15.[24] The Russians achieved both strategic and tactical surprise as the Finns had expected to be left alone until the defeat of Germany, when the situation in Finland would be sorted out by the victorious Allies. Mannerheim wrote that "it seems, from a military point of view, strange that the Russians attacked Finland at all" since "there could be no doubt that the Finnish question would find its solution in the defeat of German arms." He apparently neglected the fact that wars are fought for political objectives.

The Soviet objective was rather simple. The Finnish Army was to be destroyed, forcing Finland to capitulate. To achieve this, Stalin demanded the attack to be exceptionally violent and quick. The Soviets expected to defeat the Finnish forces on the isthmus and capture Viipuri, the second largest city in Finland, within 12 days. They would then press on north and west and have the capital of the country in their hands by the middle of July. This would allow forces to be transferred to participate in the offensive against Army Groups North and Center when Operation *Bagration* began (it was scheduled to begin on June 22, 1944).

The full offensive began at 0500 hours on June 10. Preparatory fires by Soviet artillery and aircraft were exceedingly violent. The main effort was directed at the Finnish right flank along the Gulf of Finland. Several writers report that the artillery and air preparation was the heaviest of the war on the Eastern Front up to then, surpassed only by the storm of fire unleashed in the Soviet crossing of the Oder–Neisse line in their final drive on Berlin in 1945. It is reported that the Soviets deployed 200–300 pieces of artillery for each kilometer of front.[25] The eight-mile (13km)-wide front of the 10th Finnish Division, which bore the brunt of the initial attack, was hit by 220,000 artillery shells within a couple of hours.[26] The Soviet offensive stayed on schedule until their forces reached the area to the northwest of Viipuri.[27] Here, Finnish forces brought in from other areas of the country managed to stop the Soviets.

As soon as the magnitude of the Soviet summer offensive became evident, the Finnish military leadership realized that they could avert catastrophe only with help from Germany. The only other alternative was to seek peace with the Soviet Union. Both avenues were tried—simultaneously. The two avenues were actually linked since the Finns had concluded that the only way they could get acceptable terms from the Soviets would be by stabilizing their fronts. In their desperate situation, the Finns were prepared to use German aid for purposes that were against the interests of their brothers-in-arms.

The Germans may well have realized what the Finns were up to in view of their many flirtations with the West and the Soviet Union over the past two years, but there was not much they could do about it. Not providing the requested aid would only lead to Finland leaving the war. This would remove some of the main pillars of Hitler's strategic concerns in the north: Finland would no longer be tying down Soviet forces; the Twentieth Mountain Army would be trapped; the Soviet Baltic Fleet could reach the open Baltic; and the nickel shipments would cease. This explains Hitler's generosity in giving assistance despite Germany's own precarious situation.

Hitler lifted the military equipment embargo on June 13 and began massive deliveries of anti-tank weapons. The Finnish request stated that the last defensive line could be held only if these requests were approved and delivery expedited. Besides weapons, ammunition, and supplies, the Germans sent the 122nd Infantry Division from Army Group North, and the 303rd Assault Gun Brigade. They also agreed to make available Luftwaffe assets—Detachment "Kuhlmey," named after its commander, Colonel Kurt Kuhlmey (1913–93), a famous Stuka pilot who later became a major general in the West German Air Force. The detachment consisted of one fighter group and a group and squadron of Stuka ground-support aircraft. These 70 aircraft came from the First and Fifth Air Fleets. This was a very large commitment in view of the fact that the Sixth Air Fleet supporting Army Group Center had only 40 flyable fighters on June 22, 1944, due to lack of spare parts and aviation fuel.[28] The air support was immediate. The Germans flew 940 sorties in support of the Finnish Army on June 21. This was very substantial aid considering the desperate situation in which the Germans found themselves. The Western Allies had landed in Normandy while the greatest Soviet offensive of the war was launched on June 22. The 122nd Division and the Assault Gun Brigade were sorely needed by Army Group North. It shows that Hitler's actions were still driven by his concern for Finland and the Baltic Sea.

While the Finnish military were seeking German help, the Finnish political leaders were trying to find a way out of the war. An unofficial feeler was delivered to the Soviet ambassador in Stockholm on June 22. The feeler resulted in an answer from Moscow the following day. It demanded that as a pre-condition for receiving a Finnish delegation, the Finnish President and Foreign Minister sign a declaration to the effect that

Finland was ready to surrender.[29] The Finns were not prepared to accept this demand.

German military and economic assistance up to now had been provided without any preconditions, despite German worries that Finland might seek a separate peace. The Germans now decided that the time was ripe for binding Finland irrevocably to Germany. On June 22, as the Finns were telling the Soviets that they were ready to exit the war and asking for conditions, Hitler's Foreign Minister, Joachim von Ribbentrop (1893–1946), arrived in Helsinki. Ribbentrop basically demanded a political alliance between Germany and Finland, in which Finland would firmly obligate itself to continue the war at Germany's side in return for German aid. Ribbentrop was willing to accept a letter signed by President Ryti in lieu of a document ratified by the parliament, which would probably not have passed.[30] The German position was strengthened the following day—June 23—when the Finns received the Soviet answer basically demanding unconditional capitulation. Hitler added pressure by a directive which stated plainly that without a public declaration of Finland's attitude, German assistance to Finland would end.

Finland did not have much choice. Its leaders basically had to accept the Soviet demand for an unconditional surrender or the German demand for a binding alliance. Mannerheim made it clear to the country's political leaders that Finland could not continue the fight without German armament assistance. This was underscored by the news from the fronts where the Soviets were continuing their attacks. In his memoirs Mannerheim makes no secret of the fact that giving his support for the alliance with Germany which resulted from the Ribbentrop visit was not done to "enable the country to continue the war, which had to be regarded as lost, but to stabilize the position and create a basis for peace negotiations."[31]

It may well have been the Finnish intention all along not to submit the issue to a parliamentary vote, since not doing so could afford the Finns a loophole in later abrogating the agreement. This was also the view of Mannerheim, who wrote that such an understanding "would not bind the people of Finland," and that under a future President, "Finland would be free to act as the situation demanded."[32] The letter to Hitler stated that neither President Ryti nor a government appointed by him would make a separate peace with the Soviet Union

There was a price to pay for the new agreement. The United States severed diplomatic relations with Finland on June 30. The breaking of relations, however, did not result in a declaration of war. While Ribbentrop returned to Germany in triumph, he brought with him a Finnish agreement that was unenforceable. Ziemke observes correctly that the high-handed pressure tactics by Ribbentrop ended up obscuring the generosity that the Germans had shown despite their own predicaments. The Finns concluded they had been subjected to blackmail, and it removed some of their own feelings of guilt in what they were about to do.[33]

Finland Withdraws from the War

President Ryti submitted his resignation on July 31. The parliament quickly drafted a new law that would allow Mannerheim to become President without an election. He was viewed by both the politicians and the public as the only person with enough prestige to rally the nation. The stage was now set for a full reversal of Finnish policy. The announcement of an armistice between the USSR and Romania on August 24 also increased the pressure for Finland's withdrawal from the war. Vehviläinen writes that the Finns had received a communication from the Soviet Union via Stockholm that they should act speedily, that the terms would be reasonable, and that it was not the goal of the Soviet Union to terminate Finland's independence.[34]

The decision to sue for peace was made on August 24. The Soviets were also told that Finland had repudiated the Ryti–Ribbentrop Pact, although Germany was not informed until the following day. On August 29 the Soviet Union sent its conditions for accepting a peace delegation. First, Finland had to make an immediate public declaration that it was breaking diplomatic relations with Germany. Second, Finland had to demand publicly that Germany withdraw its troops from Finland by September 15. Those that were not withdrawn by that date were to be disarmed and handed over to the Soviets as prisoners. Finnish troops were also required to withdraw to the 1940 border; Pechenga in the north, with the only Finnish access to the Atlantic, was to be handed over to the Soviets, but reparations were cut in half.

A majority in the parliament voted to accept the terms. A recommendation to sever diplomatic relations with Germany was also approved. The

Finnish Foreign Minister notified Ambassador Blücher that evening that Germany had to remove its troops from Finland by September 15. Having accepted the Soviet demands, the Finns sent an armistice delegation to Moscow. It was also authorized to negotiate a peace settlement. Mannerheim proposed to Stalin that a ceasefire take effect at 0700 hours on September 4. Through a misunderstanding, or possibly to underscore their victory, the Soviets did not cease fire until 24 hours later.[35]

NOTES

1. Harrison E. Salisbury, *The 900 Days: the Siege of Leningrad*, (New York: Avon Books, 1970) p.117.
2. Fritz, *op. cit.*, p.384.
3. Carruthers and Erickson, *op. cit.*, p.189. Salisbury, *op. cit.*, pp.117–18 and note 1; Haupt, *op. cit.*, Appendixes 1–8, pp.364–84; and Fritz, *Ostkrieg*, *op. cit.*, p.382 give slightly different figures.
4. Salisbury, *op. cit.*, p.118 and Fritz, *op. cit.*, pp.382–83.
5. Ziemke, *Stalingrad to Berlin*, pp.250–51.
6. *Ibid*, p.251.
7. Kinzel had seen a rapid rise in rank. In the spring of 1942 he was the officer Colonel Gehlen replaced as Chief of FHO. At that time he was a colonel.
8. Army Group North, Ia, *Kriegstagebuch*, dated January 6, 1944.
9. Fritz, *op. cit.*, p.384.
10. Army Group North, Ia, *Kriegstagebuch*, message to Chief of the Army General Staff (Zeitzler) dated January 20, 1944.
11. Ziemke, *Stalingrad to Berlin*, p.256.
12. Army Group North, Ia, *Kriegstagebuch*, message to General Zeitzler dated January 29, 1942.
13. *Ibid*, Ia, dated January 31, 1942.
14. Some writers have credited Hitler with the development of this doctrine, while others maintain it was the brainchild of General Model.
15. Ziemke, *Stalingrad to Berlin*, citing a message from OKH to Army Group North, dated February 6, 1942.
16. Model's appointment resulted in a situation that tells much about Model's nature and ambition. He had just prepared a study that had resulted in an offer to transfer two divisions to Army Group South. After his new appointment became known he quickly revised the study to offer five divisions immediately and another one to follow later. Model telephoned Army Group North to initiate the transfer immediately. This caused General Zeitzler to intervene and he eventually convinced Hitler to a promise of only one division at some point in the future.

17. Mannerheim, *op. cit.*, p.467.
18. Trevor-Roper, *op. cit.*, pp.218–24. The document is dated November 3, 1943, and is the last consecutively numbered directive. These directives, starting on August 31, 1939, were a means by which the OKW published its decisions on strategy. From now on this headquarters continued to issue instructions, but in the form of orders.
19. Megargee, *op. cit.*, p.209.
20. Warlimont, *op. cit.*, p.403.
21. *Ibid*, p.411.
22. S. M. Shtemenko, *The Last Six Months: Russia's Final Battles with Hitler's Armies in World War II*, translated from the Russian by Guy Daniels (New York: Doubleday & Company, Inc., 1977), p.345.
23. *Ibid*, pp.345-60.
24. Westerlund, Göran. *Finland överlevde. Finlands Krig 1939–1945 i ord och bild.* (Helsingfors: Schildts Förlag, 2007) p. 154.
25. Ziemke, *The German Northern Theater of Operations*, p. 280 and Mannerheim, *op. cit.*, p.476 .
26. Westerlund, *op. cit.*, p.163.
27. For a detailed account of the ferocious battles that were fought in the six-week period following June 10, see Lunde, *Finland's War of Choice*, Chapters 9 and 10.
28. Kurt von Tippelskirch, *Geschichte des Zweiten Weltkriges* (Bonn: Athenaeum, 1956) p.462.
29. Vehviläinen, Olli, *Finland in the Second World War: Between Germany and Russia*, translated by Gerard McAlester (New York: Palgrave Publishers Ltd, 2002) p.139.
30. Blücher, *op. cit.*, p.371.
31. Mannerheim, *op. cit.*, p.482.
32. *Loc. cit.*
33. Ziemke, *The German Northern Theater of Operations*, p. 283.
34. Vehviläinen, *op. cit.*, p.145.
35. Mannerheim, *op. cit.*, pp.497–98.

5

Summer of Disasters

Changes in the Soviet Military

The Soviet military juggernaut had undergone a tremendous change between 1941 and 1944. It had become more mechanized, modern, and better equipped, thanks in large measure to the Lend-Lease program. This enabled the Soviets to avoid encirclements and to employ that tactic against their opponent, who was slowly losing his mobility.

It is difficult to overstate the importance of the Lend-Lease program and the Murmansk convoys in this change of fortune. As far as overall aid going by all routes, Richard Woodman makes the following listing:

> Between March 1941 and December 1945, the United States of America contributed to Russia: 14,795 aircraft; 7,537 tanks; 51,503 jeeps; 35,170 motor bicycles; 8,700 tractors; 375,883 trucks and lorries, 8,218 anti-aircraft guns; 131,633 sub-machine guns; 345,735 tons of explosives; 1,981 locomotives; 11,155 railway wagons and trucks; 540,000 tons of steel rails; in excess of 1 million miles of telephone cable; food shipments to the value of $1,312 million; 2,670,000 tons of petrol; 842,000 tons of chemicals; 3,786,000 tyres; 49,000 tons of leather; and 15 million pairs of boots.[1]

This massive amount of equipment was in addition to the Soviet Union's own considerable production of war materials. For example, in the period covered by Lend-Lease the Soviets are alleged to have produced 90,000 of their own tanks, 29,000 in 1944 alone. The importance of Lend-Lease shipments in relation to home production had, however, begun to fall in 1944 compared to the previous year, except for raw materials.[2] The Soviets were slow to recognize the importance of the Lend-Lease program to their war effort. Nikita Khrushchev (1894–1971) writes that Soviet "historical works were written out of a false sense of pride."[3] He goes on to state, "Just imagine how we would have advanced from Stalingrad to Berlin without them [US vehicles]! Our losses would have been colossal because we would have no maneuverability . . ."[4]

By 1944 the conditions of the armies on the Eastern Front were basically reversed from what they were in 1941. In 1941 the Germans went into Russia with experienced and battle-hardened troops with the best military equipment in the world. They had superior mobility, firepower, and air support. By 1944 the Russians enjoyed these advantages and the Germans had lost their edge. Robert Citino also points out correctly that the improvement in communications since the beginning of the war led to increased centralization of decisions in battle. It allowed higher commanders, especially Hitler, who distrusted his generals, to intervene increasingly in operational matters and to maintain virtually absolute personal control over decisions at the front.[5]

Operation **Bagration***—Build-up and Plans*

While Operation *Bagration* dwarfed all other operations in World War II, it lacked a dramatic and popular focal point like Normandy, Stalingrad, or Leningrad. It was initially relegated to a few paragraphs in the more popular accounts of World War II. However, the near destruction of two German army groups on the Eastern Front was an event too large and important to ignore or minimize, and the literature is now recognizing its crucial significance.

Planning for *Bagration*, also known as the Belorussian Offensive, began in the spring of 1944, and knowledge of the operation was severely limited.[6] It was decided to launch the offensive on June 22. While this had symbolic importance since it marked—to the day—the three-year anniversary of the German invasion (Operation *Barbarossa*), it can be safely assumed that the pragmatic Soviet leader had other reasons for delaying his offensive for almost a month after the planned date for Allied landings in France.

The Soviet armies involved in bloody fighting during the winter and early spring had made spectacular advances, particularly in the south. They had, as we have seen, also driven the Germans away from the immediate area around Leningrad. The armies needed time to reorganize and be supplied before undertaking another major effort. Stalin was also skeptical about the planned American–British landings in France. A delay gave Stalin a chance to see how that operation developed before beginning his own offensive in Belorussia. As previously described, he also used the interim to deal with the Finns.

If the Normandy landings were successful, they might draw off German forces from the East, and the delay would thus benefit the Soviets. While the German Army in 1944 was only a shadow of that which existed in 1940–41 in terms of troop quality and leadership, it was still a potent force. If the landings in France ended in a fiasco, Stalin had to assume that the Germans would move the bulk of their 50 infantry and 10 armored divisions then in France and the Low Countries to the Eastern Front. A resurgent Wehrmacht with a major victory under its belt would be tough to deal with. The prospect of possibly having to cope alone with Germany for another year or two must have worried Stalin and his military leaders. They were acutely aware of the fact that the distance from the rail-junction city of Orsha—still in German hands—to Moscow was only roughly 250 miles (400km) while their own frontlines were 750 miles (1,200km) from Berlin.

Such German redeployment—from the West to the East—would also alter the space/force ratio, an element that increasingly plagued the Germans. As the German armies in the East were bled white from 1941 to 1944, the space/force ratio increasingly swung to the advantage of the Soviets with their seemingly endless manpower pool. That ratio could only change by a significant increase in German force levels or a withdrawal to shorter defensive lines. As the Germans were forced back to Poland and towards the German border, therefore, the Soviet planners were no doubt aware that the space/force ratio could change to the advantage of the Germans.[7]

In the spring of 1944 the Soviets had 12 fronts facing the Germans and their allies along a 2,000-mile (3,200km) front. The strength of the Soviet Army on the Eastern Front in the spring of 1944 stood at 6,077,000. The Germans had four Army Groups and an independent army (from north to south these were the Twentieth Mountain Army, Army Group North, Army Group Center, Army Group North Ukraine, and Army Group South Ukraine) with a total strength of 2,250,000 facing the Soviet fronts.

Army Group Center was commanded by Field Marshal Ernst Busch, not a particularly capable commander. His appointment, like many others in this period, was due primarily to his unquestioned loyalty and obedience to Hitler. His forces occupied a huge bulge extending eastward north of the Pripet Marshes close to the headwaters of the Dvina and Dnieper Rivers east of Vitebsk—the historic Russian invasion gate. This salient developed as a result of the misfortunes of the neighboring German army groups, particularly the disastrous events that occurred in the southern sector in the wake of Stalingrad, Kursk, and the withdrawal from the Caucasus. The Soviets had advanced to the border of Romania and past Kovel near the Polish border in northwestern Ukraine, while Army Group North had been driven away from Leningrad to the Panther Line.

While numerically the strongest army group on the Eastern Front—slightly over 700,000 troops in 51 divisions, including reserves and rear security divisions[8]—Army Group Center held the longest front by far: about 500 miles (800km). It was, therefore, a thinly held line that its four armies occupied—Second, Ninth, Fourth, and Third Panzer. By comparison, Army Group North Ukraine occupied a 224-mile (360km) front with 45 divisions (including ten Hungarian). The space/force ratio favoring the Soviets was therefore much greater in Army Group Center's area.

The air-support resources were also out of balance between Army Group Center and Army Group North Ukraine. The Sixth Air Fleet which supported Army Group Center had 775 aircraft, but 370 of these were long-range bombers of very limited value in support of defensive operations. The Fourth Air Fleet supporting Army Group North Ukraine had a total of 845 aircraft, of which 670 were fighters or ground-support aircraft.[9] This air situation was the "paper" strength and it was actually much worse than depicted by these raw numbers. According to the Fourth Army commander, General Kurt von Tippelskirch, there were only 40 German fighter aircraft flyable in the Sixth Air Fleet on June 22 because spare parts and gasoline to keep them in the air were lacking.[10]

Stavka (Soviet High Command) had not settled on striking at Army Group Center without considering other options.[11] One option studied was a strike into the Balkans, a continuation of the successful drive earlier in the year that brought the Soviets into northeast Romania. This option was rejected because it would leave much of western Russia in German hands and the attacking forces would be dangerously exposed on their northern flank. A second option called for a northwest strike from northern Ukraine across Poland to the Baltic Sea. This was promising as it could result in trapping both Army Group Center and Army Group North. It was ultimately rejected, however, since it was a long and perilous drive with dangerously exposed flanks, and viewed as beyond the Soviet Army's logistic and maneuver capabilities. In April 1944 Stavka settled on the strategic objective of destroying Army Group Center. Success would bring the Soviets to the border of Poland and East Prussia and in an ideal position for future operations. Pressure would be maintained on other fronts.

The Eastern Intelligence Branch of the OKH made its own examination of Soviet options in early May. One was almost identical to the second option considered by the Soviets—a drive from Kovel in a north-northwest direction. The OKH rejected it for much the same reasons as the Soviets. The second option given serious consideration by OKH involved a Soviet offensive through Romania and Hungary into the Balkans. While the Soviet and German appraisals were similar, they differed in their all-important conclusion. The Germans concluded that the offensive would be launched against Army Group North Ukraine, commanded by Model. The German intelligence estimate also concluded that Army Group Center's area north of the Pripet Marshes would remain quiet.

Having settled on a strategic objective, the Soviets resorted to a vast strategic and tactical deception program. First, Stavka ordered the entire Red Army to assume a defensive posture on April 19. The Soviet main deception effort was to try to make the Germans believe that the resumption of the strategic offensive would come in July against the southwestern part of the front, with the main effort against Army Group North Ukraine. The Soviets apparently knew that the Germans expected the strategic offensive to take place in the Ukraine, not Belorussia, and it therefore became the task of the deception effort to reinforce existing enemy beliefs.[12]

The Soviets had to achieve surprise while undertaking a massive build-up of forces.[13] They assembled 1,200,000 frontline troops to throw against Army Group Center. These were backed up by another 1,200,000 troops farther to the rear under Stavka control, to be used as an exploitation force after the offensive began to roll. The build-up of forces opposite Army Group Center began in early May and gathered steam as time passed. In just the first three weeks of June, 75,000 railroad carloads of troops and supplies were brought into the area opposite the German army group. The four fronts opposite Army Group Center received an increase in personnel of 60 percent during May and June. The number of tanks and assault guns was tripled and the number of indirect-fire weapons was nearly doubled. Air strength was also increased.

In the most massive build-up of the war, the Soviets assembled some 4,000 tanks, 24,400 indirect-fire weapons, and 5,300 aircraft, giving them armor, artillery, and air superiorities of 10:1 at the assault points.[14] The Soviet air force had full air superiority, bordering on dominance, and kept German reconnaissance aircraft at a distance except in areas they wanted the Germans to observe.

It was not until the end of May that the Germans began to detect an increase in Soviet force levels in the Army Group Center sector, and the number of reports increased rapidly in June. These increasing signs of trouble, however, received only cursory interest at Army Group Center, while OKH viewed the build-up as a Soviet deception. Busch failed to react except for an increased concern for the curve in the front of General Walter Weiss' (1890–1967) Second Army on his right flank. The Germans had already played directly into Soviet hands in May when much of Army Group Center's strength was given to Model's Army Group North Ukraine.

Zeitzler, OKH's Chief of Staff, had proposed the formation of a reserve army, drawing on units from Army Group Center and Army Group North. He recommended using the proposed reserve army, with LVI Panzer Corps as its nucleus, to launch a spoiling offensive. Model saw in this proposal a chance to conduct an active defense and also acquire substantial additional forces for his army group. Zeitzler, who had replaced Halder as Army Chief of Staff in September 1942, was probably chosen by Hitler because he was far more pliable than Halder. This deficiency would soon become glaringly apparent.

Model proposed to Hitler that he be assigned LVI Panzer Corps for offensive operations, knowing that this would sit well with the Führer. Thus, LVI Panzer Corps was transferred to Army Group North Ukraine on May 20. Busch did not protest Hitler's order despite the fact that he had heavily reinforced the Panzer corps. The movement of the boundary resulted in a 28-mile (45km) reduction in Army Group Center's sector, but this miniscule reduction came at a high price. Army Group Center lost 15 percent of its divisions, 23 percent of its assault guns, and a staggering 50 and 88 percent, respectively, of its artillery and tank strength.[15]

Zeitzler convened a high-level meeting on June 14, 1944, at OKH headquarters at Rastenburg in East Prussia. The participants were to receive Hitler's and OKH's assessment (one and the same) of the situation and what to expect during the summer of 1944. Zeitzler was somewhat apologetic for having brought the Chiefs of Staff of Army Group Center and its armies to the meeting, since the subject would not be of particular concern to Army Group Center![16] Zeitzler announced that OKH had concluded that the Soviets would continue their offensive against the southern army groups, with Army Group North Ukraine absorbing the brunt of the Soviet offensive. This conclusion must rank as one of the most calamitous misreadings of enemy intentions in World War II. (It is surprising that it is not covered in John Keegan's excellent book *Intelligence in War*.[17])

The final Soviet operational directive was provided to the front commanders on May 31. The offensive was to be launched on a 310-mile (500km)-wide front from just south of Polotsk, on the boundary between Army Group Center and Army Group North, to Rogatchev, near the boundary between the Fourth and Ninth Armies. Stalin had assigned the code-name *Bagration* to the operation.[18] Marshals Georgi K. Zhukov (1896–1974) and Polkovnik Vasilevsky (1895–1997) were each responsible for operational planning, coordination, and direction of two fronts. Zhukov was assigned the two southern fronts, Second and First Belorussian, while Vasilevsky had the two northern fronts, First Baltic and Third Belorussian. Our focus will be primarily on the two northern fronts as their actions impacted most on the German forces in the Baltic.

Unlike many operational plans, the Soviet plan worked so well that it is not necessary to discuss it in detail as it unfolded as planned. The initial tasks of the four fronts were to isolate and reduce four communications centers in the rear of the German lines: Vitebsk, Orsha, Mogilev, and Bobruysk. The operations against Vitebsk were primarily the responsibility of the First Baltic Front under General Ivan K. Bagramyan (1897–1982). The Third Belorussian Front, under General Polkovnik Chernyakovsky, would assist the First Baltic Front by enveloping Vitebsk from the south with the Fifth and Thirty-Ninth Armies before heading toward Senno. Another assault group from the Third Belorussian Front, consisting of the Eleventh Guards and Thirty-First Armies, would attack toward Orsha. Cavalry-Mechanized Group Oslikovsky would undertake a rapid advance west past Senno.[19]

The second phase of the Soviet operation involved deep armor-led drives against Minsk from both the northeast and southeast designed to isolate the Fourth German Army. Strong forces (from Third Belorussian Front) would bypass Minsk on the north and head for Molodechno, while equally strong forces (from First Belorussian Front) would head for Baranovichi southwest of Minsk. These drives would not only isolate Fourth Army but would block the escape routes from Minsk, which were restricted by vast areas of forests and swamps.

On the German side, the far left flank was held by General Georg-Hans Reinhardt's (1887–1963) Third Panzer Army from both sides of Vitebsk to near Polotsk, where it tied into General Christian Hansen's (1885–1972) Sixteenth Army of Army Group North. On its right, Third Panzer tied into Fourth Army north of Orsha. Fourth Army, which held a 25-mile (40km)-deep and 84-mile (135km)-wide bridgehead east of the Dnieper River, tied into Ninth Army north of Rogatchev. Ninth Army held a front that curved southwestward along the Prut and Dnieper Rivers to the area south of Zhlobin, where it bent westward over the Beresina River to the lower Pitch and Pripet. Second Army held the longest sector along the Pripet River to where it tied into the left flank of Army Group North Ukraine north of Kovel.

The Attacks

An avalanche of Soviet forces struck Army Group Center on the morning of June 22, 1944, although the Soviets claim it started a day later.[20] It may be, as Chris Bellamy suggests, that some of the attacks began on June 22, but that the full fury was not unleashed until the 23rd.[21] The estimated

143,000 partisans in Belorussia had begun attacks against Army Group Center's lines of communications on June 20, but paused when the Soviets launched diversionary attacks in the south. The reinforcements that the Germans sent south were allowed to proceed unmolested. When they tried to return after the main blow fell on Army Group Center, the partisans went into action and virtually paralyzed traffic in the German rear area.[22]

The main Soviet attacks proceeded according to plans. The First Baltic and Third Belorussian Fronts quickly pierced the pulverized German frontlines on both sides of the city of Vitebsk and proceeded with its envelopment. Third Panzer Army, on the left flank of Army Group Center, was caught completely by surprise by the Soviet Sixth Guards Army, and its front was torn open. In this phase of the operation the Soviets employed their vast air superiority primarily against German artillery, which was established in open positions near the front so that the guns could be used in a direct-fire role. This positioning left the German guns very vulnerable to air attack.

On the second day of the operation, the Soviets again overwhelmed Third Panzer Army north of Vitebsk and proceeded to encircle the city from the north, trapping five German divisions. Hitler's (and Busch's) fixation on a rigid defense and holding on to areas designated as "fortified places" began playing havoc with any efforts by the armies to mount a coherent defense. The German defenders were not allowed to order the construction of lines in the rear, or even discuss withdrawal preparation plans in case of an enemy breakthrough.[23]

Starting in 1943, Hitler increasingly resorted to ordering troops to hold positions in hopeless situations, and this habit continued on an accelerated pace until the last days of the war. These orders became virtual death sentences for German units.[24] Liddell Hart writes the following about Hitler's rigid defense mindset: "Each time the Germans were tied to the defence of a fixed point by Hitler's orders, an eventual collapse was the costly penalty. The weaker the defending side, the more essential it becomes to adopt mobile defence. For otherwise the stronger side can make space its ally and gain a decisive advantage through outflanking manoeuvre."[25]

Liddell Hart's statement above assumes that the Germans had the ability to maneuver. As stated at the beginning of this chapter, the German Army had lost much of its earlier mobility, and the Luftwaffe had completely lost its ability to effectively contest Soviet air superiority. We have also seen that Rommel had concluded in April 1944 that mobile defense was no longer an option because of Allied air superiority. Trying to withdraw under these circumstances invited disaster unless it had been well preplanned. This situation must be weighed against the fact that the Luftwaffe no longer had the capability to supply encircled forces, and there were no forces available to break encirclements. This quandary for the Germans intensified as the war went on.

The Third and Second Belorussian Fronts were tearing through the Fourth Army's frontlines and heading for Orsha and Mogilev. A message from Busch reported that he saw no way of restoring the front of Third Panzer Army without giving up Vitebsk or receiving reinforcements, but Hitler was not willing to give up that city, and OKH was not willing to bring units north from Army Group North Ukraine because that headquarters still expected the main attack to fall there. Busch himself resisted taking units from Weiss' Second Army for the same reason. Decision-making had become paralyzed at the highest levels. There was great uncertainty and fear of making timely decisions, when bold and rapid decision-making was exactly what was needed. Hitler's vacillating attitude and frequent change in decisions seriously undermined efforts at the front and caused many tragedies and the loss of untold numbers of soldiers.

On June 24, Fourth Army's left flank corps was beginning to disintegrate under powerful attacks, and the First Belorussian Front penetrated the Ninth Army's lines near its northern boundary. The Soviets reached Senno in the Third Panzer Army sector, where they turned south behind Fourth Army's left flank. Hitler finally gave permission to withdraw four of the five divisions trapped at Vitebsk, but it was too late. Tippelskirch, commander of Fourth Army, requested permission to abandon the bridgehead east of the Dnieper River, but Busch refused. The following day Tippelskirch took matters into his own hands and ordered the withdrawal. On June 25, Ninth Army, in danger of having its main force trapped between the Dnieper and Beresina Rivers, also requested permission to withdraw before it was destroyed. Busch again refused.

By the morning of June 26, Army Group Center appeared to be falling apart. It had committed all its reserves without being able to stop the Soviet advances. Vitebsk was encircled and the forces there were lost. Third Panzer

Army was driven back on the Dvina and Ulla Rivers, 50 miles (80km) west of Vitebsk. The right flank corps of Third Panzer Army—badly mauled remnants of five divisions—was in full retreat west and south of Senno and had lost contact with the rest of the army. In Ninth Army's sector, the Soviet armies were pushing toward Bobruysk and fanned out on both sides of that city. The lead Soviet elements in the south were only 3 miles (5km) from the city on June 26. Repeated requests by Ninth Army to be allowed to withdraw to Bobruysk and the Beresina River were denied until the morning of June 27. But before the army could react to this approval and thereby establish contact with the Fourth Army, new orders arrived forbidding any withdrawal.

OKH and Busch changed their minds again in the afternoon. General Hans Jordan (1892–1975), commander of Ninth Army, was given permission for a breakout to the north, but the permission was accompanied by an order to hold Bobruysk. The speed of events had by now overtaken the vacillating attitude of the army group and OKH. Bobruysk was encircled by 10 Soviet divisions, trapping two German corps of about 70,000 men in or east of the city. Panic ensued among the thousands of leaderless German troops in Bobruysk, as they milled around in confusion.[26] Ninth Army headquarters, located outside the pocket, transferred its one remaining operational corps to the Fourth Army and withdrew to Marina Gorka, where it tried to hold open an avenue of escape for the Fourth Army using parts of the 12th Panzer Division. The Ninth was the first German army to be ground to pieces in the Soviet offensive.

Things were not going much better for the other armies. General Konstantin Rokossovsky's (1896–1968) First Belorussian Front was also driving toward Minsk and the city of Slutsk to its south. The Second Belorussian Front forced a crossing of the Dnieper north of Mogilev on June 26, and Tippelskirch was forced to consider a withdrawal of his army by a single road through the swamps and forests between the Prut and Beresina Rivers. Tippelskirch sent a blunt message to Busch on June 27, which basically asked if the army group wanted Fourth Army to fight its way west or be encircled. Tippelskirch was told that if Fourth Army had to fall back, it was to establish a line on the Prut River, but the "fortified places" of Mogilev and Orsha were to be held at all costs. By the time he received this message, the Soviets were already in Orsha. Tippelskirch ordered a withdrawal when the Soviets began enveloping his southern flank.

Fourth Army headquarters moved from Belynichi to Beresino on June 28 over the same road the army would have to use—a road clogged by burning vehicles and dead horses from Soviet air strikes. It took nine hours to cover the 30-mile (50km) distance. When Tippelskirch reached Beresino, he found a message from Busch ordering him to get behind the Beresina River quickly. An order from OKH (Hitler) gave permission to withdraw from Mogilev—that place had not been heard from since the previous day and had already fallen to the Soviets.[27] In his report to Zeitzler on June 28, Busch noted that Jordan's Ninth Army had collapsed, the Fourth was retreating, and that Third Panzer had only one corps left of its original three. Despite this disastrous situation, Busch promised to hold a line in the vicinity of Beresino, notwithstanding the fact that the remnants of Third Panzer and Ninth Armies were already west of that line.

It was finally dawning on OKH that the offensive against Army Group Center was on a greater scale than expected, with Minsk as a probable objective, but still they clung to the belief that another, more powerful offensive would strike Army Group North Ukraine.[28] OKH proposed to pull Army Group North back to a line running from Dvisk to Riga in order to shorten the front and gain divisions to use in the Army Group Center area. Hitler ignored the OKH proposal and instead relieved Busch and appointed Model to command both Army Group Center and Army Group North Ukraine. In view of the disastrous situation, this was not a bad arrangement. Model was held in high esteem, and with him in command of both army groups it would be easier to shift forces between them. However, it did nothing to correct the problems in space/force ratio, which the OKH proposal to withdraw Army Group North would have done.

Soviet aircraft knocked out the only bridge across the Beresina River on June 29, while the First and Third Belorussian Fronts were outflanking what was left of the German Fourth Army from north and south. Soviet tanks and artillery came within range of the bridge-site over the Beresina on June 30. Model was desperately trying to get some divisions from Army Group North, which could only spare these forces by pulling back its right flank. Hitler simply ignored Model's request. Hitler still appears to have been motivated by his desire to keep Finland in the war. Both ground and air reinforcements were on their way to that country. He was also unwilling to give up the shale oil fields in Latvia.

The tanks and motorized units from Rokossovsky's First Belorussian Front drove past Slutsk and Borisov toward Baranovichi and Molodechno. This caused Jordan's Ninth Army headquarters to leave Marina Gorka and head for Stolbtsy, half-way between Baranovichi and Minsk. It hoped to hold a crossing over the Neman River, the last escape route from Minsk where a panicky situation already existed. The Fifth Guards Tank Army was getting perilously close in the north. Trying to organize a force of stragglers to defend the town proved impossible. General Jordan directed his only remaining Panzer division against Stolbtsy from Marina Gorka, but the Soviets had already captured the town.

With the exception of a rearguard, Tippelskirch's Fourth Army was across the Beresina River while his headquarters hurried to Molodechno to try to hold the railroad line running west from that town. Troops from the First and Third Belorussian Fronts took Minsk on July 3. Ninth Army tried unsuccessfully to open the bridge at Stolbtsy while the Soviets drove toward Baranovichi the following day. After that, the only German troops to escape were individuals and small groups that made their way through the dense Nalibocka Forest. Ninth Army managed to hold open the pocket around Minsk long enough for perhaps 10,000–15,000 of its troops to escape. Jordan's headquarters had ceased to function by the time it reached Baranovichi, and could no longer exercise control of the divisions arriving from Second Army. The headquarters was moved to the rear to reorganize and re-equip.

After 12 days of combat, Army Group Center was utterly shattered. Fourth Army's strength at the beginning of the operation was 165,000 men. It had lost 130,000 of these by the time Minsk fell. Third Panzer Army lost 10 divisions. In all, Army Group Center lost 25 divisions.[29] Past experience led the Germans to believe that the Soviets would pause to re-supply and re-organize; the Soviets had advanced 130 miles (210km) since the start of the offensive and this was further than they had in one leap on previous occasions. Model hoped to establish a defensive line between the cities of Baranovichi and Molodechno. To do so, he needed additional forces to close two gaps on his left flank. A 50-mile (80km) wide gap had developed between the right flank of Sixteenth Army of

Army Group North at Polotsk and the left flank of Third Panzer Army. A gap of similar size had opened between the troops of Fourth Army trying to establish a line at Molodechno and the right flank of Third Panzer. There was an acute danger that the Soviets could encircle and destroy what was left of Third Panzer Army. This would open the road to Riga and East Prussia, and pin Army Group North against the Baltic.

Lindemann, commander of Army Group North, had no troops to spare to help Model seal the gaps as long as he was forced to hold Polotsk. On July 3, Lindemann was given permission to withdraw a short distance from Polotsk and was ordered to attack southwestward to establish contact with Army Group Center. Lindemann replied that with the few troops made available by the short withdrawal he could still not attack. Hitler promptly relieved Lindemann and appointed General Johannes Friessner (1892–1971) to take command. General Friessner had commanded what was known as the Narva Detachment in Army Group North. Friessner was able to stretch his front westward and narrow the gap between Army Group North and Army Group Center to about 19 miles (30km). He intended to close this gap with a southward attack by three divisions.

The pause in the Soviet offensive that the Germans had expected did not occur. Stavka ordered the offensive to continue without cessation on a broad front. The First Baltic Front was ordered to advance toward Dvinsk; the Third Belorussian Front was aimed at Molodechno and the Neman River; the First Belorussian Front advanced on Baranovichi and then on to the city of Brest; and the Second Belorussian Front remained behind in the Minsk area to conduct mopping-up operations.

The rapid Soviet advance on a wide front nullified Model's plans to establish a defensive line from Mododechno to Baranovichi. On July 6 the Third Belorussian Front had penetrated the narrows south and east of Molodechno, and the road to Vilnius was wide open. Weiss' Second Army was able to hold Baranovichi for only a couple of days before it fell to the Soviets on July 8.

General Friessner's attack from the north ran into the Fourth Shock and Sixth Guards Armies from the First Baltic Front advancing towards Dvinsk. Friessner now proposed that Sixteenth Army withdraw to the Lithuania position, from Kraslava to Ostrov. Hitler relented, but his solution—a withdrawal halfway to the Lithuania position–-only made things worse.

With no prospects of stopping the Soviets anywhere, Model requested a meeting with Hitler on July 9. Hitler was adamant about not withdrawing Army Group North. Instead, he promised immediately to make available to Model a Panzer division from Germany and two divisions from Army Group North, followed by two divisions later. With these reinforcements, Third Panzer Army was to attack northward to close the gap between it and Army Group North. Nothing came of this plan. Friessner informed Hitler on July 12 that he intended to attack south toward Third Panzer Army, but emphasized that the effort would be useless since the First Baltic Front under General Bagramyan would continue its westward drive. He pointed out that his own front was unstable, and he urged a withdrawal of Army Group North to a line running from Riga to Kaunas. If his proposal was not approved, Friessner asked to be relieved of his command. Hitler rejected Friessner's proposal and countered with a plan to assemble five Panzer divisions behind Kaunas to drive north to close the gap between the two army groups.

The following day, Model informed OKH that he would try to stop the Russians along a line from Kaunas along the Neman River to Brest, but to do so he needed the Panzer divisions that Hitler had planned for the northward drive. Even counting the new units arriving, he would only have 16 divisions near full strength to counter 160 Soviet divisions and brigades. At a conference at Rastenburg on July 14, Hitler agreed to let Model have the divisions to first stop the Soviet offensive and then use them offensively to plug the gap between the two army groups. The logical solution of withdrawing Army Group North was again rejected.

The Germans managed to restore some semblance of order in the Army Group Center area after the middle of July. The Fourth Army and Third Panzer Army were able to establish a line from Ukmerge through Kaunas and along the Neman River south of Grondo, while the Second Army continued a left flank pivot as it withdrew toward Bialystok, as ordered by Hitler earlier. Ninth Army was still in the rear reorganizing and preparing defensive works to protect East Prussia. The Germans were helped immeasurably by the fact that the Soviets, after advancing more than 200 miles (320km), were outrunning their supplies. Railroads, bridges, and roads had to be rebuilt or repaired in the area devastated by the offensive before another sustained drive could be undertaken.

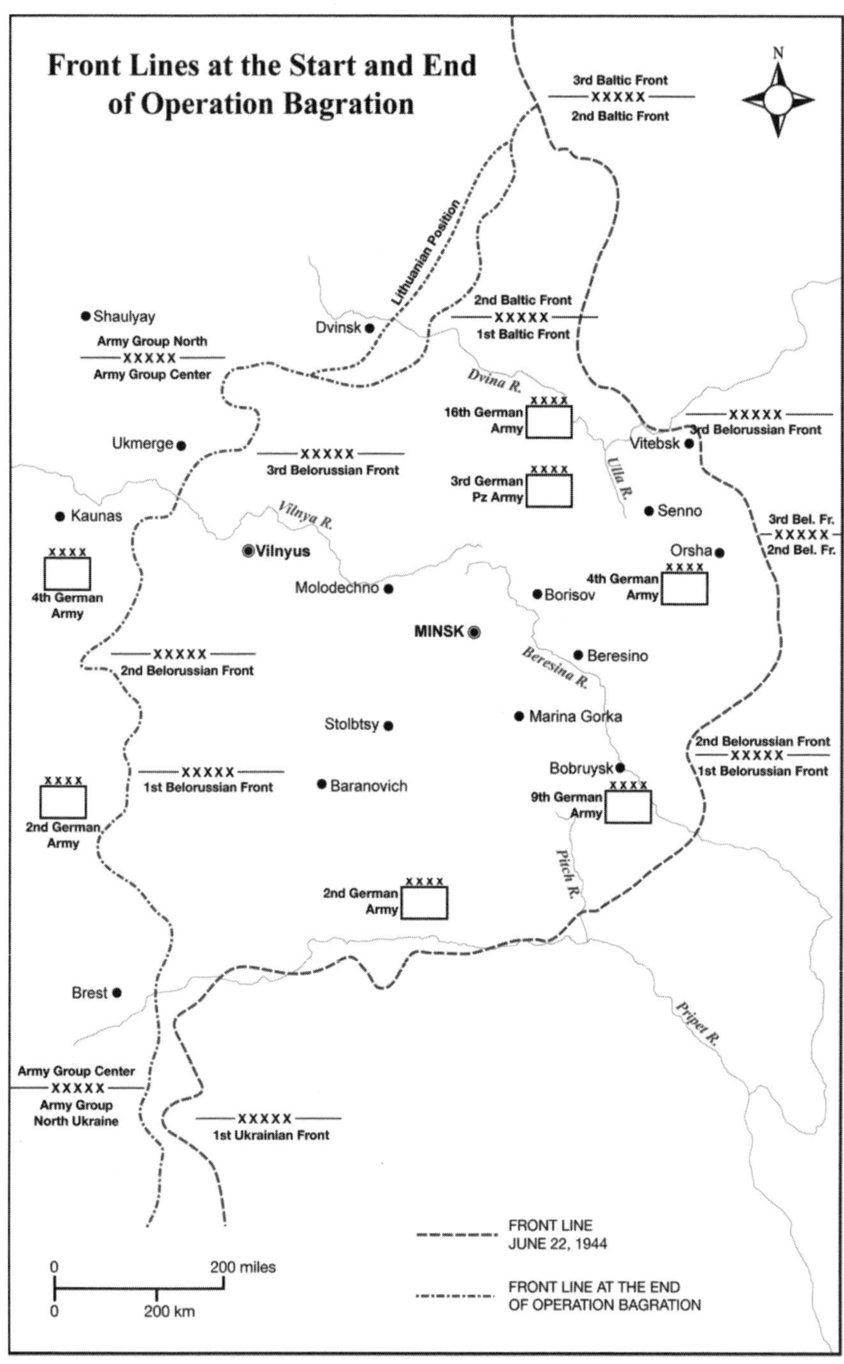

Front Lines at the Start and End of Operation Bagration
N
3rd Baltic Front
XXXXX
2nd Baltic Front
Lithuanian Position
2nd Baltic Front
XXXXX
1st Baltic Front
Shaulyay
Army Group North
XXXXX
Army Group Center
Dvinsk
Dvina R.
XXXX
16th German Army
XXXXX
3rd Belorussian Front
Vitebsk
Ukmerge
XXXXX
3rd Belorussian Front
XXXX
3rd German Pz Army
Ulla R.
Senno
Kaunas
Vilnya R.
3rd Bel. Fr.
XXXXX
2nd Bel. Fr.
XXXX
4th German Army
Vilnyus
Orsha
Molodechno
XXXX
4th German Army
Borisov
MINSK
Beresino
Beresina R.
XXXXX
2nd Belorussian Front
Stolbtsy
Marina Gorka
2nd Belorussian Front
XXXXX
1st Belorussian Front
Bobruysk
XXXX
XXXXX
1st Belorussian Front
Baranovich
XXXX
9th German Army
2nd German Army
Pitch R.
XXXX
2nd German Army
Brest
Pripet R.
Army Group Center
XXXXX
Army Group North Ukraine
XXXXX
1st Ukrainian Front
FRONT LINE JUNE 22, 1944
FRONT LINE AT THE END OF OPERATION BAGRATION
0
200 miles
0
200 km

The famous unsuccessful attempt on Hitler's life was made at Rastenburg on July 20 by an anti-Hitler conspiracy within the army. The conspiracy was quickly shattered and resulted in a number of new officers being placed in key posts, mostly on the Western Front. The only changes that affected the Eastern Front were not a result of the assassination attempt. On July 21, General Heinz Guderian was appointed successor to Zeitzler, who had reported sick three days earlier.

Army Group Center radio monitors intercepted a Soviet order to their tank units north of Vilnius. The messages instructed the Soviet units to attack in the gap between Army Groups Center and North. This raised the distinct possibility of another great disaster and initiated the next phase of the Soviet offensive—pressure against the flanks as the advance in the center began to have supply problems. Model told OKH that he could not assemble an attack force in time to stop the Soviet drive, and that Army Group North had to manage on its own.

The conditions in Army Group North were dire. It was trying to get into the Lithuanian positions, but these were already in jeopardy. Friessner had no reserves left and warned that the front was about to collapse. This dangerous situation resulted in a meeting on July 18 between Hitler, Göring, Zeitzler, Model, and Friessner. The only forces Hitler had to offer were two assault gun brigades intended for Finland. Here was one of those rare occasions when Göring spoke up against Hitler's plans. He observed that the only way to generate sufficient forces and keep Army Group North from being encircled was to withdraw behind the Dvina River and establish a line between Riga and Kaunas. Hitler agreed that this was the simplest solution, but noted that this would cost Germany the Latvian oil, Swedish iron ore, and Finnish nickel.[30] As it turned out, the Latvian oil and Finnish nickel supplies would be lost within a month. Hitler insisted that Army Group North stay in place by every possible means. Zeitzler thereupon offered his resignation. When this offer was refused, he reported sick.

The Soviet pressures against the northern flank of Army Group Center took the form of a drive into the gap between that army group and Army Group North, with Riga as the objective. Bagramyan's First Baltic Front was given two fresh armies: Second Guards and the Fifty-First. These had just arrived from the Crimea.

In the north, Third Panzer Army was hard pressed around Kaunas. Between July 18 and 21, the First Baltic Front had created several bridgeheads across the Neman River while other forces were pushing the left flank of Third Panzer Army south. The division on the left flank began to disintegrate under continual attacks by six divisions of Second Guards Army. A 47-mile (75km) gap had developed on the left flank of Third Panzer Army, and Second Guards Army poured through it on July 22, its spearheads reaching a point 43 miles (70km) behind the Germans by evening. Third Panzer Army was virtually ineffective, its frontline strength having fallen to 13,850 men.[31]

General Hansen's Sixteenth Army, on the right flank of Army Group North, had withdrawn to the Lithuania position on July 19, but it could not hold, so Friessner ordered a further 9-mile (15km) withdrawal on July 22. Friessner warned OKH that further withdrawals would be necessary to save the army group from destruction. Hitler's solution was to move General Ferdinand Schörner, commander of Army Group South Ukraine, to take over the command of Army Group North while Friessner assumed command of Army Group South Ukraine.

Bagramyan's motorized columns, which had passed Third Panzer Army's left flank, turned north and, in a 50-mile (80km) night dash, captured Jelgava and cut the last rail link to Army Group North. Third Panzer Army, itself in trouble, did not have adequate forces to halt the Soviet advance. Nine rifle divisions and two Guards tank corps fell on the right flank of Third Panzer Army south of Kaunas on July 29. On the same day, Rokossovsky's tanks drove north past Warsaw.

Third Panzer Army's flank collapsed on July 30 and the Soviets advanced to Mariampol, only 19 miles (30km) from the East Prussian border. General Georg-Hans Reinhardt, commander of the Third Panzer Army, sought permission to withdraw from Kaunas where two of his divisions were being encircled and pulverized. Model said he could not grant that permission and it was useless asking OKH. Taking matters into his own hands, Reinhardt withdrew his troops during the night behind the Nevayazha River, 9 miles (15km) to the west.

Rokossovsky's armored columns easily penetrated the thin screening line established by Ninth Army, and reached the east bank of the Vistula at Deblin and Pulawy. Motorized Soviet columns were pouring west from

Panevezhis behind Third Panzer Army. On July 31, Soviet mechanized forces reached the Gulf of Riga, trapping Army Group North.

There were finally signs that the Soviet offensive was running out of steam. They did not try to expand on their breakthrough to the Baltic Sea, the tanks in the Warsaw area ground to a halt—apparently short of fuel—and Ivan Chernyakovsky's (1906–45) Third Belorussian Front did not move against East Prussia through the gap between Mariampol and Kaunas, although it captured Vilkavishkis, 8 miles (13km) from the border. The Soviets, having advanced in some places more than 145 miles (235km) since the capture of Minsk, and about 350 miles (570km) in all, had finally outrun their supplies. Logistics had dammed the flood.

Model took advantage of the Soviet slow-down. He managed to seal the Soviet bridgeheads across the Vistula and establish a continuous front from around Shaulyay to the Vistula near Pulawy. But the 410-mile (665km) wide front was thinly manned—just 39 German divisions and brigades faced one-third of the Soviet strength on the Eastern Front.

Model sent Hitler a somewhat optimistic report on August 3. After completing a number of containment operations and counterattacks with newly arrived units by August 15, he would assemble sufficient forces to attack and re-establish contact with Army Group North. The most urgent issue on the Eastern Front in early August was to keep Army Group North from collapsing. Schörner told Hitler on August 6 that his army group would hold until contact with Army Group Center was restored, provided that happened soon since his exhausted troops were under relentless pressure. Schörner told Guderian that if the relief did not come quickly, he would pull back to a line from Riga to Kaunas, if still possible.

August 16 was an eventful day. The Third Belorussian Front threw three armies against the right flank of Third Panzer Army just as the relief attack from Shaulyay toward Army Group North with two under-strength Panzer corps began. Then Model was ordered to take over as commander on the Western Front. General Reinhardt, as senior army commander, took over the army group on August 15 and his former position as commander of the Third Panzer Army was given to General Erhard Raus (1889–1956). As August ended, it was evident in the zones of Army Groups North, Center, and North Ukraine that the Soviet armies had taken up a defensive posture, thereby bringing the offensive to a close. The Soviets had a large bridgehead on the Vistula at Baranow and smaller ones at Magnuszew, Serock, and Rozan.

The German Army never recovered from the disaster between Vitebsk and Warsaw. The virtual destruction of three armies of Army Group Center was the most calamitous defeat suffered by the Germans in the war, and the loss of experienced officers and non-commissioned officers (NCOs) could not be made good at this stage of the war. By the end of 1944 the Soviets had restored their pre-1941 frontiers except for Courland. They could sit calmly on the Vistula, reorganizing and re-supplying their forces, supremely confident of their ability to drive to the Oder and Neisse Rivers and on to Berlin. The demoralized Germans—now coping with a full-fledged two-front war—could only mount a weak defense along the Vistula. Operation *Bagration* had sealed their fate.

NOTES

1. Richard Woodman, *The Arctic Convoys 1941–1945* (London: John Murray Publishers Ltd., 1994) p.444.
2. Carruthers and Erickson, *op. cit.*, p.175 and John Erickson, *The Road to Berlin* (London: Cassell, 2004) p.405.
3. Nikita S. Khrushchev, *Khrushchev Remembers*, translated from the Russian by Strobe Talbott (New York: Bantam Books, Inc., 1971) p.237.
4. *Loc. cit.*
5. Robert M. Citino, *Death of the Wehrmacht* (Lawrence, Kansas: University Press of Kansas, 2007) pp.303–09.
6. Paul Adair, *Hitler's Greatest Defeat: Disaster on the Eastern Front* (London: Rigel Publications, 2004) p.52.
7. Liddell Hart, *History of the Second World War*, p.569 writes that the operations in the East in 1944 "provided the clearest possible demonstration of the decisive importance of the ratio between space and force."
8. Chris Bellamy, *Absolute War: Soviet Russia in the Second World War* (New York: Alfred A. Knopf, 2007) p.613, notes that Army Group Center had 1.2 million men in 63 divisions. This may be a figure from an earlier date since the Germans give the strength of the army group in May, apparently before it lost the 56th Panzer Corps to Army Group North Ukraine on May 20, at 792,196. Ziemke lists 51 divisions and this includes three Hungarian and five security divisions (Ziemke, *Stalingrad to Berlin*, p.319).
9. British Air Ministry, *The Rise and Fall of the German Air Force* (London: Public Record Office, 2000) p.357.

10. Tippelskirch, *op. cit.*, p.462.
11. Adair, *op. cit.*, p.49.
12. *Ibid*, p.59.
13. Ziemke, *Stalingrad to Berlin*, p.319, writes that the build-up was accomplished with a minimum redeployment of units and was accomplished largely by reinforcing units already at the front.
14. S. P. Platonov, *Vtoraya Mirovaya Voyna, 1939–45* (Moscow: 1958) p.587 and volume 4, p.163 of the six-volume official Soviet history of the war, *Istoiya Velikoy Otchestvennoy Voyny Sovetiskogo Soyuze 1941–1945* (Moscow: 1950-53) as cited in Ziemke, *Stalingrad to Berlin*, pp.314–15.
15. Army Group Center, *Kriegstagebuch*, May 29, 1944, as cited by Ziemke, *Stalingrad to Berlin*, p.314.
16. *Ibid*, June 14, 1944.
17. John Keegan, *Intelligence in War: Knowledge of the enemy from Napoleon to Al-Qaeda* (New York: Alfred A. Knopf, 2003).
18. Pyotr (Peter) Bagration was a fellow Georgian, a general who was mortally wounded in the battle of Borodino against Napoleon in September 1812.
19. According to Ziemke, *Stalingrad to Berlin*, p.318, note 16, this was a type unit that first appeared in the summer of 1944. These units normally consisted of a tank or mechanized corps and a cavalry corps and were named after their commanders. They were intended for exploitation and pursuit operations.
20. The first Soviet communiqué mentioned June 23 as the start date and most Soviet accounts use this date. It seems, however, that the Germans should be aware of when all hell broke loose and therefore June 22 is used as the start date.
21. Bellamy, *op. cit.*, p.613.
22. *Ibid*, pp.612–13.
23. Liddell Hart, *The German Generals Talk*, pp.218–19.
24. Carruthers and Erickson, *op. cit.*, p.151.
25. Liddell Hart, *Strategy*, p.297.
26. Ziemke, *Stalingrad to Berlin*, p.322.
27. General Tippelskirch's highly decorated son, Adolf-Hilmar von Tippelskirch, was killed at Mogilev on June 28, 1944.
28. Ziemke, *Stalingrad to Berlin*, p.324.
29. *Ibid*, p. 325.
30. Army Group North, *Kriegstagebuch*, report on a lecture by Hitler at Wolfsschanze on July 18, 1944. In MS # P-114a, part V.
31. Ziemke, *Stalingrad to Berlin*, p. 333.

Adolf Hitler discusses the situation on the Eastern Front with Hermann Göring, left, commander of the Luftwaffe, and Wilhelm Keitel, right, head of Oberkommando der Wehrmacht (OKW).
Courtesy Krigsarkivet, Stockholm (The Military Archives of Sweden)

German civilians killed by Soviet troops at Nemmersdorf, East Prussia.
Courtesy Bundesarchiv, Bild 101I-464-0383I-26; photographer, Kleiner

Generaloberst Lothar Rendulic, who had just been awarded the Oak Leaves and Swords from the Führer, is seen here inspecting troops and fortifications in Norway.
Courtesy Bundesarchiv, Bild 183-J28650; photographer, Bauriedl

The documentary *Tag der Befreiung* (Liberation Day) premiered at an International Film Festival to mark the 30th Anniversary of the fall of the Nazi Regime. Original footage from the film shows Marshall G.A. Zhukov at a command post at the Oder Front in 1945. Gerhard Jentsch and Wolfgang Bartsch directed the film at the DEFA-Studio.
Courtesy Bundesarchiv, Bild 183-P0402-011; photographer, o.Ang

A machine gun position on the perimeter of the Courland Pocket. For several weeks German units successfully withstood considerable pressure from repeated assaults by Soviet forces. *Courtesy Bundesarchiv, Bild 146-1978-062-11; photographer, Bachem*

Lower Silesia Front, March 1945. Panzergrenadiers accompanied by Panther tanks move into a new position. *Courtesy Bundesarchiv, Bild 183-H28356; photographer, o.Ang*

Armed with Panzerfausts, volunteers from the Panzergrenadier-Division "Grossdeutschland" advance on the Memel bridgehead to retake a market town occupied by the Soviets.
Courtesy Bundesarchiv, Bild 146-1995-081-15A; photographer, Otto

During the struggle for the Soviet bridgehead north of Küstrin, Wehrmacht Panther tanks deploy to their starting positions near the town of Ortwig.
Courtesy Bundesarchiv, Bild 183-H28153; photographer, o.Ang

East Prussia Volkssturm being trained by the "Großdeutschland" Division. Wehrmacht propaganda repeatedly lauded the efforts of the Volkssturm battalions in holding back the advancing Soviet army. New battalions were hastily formed and trained by returning veterans from the fighting on the eastern front. Aging World War I veterans and youth whose only prior experience was army-sports and fitness camps were taught how to handle modern weapons. *Courtesy Bundesarchiv, Bild 183-J30793; photographer, Ernst Schwahn*

Pomerania, February 1945. The Germans threw everything they had into defending the Pomeranian town of Pyritz including a company of Hitlerjugend Volksstturm. Here the men are in conversation with a H.J.- führer of the regional leadership. *Courtesy Bundesarchiv, Bild 183-J28536; photographer, o.Ang*

At the beginning of March 1945, German infantrymen retreat at twilight before the advancing Soviet army. *Courtesy Bundesarchiv, Bild 183-J28759; photographer, o.Ang*

A bitter struggle outside Scherl in Upper Silesia. During their counter-offensive, German soldiers successfully held off a breakthrough attempt by Soviet forces. *Courtesy Bundesarchiv, Bild 183-J28729; photographer, Casper*

Near Scherl, the view from a heavy flak battery immediately after the position was hit by Soviet forces attacking under the cover of fog. Closing in as near as 50 meters they were held off by flak and Panzerfausts. *Courtesy Bundesarchiv, Bild 183-J28733; photographer, Ellerbrock*

A destroyed German assault gun on the Samland Peninsula near Königsberg, East Prussia. Königsberg itself surrendered on April 9, 1945, after a three-month siege by Soviet forces.

East Prussia—A troop ship evacuating German forces across the Baltic Sea.
Courtesy Bundesarchiv, B 145 Bild-P057338; photographer, o.Ang

On board a transport ship during its journey across the Baltic. The Germans tried to evacuate as many men as possible, albeit in an effort that came too late to affect the course of the war.
Courtesy Bundesarchiv, B 145 Bild-P057335; photographer, o.Ang

6
Army Group North Trapped

The Loss of the Narva–Pskov Line

Operation *Bagration*, which decimated Army Group Center, had completely outflanked Army Group North during the summer and driven back its right flank, the Sixteenth Army under General Hansen. We saw in the previous chapter that General Friessner had requested permission to withdraw to the Lithuanian positions running from Kraslava to Ostrov. However, since Hitler agreed only to a shorter withdrawal, the Lithuanian positions themselves were soon in jeopardy.

At a high-level meeting on July 18, despite the unanimous agreement of others in attendance, including Göring, that withdrawal was necessary, Hitler again refused to allow any withdrawals of Army Group North. He again emphasized the importance of Finland, the Latvian oil fields, supply of nickel from northern Finland, supply of Swedish iron ore, and the loss of the submarine training areas as his reasons.[1] Within a short time he would have to come up with other grounds, since most of these, in any case, were about to be lost.

The Sixteenth Army was struggling to get into the Lithuanian positions on July 19. Since it was soon obvious that they could not be held, Friessner ordered a further 9-mile (15km) withdrawal on July 22. This came with a warning to OKH that further withdrawals would be necessary to save Army Group North from destruction.

The heavily reinforced First Baltic Front under General Bagramyan drove through the gap (Baltic Gap) between Army Group North and the northern flank of Army Group Center, with Riga in the Sixteenth Army sector as the objective. Bagramyan's motorized columns turned north behind Third Panzer Army's left flank and captured Jelgava after a 50-mile (80km) night advance. This cut the last rail link between Army Group North and Germany. Soviet mechanized forces reached the Gulf of Riga on July 31. Army Group North was trapped.

At this point (August 9, 1944) Army Group North held a very irregularly shaped front from Narva in the north, which was the left flank of the Eighteenth Army, to Lake Peipus in the southwest and along its western shore and that of Lake Pskov before curving southwest to where it tied into the Sixteenth Army northeast of Riga. Narva and Pskov were still held by the Germans. Sixteenth Army covered Riga and tied into Army Group Center north of Jelgava, although a gap existed where the First Baltic Front had penetrated to the Baltic coast.

The Finns, who were still in the war, had directed a general inquiry to the Germans about the situation in the Baltic area; accordingly, on August 3, OKW sent General Schörner to make a personal report to Mannerheim. The Finnish inquiry was no doubt prompted by the fact that after the Soviets broke through to the Baltic at the end of July, the telephone communications between Finland and Germany were broken and Lufthansa had suspended its flights to Finland.

Schörner was undaunted by the catastrophic situation of the army group he had taken over on July 23. He promised Mannerheim that the Baltic area would be held, that his troops would be supplied by air and sea, and that armored forces from East Prussia would break the encirclement. Mannerheim probably did not believe these promises, but they were kept, at least for a while. Schörner's arguments did not convince Mannerheim to remain in the war, but it gave him the time needed to negotiate an end before Finland was completely isolated.

While ferocious fighting had taken place between Narva and Pskov ever since the occupation of the Panther Line, space does not allow it to be covered here, like the fighting in many other areas. Nevertheless, it must be noted that the Germans and volunteers from several other countries, including Estonia, Norway, Denmark, the Netherlands, and Belgium, acquitted themselves well against vastly superior Soviet forces.[2] The Germans finally lost Pskov on July 24 and Narva on July 26.

A German attack to open a corridor to Army Group North, executed under the cover name Operation *Doppelkopf* (Double Head), began on August 16. With naval gunfire support from the heavy cruiser *Prinz Eugen* and two destroyers, two Panzer brigades from General Raus' Third Panzer Army captured Tukums on the Gulf of Riga on August 20—thus breaking the encirclement of Army Group North. The narrow corridor to Army Group North along the coast was widened to 22 miles (35km) over the next few days.

The obvious and logical decision now would have been for Army Group North to carry out a retreat through Army Group Center to the south towards the German border before the corridor to Tukums was again closed. A suggestion to this effect, supported by General Guderian, was made by General Reinhardt, the new commander of Army Group Center, but it was rejected by Hitler.

Keitel's Mission to Helsinki

Still trying desperately to keep Finland in the war, Hitler sent Generalfeldmarschall Keitel to Helsinki on August 17. He brought an oak leaf cluster for Mannerheim and a Knight's Cross of the Iron Cross for General Erik Heinrichs (1890–1965), Mannerheim's Chief of Staff.

The German military situation at the time of Keitel's visit was not one that could give the Finns any confidence. The Allies had broken out of Normandy, landed in southern France, and encircled Army Group B in France; the liberation of Paris was imminent, the Germans had been driven back to the Gothic Line in Italy, and the Soviets were on the outskirts of Warsaw. Few observers would have guessed that the war would last almost nine more months. Keitel's mission was to reassure the Finns that Germany would continue to provide both military and economic aid. Mannerheim, now both Head of State and military Commander-in-Chief, used the opportunity provided by Keitel's visit to abrogate the Ryti–Ribbentrop agreement. While the Finns had managed to stabilize the military situation, they could not endure a second bloodletting. The pact between Ryti and Ribbentrop had been made under dire circumstances, and Finland felt that Ryti's resignation invalidated the agreement and that Finland would only fight as long as it served its own interest to do so.[3]

Keitel was surprised by this blunt announcement. While he rejected the premise, he pointed out that he was not authorized to concern himself with political matters. The official notification that Finland had abrogated the Ryti–Ribbentrop Pact was not provided to Germany until August 26, 1944.

Soviet Regrouping

In August, Marshal Vasilevsky took over the planning and coordination of the three Baltic fronts. Marshal Govorov's Leningrad Front remained under the direct control of Stavka. The Second and Third Baltic Fronts had regrouped at the beginning of August and resumed their attacks on August 5 with great ferocity between Lake Peipus and Dvina. The Soviets kept hammering away at the fronts of the Eighteenth and Sixteenth Armies. The Germans had prepared a plan named *Aster* for the eventual withdrawal from Estonia. Though planning was approved by General Schörner, it was referred to as a "map exercise" in order not raise Hitler's well-known concerns about any planned withdrawals.[4]

Even the ever-optimistic Schörner was beginning to waver. On September 15 he requested permission to evacuate Estonia, stating ominously that this was the last chance to get away from the trap that was forming.[5] Hitler used several arguments in his opposition to Schörner's request. He expressed worries that III Panzer Corps on the left flank on the Gulf of Finland would not be able to get away, and argued that the navy would lose its training areas. Hitler also raised a new objection. He stated that the Soviet Union had floated peace feelers and insinuated that Germany needed the Baltic area as a bargaining chip. This was one of those arguments that Hitler resorted to in order to override the objections of his generals. Nevertheless, Hitler gave a conditional approval for the withdrawal which was not scheduled to begin for another two days.[6]

On the face of it Hitler's new objection to a withdrawal seems preposterous, but it may contain a grain of truth. The Japanese ambassador to Germany, General Hiroshi Oshima (1886–1975), came to see Hitler on September 4, 1944. The Japanese believed, now that the Soviets had regained the territories lost since 1941, that it was not out of the question for a negotiated peace agreement to be reached between the Soviets and the Germans. Japan was willing to broker such an effort. Japan's own interest in brokering a peace was that this would allow the Germans to devote all their military strength against the Allies and therefore take some pressure off the Japanese in the Pacific.

Although Hitler flatly turned down the offer, Oshima did not give up. He approached Joseph Goebbels' (1897–1945) Propaganda Ministry with the suggestion, knowing that in this way it would again be brought to Hitler's attention. Goebbels passed the information to Bormann and Himmler and also prepared a memorandum for Hitler. Hitler read the memorandum, but put it aside without comment and Goebbels was never given an audience to discuss it.[7]

The Austrian military historian Heinz Magenheimer maintains that there were a number of peace feelers between the Soviet Union and Germany in the period 1942–43.[8] Several officials in Germany—such as Joseph Goebbels and Alfred Rosenberg—are alleged to have been involved, as was Mussolini and his Foreign Minister, Count Gian Galeazzo Ciano (1903–44). It looks as if some, if not most, of the informal discussions took place in Sweden. It further appears that the Soviets were only interested if Germany withdrew to the pre-*Barbarossa* borders. Hitler was seemingly never in favor of the scheme, as he insisted in dealing from a position of strength and would not entertain a withdrawal from the occupied parts of the Soviet Union, particularly the Ukraine. There is no reference to any peace feelers in 1944 other than that of the Japanese described above.[9]

In September, Govorov's Second Shock Army began a northward drive south of Tartu (Dorpat), the second largest city and cultural hub of Estonia about 110 miles (175km) southeast of Tallinn, the political and financial center of the country. The objective was to destroy Army Detachment Narva on the left flank of Army Group North.[10] The Second Shock Army hit Army Detachment Narva on September 17 and it began to lose hold of the area between Lake Peipus and Vortsjärv.

Schörner altered the withdrawal plan, ordering III Panzer Corps to make an overland march from the Narva River to Pernau on the Gulf of Riga, a distance of 118 miles (190km). He required that they reach their destination by September 20. The heavy equipment and baggage was evacuated through Tallinn or shipped across the straits to the Estonian islands. Both the Eighteenth and Sixteenth Armies retreated under heavy pressure. The Soviets had hoped to split the armies into pockets, but they remained intact despite desperate fighting and heavy losses. The retreat continued, first to the Wenden and Dvina positions and then to the Segewold (Eighteenth Army) and Mitau East positions (Sixteenth Army)—25 miles (40km) south of Riga—which Soviet spearheads reached on September 15. The withdrawal of Army Detachment Narva and Eighteenth Army to the Wenden position had been planned for in the earlier mentioned exercise *Aster*. These positions basically formed a 37–62-mile (60–100km) deep bulge around the city of Riga, with the Courland Peninsula to the west.

Latvian Oil

With Finland's departure from the war, the structure of Hitler's justifications for his actions in the north began unraveling. There is no doubt that oil was in critical short supply in Germany during the last two years of the war. The Latvian oil fields were lost with the Narva positions, although they had never figured very prominently in German fuel requirements. Some of that oil was used by the German railroad and some by the navy. However, as late as the beginning of July, Hitler had prohibited giving up Estonia by pointing out the importance of this oil region for the conduct of the war.[11]

In 1940 the annual Latvian shale oil production reached 1.7 million tons (about 11.9 million barrels), but most of it was used domestically, particularly in the cement industry. Only 6.4 percent of the production was exported in 1938.[12] The best information available to me indicates that in the period 1942–43, Germany received about one million barrels on an annual basis from the Latvian fields. Germany started the war with a total stockpile of 15 million barrels, to which was added 5 million from the captured territories in 1940. During the war the Germans had three sources of fuel: 1) imports, 2) domestic production, and 3) synthetic petroleum produced from coal.

In summer 1942 the Germans had tried to capture the Russian oil fields. They did seize Maikop, but the Soviets had done such a good job of destroying the facilities that Germany did not get a drop of oil from the fields by the time they were forced to withdraw in January 1943. The much larger Russian fields at Grozny and Baku were never captured. Romania became the chief supplier of oil, the amount reaching 13 million barrels annually by 1941, and this level was maintained through 1943. The Romanian oil fields were being depleted and the air raids on Ploesti in August destroyed 50 percent of the country's refinery capacity.[13]

In order to become more energy independent, the Germans undertook a massive expansion of domestic production. This caused an increase in crude output from 3.8 million barrels in 1938 to 12 million in 1944. However, it was the synthetic fuel plants that produced most of Germany's oil. This source of fuel increased from 10 million barrels to 36 million barrels in 1943, which represented 50 percent of all sources.[14] This ratio grew to about 57 percent in 1944.

By themselves these figures are somewhat misleading. While they show where the oil came from and a dramatic increase in synthetic fuel and domestic production, the percentages increased as much from the decline of other sources as they did from actual increases. Figures provided by Earl F. Ziemke give a different picture of the situation.[15] The massive Allied bomber offensive in September 1944 so heavily damaged all synthetic oil plants that production had to stop. This was the same month that Speer's aircraft production reached almost 3,000—a new high. In June 1944, at the time of the Normandy invasion, the Luftwaffe had consumed 90 million gallons and its entire future supply dropped to 95 million gallons. These alarming statistics explain why Hitler sent his best forces from the West after the Ardennes Offensive to the oil field region in Hungary rather than to shore up the Oder/Neisse Front.

Tank and vehicle production also reached new highs, but again the figures are misleading. The steel mills in the Ruhr were heavily bombed and little steel reached the factories thereafter, and the area would soon be lost to the Allies. The other industrial area in Silesia would soon fall to the Soviets. Much of the vehicle production actually involved the repair and reconditioning of damaged vehicles.

In late June 1944, Göring promised an additional 800 fighter aircraft if Field Marshal Hugo Sperrle (1885–1953), supreme commander of the Luftwaffe in the West, could come up with crews. All he could promise Hitler was 500 crews. This infuriated Hitler and led to the dismissal of both Rundstedt and Sperrle.[16] It made little difference how many aircraft and tanks Speer produced, since there was a dramatic shortage of trained crews. The German fighters put up a determined fight against the bombers, but in a three-day period from January 13 to 15, 1945, German aircraft shot down only 57 Allied aircraft while their own losses in fighters was an astonishing 236.[17] The losses were primarily due to the lack of training.

Nickel Supply and the Soviet Baltic Fleet

The nickel supply from northern Finland was also in question since the fate of the Twentieth Mountain Army was itself uncertain. On September 2, 1944, Hitler told Albert Speer, "If the source of nickel in northern Lapland is lost, our armaments production will be finished in a few months."[18] In a memorandum on September 5, 1944, Speer concluded that the nickel stockpiles already in Germany would last until January 1946, while the supply of chromium from Turkey was more problematic since it would only last until June 1, 1945. That shortage would quickly bring an end to the entire armaments production.[19]

The blockade of the Soviet Baltic Fleet also came to an end. Part of Finland's armistice agreement stipulated that the Finns would sweep the mines, provide air bases to the Soviets, put their merchant marine at Soviet disposal, and allowed temporary occupation of Hanko at the entrance to the Gulf of Finland. The Soviet Baltic Fleet had already occupied the southern coast of the Gulf of Finland and several islands off that coast. The surface fleet, however, was not immediately ready to put to sea. It had been bottled up in Kronstadt for over three years, had sustained damage, and needed to replace personnel lost during the ground war around Leningrad. However, repairs had started in late 1943 and the fleet would soon be seaworthy. The submarines were in better shape and they were already heading into the Baltic to attack German shipping along the eastern shore.[20]

In their 1943 plan for the withdrawal from Finland—Directive 50—there were two amphibious contingencies for the Germans, labeled as *Tanne West* (Fir West) and *Tanne Ost* (Fir East). *Tanne West* was a contingency plan to occupy the Åland Islands in the Gulf of Bothnia, while *Tanne Ost* was a plan to occupy the island of Suurasaari (Hogland) in the middle of the Gulf of Finland between Estonia and Finland. *Tanne West* was dropped because it could cause an unfavorable reaction from Sweden and because of personnel shortages. The seizure of Suurasaari was initially to be an army operation under the direction of the OKH. A regiment from the 58th Infantry Division was sent to Tallinn (Reval) for this purpose in June 1944. This unit had to be transferred to Army Group North in early July. Hitler then gave the mission to the navy, which had argued strongly for it, on July 9, 1944.

The navy began preparing for *Tanne Ost* and Grand Admiral Dönitz implied in a meeting with Hitler that the Estonian coast was of decisive importance for the war since it provided security for his submarine fleet.[21] He was no doubt alluding to keeping the Soviet Baltic Fleet from reaching the open waters of the Baltic and thereby jeopardizing the training areas for his new submarines.

A German naval force sailed for Suurasaari on September 14 under the command of a navy captain. It consisted of a makeshift regimental-size collection of navy and army personnel, scraped up in Tallinn. The landing took place on September 15 and it was a total fiasco. The Finns resisted, killing 153 Germans and taking 1,231 prisoners, including 175 who were wounded. The Finns suffered 36 killed, 67 wounded, and eight missing.[22] The absurdity of this operation is underscored by the fact that the Narva front was ordered withdrawn on September 16, meaning that even if the Germans had succeeded in seizing the island, it would have had to be evacuated.[23] In the words of one author, "The most senseless German operation of the year 1944 was over!"[24]

The failed German operation had a detrimental effect on the understanding the Germans had with the Finns to facilitate the withdrawal of the Twentieth Mountain Army.[25] The feeling of bitterness it caused contributed to the outbreak of fighting between the former brothers-in-arms. Even Warlimont, Deputy Chief of Staff for operations at OKW, writes that there was no longer any need to consider the Finns after they quit the war. He notes that despite strong arguments from Guderian, Hitler "clung doggedly to his tactics of holding on at all costs in the northern sector of the Eastern Front."[26]

Withdrawal to and Entrapment in Courland

The German Navy began embarking German personnel from Tallinn on September 17, 1944, including those from III SS-Panzer Corps, who had arrived there in coastal steamers and small motor craft. The evacuation was completed on September 22 with little interference from the Soviets, whose spearhead was just reaching the city. German ships evacuated a total of 37,831 soldiers, 13,049 wounded, 20,418 civilians, and 931 prisoners of war.[27]

The occupation of the Segewold positions near Riga was completed in the evening of September 26. Some divisions were moved directly into

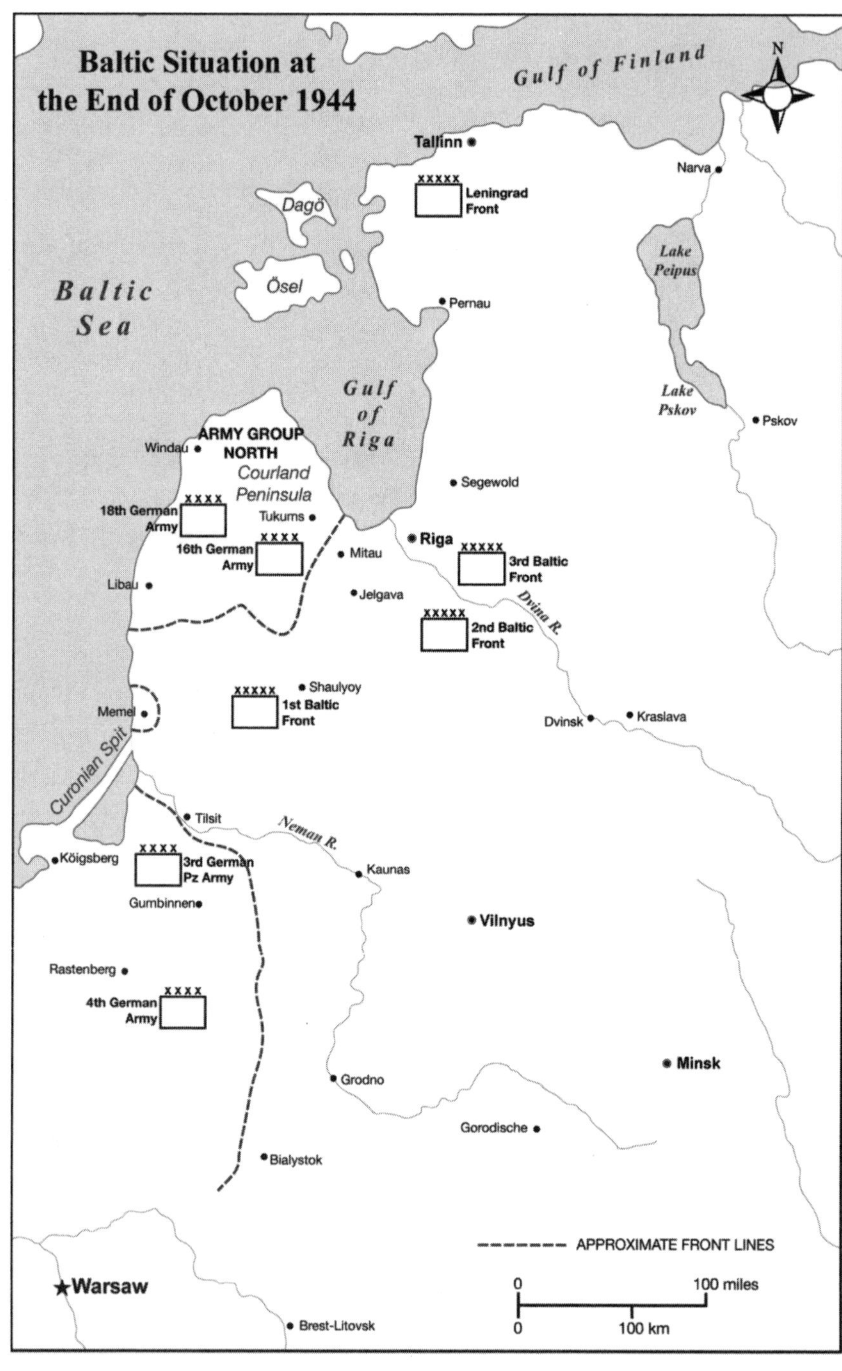

Baltic Situation at the End of October 1944
Gulf of Finland
N
Tallinn
Narva
XXXXX
Leningrad Front
Dagö
Ösel
Lake Peipus
Baltic Sea
Pernau
Gulf of Riga
Lake Pskov
Pskov
Windau
ARMY GROUP NORTH
Courland Peninsula
Segewold
XXXX
18th German Army
Tukums
XXXX
16th German Army
Riga
XXXXX
3rd Baltic Front
Mitau
Libau
Jelgava
Dvina R.
XXXXX
2nd Baltic Front
XXXXX
Shaulyoy
1st Baltic Front
Memel
Dvinsk
Kraslava
Curonian Spit
Tilsit
Neman R.
XXXX
Köigsberg
3rd German Pz Army
Kaunas
Gumbinnen
Vilnyus
Rastenberg
XXXX
4th German Army
Minsk
Grodno
Gorodische
Bialystok
APPROXIMATE FRONT LINES
Warsaw
0
100 miles
0
100 km
Brest-Litovsk

blocking positions at the base of the Courland Peninsula, which General Schörner considered part of his rear area. Soviet forces between Riga and the Gulf of Finland at the beginning of September included 900,000 troops organized into 125 infantry divisions, five tank corps, and one mechanized corps. The strength of Army Group North on September 1 was 571,579 soldiers and 42,833 volunteers.[28]

General Schörner ordered the start of an evacuation from Riga on September 26, mostly the depots established there. The Third Panzer Army of Army Group Center had been transferred to Army Group North on September 21. This transfer included responsibility for the sector held by the Panzer army. The transfer meant that Army Group North became responsible for the protection of the port of Memel. The Third Panzer Army remained part of Army Group North until October 11.

The Soviets ceased their attacks against Sixteenth Army at the end of September and turned their attention to the front of the Third Panzer Army to the south. When the Soviet attack came the main effort was made by the First Baltic Front under General Bagramyan. His mission was to cut his way through Third Panzer Army to the Baltic. The Leningrad Front headquarters had been dissolved[29] and Marshal Govorov was given command of the Second and Third Baltic Fronts. Govorov's forces were to attack on a broad front against Riga and to follow the Germans if they withdrew to the Courland Peninsula.

The First Baltic Front attacked west of Shaulyay in the direction of Memel with three armies on a 50-mile (80km)-wide front. The Third Belorussian Front on the left of the First Baltic Front made a supporting attack in the direction of Tilsit. While Schörner rushed reinforcements to the Third Panzer Army front, the Soviets achieved a clear breakthrough on October 7. On October 9 the Fifth Guards Tank Army and the Forty-Third Army reached the coast north and south of Memel. The Third Panzer Army's command post was overrun and the staff was lucky to escape to Memel, where the XXVIII Corps of the Third Panzer Army had been forced into a beachhead around the port.

Schörner told Hitler he would attack in the direction of Memel, but he had to assemble forces to carry out that assault. He recommended the evacuation of Riga and pointed out that the city was hardly worth holding, since it was already under artillery fire and Soviet submarines were operating in the Gulf of Riga. Hitler delayed a day before giving his permission. Schörner also had to worry about his rear, since Soviet forces on the Baltic islands would soon have only 19 miles (30km) of water to cross before they reached the northern end of the Courland Peninsula. Schörner needed to rush forces north to protect his backyard.

On October 11, the Third Panzer Army was again assigned to Army Group Center to protect its flank against the Soviet attack toward Tilsit. The Panzer army had only one available corps, with one being encircled at Memel and one cut off with Army Group North. East Prussia was now under direct threat. On October 16, three Soviet Armies attacked across the German border, headed toward Gumbinnen. The stump of Third Panzer Army was moved behind the Neman River. Army Group North was ordered to go over to the defensive in Courland after a report on October 21 that the first German city, Aachen in the west, had fallen to the Allies and that Gumbinnen might also be lost within a day.[30]

It is somewhat difficult to tell what the Soviets thought about the Courland Pocket, except in retrospect. Their views probably changed as time passed. Stalin wrote to Churchill on September 29, 1944, that his armies were in the process of destroying the German Baltic Army Group that was a threat to his right flank. He noted that without neutralizing Army Group North it would not be possible to strike deep into Germany.[31] There is no reason to believe that these thoughts were not genuine. The official Soviet history of World War II has virtually nothing to say about Courland except for one short sentence.[32]

Other Soviet military writers do make some observations. There seems to have been surprise and relief that the Germans allowed themselves to be trapped in the Courland Peninsula. The feeling appears to be that Army Group North could have given the Soviets considerable trouble on the German border. In a conversation with Churchill on February 4, 1945, Stalin said that German failure to make a timely withdrawal from the coastal enclaves and bypassed cities in the interior resulted in their using "untrained, badly led, and ill-equipped Volkssturm" for the defense of the Oder in small and badly trained reserve divisions.[33] The Austrian military historian Heinz Magenheimer presents persuasive arguments on these very points.[34]

Shtemenko writes that Stavka's objectives were all along to trap Army Group North and then destroy it piecemeal. He continues, "Although

GHQ [General Headquarters or Stavka] was anxious to liquidate the Kurland grouping as soon as possible, the task turned out to be extremely difficult. . . . Eventually our troops had to be content with blockading the enemy on the Kurland Peninsula."[35] This is in line with the views of Chris Bellamy, who writes:

> This left a huge pocket with thirty-three divisions trapped to the north of the westward Russian advance. Stavka assessed, probably rightly, that while this huge pocket of German troops was an annoyance; it could be contained, and was less of a priority than the main thrust to destroy Germany proper. . . . Had they been withdrawn back into Germany as well, they could have caused considerable problems for the Russians, British or Americans, or all three.[36]

Stephen Fritz and Howard Grier offer a somewhat different explanation for why Hitler allowed so many German troops, sorely needed to defend the homeland, to be entombed in Courland.[37] They both note that the decision to retire to Courland and to launch the Ardennes Offensive came within days of each other—it was actually longer. Fritz notes that Hitler hoped that the Ardennes Offensive would achieve a sudden turnaround in the fortunes of war and that this hope was also in accordance with the strategy he laid out in Directive 51 in November 1943 (see Chapter 4).[38] Success in the Ardennes Offensive would allow him to move forces to the East and could splinter the alliance against him. In this scheme of things it was important to hang on to Courland as a springboard for a new offensive.

The Ardennes Offensive was Hitler's brainchild, and his alone—Hitler's personal military staff (OKW) began planning it in September 1944. It was not until the end of October that Rundstedt, the Commander-in-Chief West, Model, the commander of Army Group B which had to carry out the operation, and General Hasso von Manteuffel (1897–1978), commander of the Fifth Panzer Army, learned about the operation. In view of the dire military situation in which Germany found itself, and the scarcity of resources, they were staggered by the lack of realism of this extremely ambitious plan.[39] Hitler's plan was basically to drive to Antwerp, thereby splitting the Anglo/American forces. He hoped that eventually the British would be faced with another Dunkirk and the Americans would also withdraw from the continent. The objections of the commanders were in vain.

Hitler's plan was wishful thinking at this stage of the war. Churchill admitted that the offensive "caused us no little anxiety," but noted that it turned out to the advantage of the Allies in the end. The Allies could replace their losses, but the Germans could not do the same, and the outcome of the Ardennes Offensive eased the subsequent fighting along the Rhine.[40] In a conversation with Churchill on February 4, 1945, Stalin labeled the Ardennes Offensive by the Germans a "stupid maneuver" that had harmed German efforts to defend their country.[41]

The speculative connection of the Ardennes Offensive and Hitler's determination to hold on to the Baltic coast has a long history, yet there is no direct evidence that they were linked. We have no statement from Hitler and no testimony by his generals to that effect, at least none known to me. There is also no solid evidence in the records that he intended to use the troops in the Courland Peninsula in an offensive role. Nevertheless, Fritz' and Grier's arguments cannot simply be brushed aside despite the fact that they are based on indirect evidence of a speculative and coincidental nature.

The OKH was clamoring for forces from the West to help shore up the Vistula front before the anticipated Soviet winter offensive. Hitler was not about to cancel the Ardennes Offensive, but he could have withdrawn the large number of troops in Courland and thereby, to a large extent, have disrupted the Soviet winter offensive. Such a withdrawal would also have freed the troops in some of the other enclaves further west. By 1945 Hitler had come up with new reasons for not evacuating the Courland Peninsula. He maintained that the forces there (and in other pockets) slowed and frustrated the Soviet drive into Germany, and that the losses in a withdrawal would be too great—in other words he viewed it as an economy of force measure while in reality it was a reckless expenditure of precious resources.

It appears that Grier agrees with Hitler's position and it is worthwhile quoting the passage that leads me to this belief:

> The results of the *Wellenbrecher* doctrine, however, were mixed. Tactically it was successful. Army Group North/Courland clearly

> tied down superior Soviet formations until the end of 1944. Even in 1945 Russian divisions in Courland outnumbered German divisions by three or four to one. German forces in East Prussia engaged approximately 10 Soviet armies until the beginning of April 1945. After that, six to seven armies remained to storm Königsberg and clear Nazi troops from Samland.[42]

The sources used for the comparative strengths are, however, unknown and I am skeptical about their accuracy. More importantly, the simple comparison of divisions, corps, and armies of different nationalities is misleading unless something is known about their relative strengths. Ziemke, in *Stalingrad to Berlin*, Appendix A, provides a chart comparing the authorized strength of Soviet and German units, and their strengths are considerably different. Similarly, according to my research, the statement that six to seven Soviet armies were used to storm Königsberg and clear the Samland Peninsula is misleading. Three Soviet armies actually participated in the fighting for Königsberg. Two of these were from the First Baltic Front—Thirty-Ninth and Forty-Third—while the Eleventh Guards Army was from the Third Belorussian Front. Another army from the First Baltic Front remained in reserve, but did not participate in the fighting. The subsequent clearing of the Samland Peninsula was conducted by three armies of the First Baltic Front, now part of the Third Belorussian Front. Again, one army remained in reserve.

Professor Percy Ernst Schramm, on the other hand, deplores the loss of the troops in the Courland Pocket as one of the "most harrowing consequences of the wave breaker doctrine."[43]

In his excellent section on Courland evacuation proposals, Professor Grier shows a healthy and correct skepticism of German naval sources.[44] Despite the self-serving comments by Dönitz at a meeting with Guderian and Hitler on March 17, 1945,[45] the German Navy had a strong axe to grind when it came to Courland and the Baltic. When the navy gave its initial time requirement for evacuating the pocket in October 1944 it was estimated to take five months. Grier rightly challenges these figures, since the ships intended for use were those belonging to the navy and did not include the many passenger vessels that were available. Finally, he points out that it only took four or five days to evacuate 32,000 men in January and correctly concludes that the navy had deliberately made things seem overly difficult in their October 1944 estimate. At the 17 March meeting, Dönitz had told Hitler that it would take 90 days to evacuate Army Group Courland. Grier notes that the army group had worked up a plan that showed that the evacuation could be carried out in 15–18 days. What this shows is that Hitler may have considered Guderian's request to withdraw Army Group Courland, but that Dönitz threw roadblocks in the way of any withdrawal except those actually ordered by Hitler.

When it comes to the value of the Courland Pocket to Germany, I consider it a wrong-headed sacrifice of precious resources. John Erickson, Percy Ernst Schramm, Heinz Magenheimer, Chris Bellamy, Heinz Guderian, Ian Kershaw, and Robert Payne are all critical of leaving Army Group North trapped in the Courland Peninsula.[46] Shtemenko wrote that it had been the objective of Stavka all along to trap Army Group North and eliminate it piecemeal, but when it proved to be a tough nut to crack they decided to keep it under siege.[47] The subsequent attacks on Army Group Courland were probably part of their siege operation. The Soviets knew that the Germans were receiving thousands of tons of supplies and equipment by sea. It was important for the Soviets to keep the supply and equipment levels of Army Group Courland low enough to prevent it from becoming an offensive threat. Since they had chosen to blockade the Germans we should be allowed to speculate that the main purpose behind the periodic attacks was to force the Germans to burn up their supplies. It should also be noted that there was no increased role for the Soviet Courland Group of Forces in the Soviet winter offensive in 1945.

Any thought that the purpose of keeping Army Group North in Courland was to use it as a launching pad for a renewed offensive in the East was purely wishful thinking. At the beginning of 1945, the Soviets had 6,000,000 troops facing 2,000,000 Germans.[48] The Soviets had total air dominance and the Germans were so short of fuel that they had lost virtually all their mobility.

While preparing the plan for the Ardennes Offensive, Hitler's personal military staff (OKW), either through inexperience or to satisfy Hitler's demands, used the daily fuel requirements of a Panzer division in an administrative move, neglecting the fact that the requirement was at least doubled for combat operations.[49] This was the worst deficiency in a flawed plan—the tanks ran out of fuel and the Luftwaffe could not perform as required. Even to come up with the 17,500 tons of fuel—which in normal times amounted to 60 hours of production—deliveries to other fronts had to be drastically reduced.[50]

The Allied Strategic Bomber Offensive against fuel installations continued unabated and virtually brought operations on all fronts to a standstill. The 11th SS-Panzergrenadier Division *Nordland* had taken part in Operation *Sonnenwende* (Solstice) despite a severe fuel shortage. (*Sonnenwende* was the unsuccessful German counterattack at Stargard in February 1945, discussed in the last chapter.) Later they were sent to reinforce the defenders of Berlin, but the division was so short of fuel that many of the Danes and Norwegians who arrived at their destination had to leave their tanks and other vehicles behind.[51] Even had the Ardennes Offensive not been a total failure, it shows a lack of understanding of military operations to believe that Army Group Courland presented an offensive threat to the Soviets under the situation described above. Logistics are what make military operations possible, and the lack of them doom such operations to failure. In the words of Andrew Roberts, the Soviets came to view the Courland Pocket as an enormous POW camp maintained and administered for them by the Germans.[52]

The Soviets expressed great pride in the operations that led to cornering Army Group North, and much credit is given to General Bagramyan. The offensive is referred to as the Memel operation, and it was no doubt a brilliant tactical maneuver. The attacks by two Soviet fronts kept the Eighteenth and Sixteenth Armies pinned down while the Leningrad Front presented a threat to their rear via the Baltic islands. Simultaneously, Bagramyan's front launched its attack in the direction of Memel, and for the final time the connection of Army Group North to East Prussia was severed, fracturing the Third Panzer Army, and creating a second German pocket around Memel.[53]

By the time Army Group North was trapped in the Courland Peninsula, it was obvious to all that many of the reasons that Hitler had repeatedly cited in his fanatical determination to hang on to the Baltic shores were no longer valid. Finland had left the war and the nickel supply from northern Finland was no longer available. However, based on what Speer told Hitler it had not been an important consideration for the German war industry for some time. The Twentieth Mountain Army was beginning its valiant winter retreat through northern Norway. However, it would not be available for the battle of the frontiers. The Soviet Baltic Fleet was no longer bottled up and it was just a matter of time before it would give the Germans major problems. The Latvian shale oil was lost, but it had never figured prominently in the German fuel situation.

With many of the underpinnings of his doctrine in the Baltic having unraveled, Hitler was now left with just two—fear of Swedish intervention on the side of the Allies and the loss of Germany's submarine training areas. These will be examined in the next chapters.

NOTES

1. Steven H. Newton, *Retreat from Leningrad: Army Group North 1944/1945* (Atglen, PA: Schiffer Military History, 1995) pp.215–16.
2. Jonathan *Trigg, Hitler's Vikings: The History of the Scandinavian Waffen-SS: The Legions, The SS Wiking and the SS Nordland* (Glouchestershire: Spellmount, 2010), pp.174–83. Trigg has written three other books on foreign nationals serving in the SS. There are also several foreign books and some are listed in the bibliography.
3. Mannerheim, *op. cit.*, pp.492–93; Blücher, *op. cit.*, pp.395–96; Erfurth, *The Last Finnish War*, p.206; and Vehviläinen, *op. cit.*, p.144.
4. Ziemke, *Stalingrad to Berlin*, p.404.
5. MS # P-114a (Sixt), Teil V, p.907, cited by Ziemke, *Stalingrad to Berlin*, p.404.
6. Jodl Diary and International Military Tribunal Documents 1809-PS and 1811-PS as cited in Ziemke, *Stalingrad to Berlin*, p.405.
7. Ian Kershaw, *Nemesis*, pp.728–30.
8. Magenheimer, *op. cit.* The sub-chapter dealing with this subject is titled "The Question of Closing Down the Eastern Front and a Separate German-Soviet Peace" and is found on pp.191-201.
9. Magenheimer's excellent work is only one of his many books and articles on military history. After reading this particular book it appears to me that he may belong to the school of historians who, among other things, maintain that Germany's attack on the Soviet Union was a "pre-emptive" action since the Soviets were themselves getting ready to attack.
10. Newton, *op. cit.*, p.258.
11. Haupt, *op. cit.*, p.261.
12. Research Paper/Report by PhD candidate Ingo Valgma at the Mining Institute of Tallinn Technical University.
13. Peter W. Becker, "*The Role of Synthetic Fuel in World War II Germany*" in *Air University Review* (July–August 1981).

14. *Loc. cit.*
15. Earl F. Ziemke, *Battle for Berlin: End of the Third Reich* (New York: Ballantine Books, Inc., 1968) p.15.
16. Guderian, *Panzer Leader*, p.334.
17. *Ibid*, p.417.
18. Albert Speer, *Inside the Third Reich*, p.405.
19. *Ibid*, p.406.
20. Bellamy, *op. cit.*, pp.624–26.
21. Haupt, *op. cit.*, p.262.
22. Ari Raunio, *Sotatoimet. Suomen sotien 1939-45 kulku kartoin* (Kustantaja: GHenimap Oy, 2004) p.187.
23. Newton, *op. cit.*, p.251. Hitler's approval of the withdrawal came with the caveat that it could be rescinded within two days.
24. Haupt, *op. cit.*, p.263.
25. Warlimont, *op. cit.*, p.472.
26. *Ibid*, p.473.
27. Haupt, *op. cit.*, p.265.
28. *Ibid*, p.258.
29. The Leningrad Front had orders to attack and occupy the Baltic islands.
30. Army Group North, *Kriegstagebuch*, Ia, Nr. 4587/44, dated October 21, 1944.
31. Haupt, *op. cit.*, p.271.
32. USSR Ministry of Defense, *History of the Great Patriotic War of the Soviet Union, 1941–1945* (Moscow: Voennoe Izdat, 1962) volume 4, p.363, and Haupt, *op. cit.*, p.328. The short 20-word sentence reads "The enemy's Kurland Group continued to block on the peninsula until the end of the war and surrendered in May 1945."
33. Winston S. Churchill, *Triumph and Tragedy* (Boston: Houghton Mifflin Company, 1953) p.348.
34. Mangenheimer, *op. cit.*, pp.266–67.
35. S. M. Shtemenko, *The Soviet General Staff at War 1941-1945*, translated from the Russian by Robert Daglish (Moscow: Progress Publishers, 1970) p.293.
36. Bellamy, *op. cit.*, p.624.
37. Fritz, *op. cit.*, pp.433–34; Grier, *op. cit.*, pp.147–51.
38. It was in accordance with the priorities established in Directive 51, but I believe the intent of that directive was to defeat an attempt by the Allies to breach the German defenses on a broad front, in other words to keep a successful landing from becoming a larger beachhead. The German attempt to defeat the landing died with the battle of the Falaise Pocket, fought from August 12 to 21 in which Army Group B consisting of two armies was encircled. The Germans lost between 80,000 and 100,000 troops, with about 50,000 of these being taken prisoner.
39. B. H. Liddell Hart, *The Other Side of the Hill* (London: Cassell, 1951) pp.446–49.
40. Churchill, *Triumph and Tragedy*, p.281.
41. *Ibid*, p.348.

42. Grier, *op. cit.*, p.140.
43. Schramm, *op. cit.*, p.160
44. Grier, *op. cit.*, pp.141–43.
45. Karl Doenitz, *Memoirs: Ten Years and Twenty Days*. Translated by R. H. Stevens in collaboration with David Woodward. (New York: Da Capo Press, Inc., 1997) pp. 399–400.
46. See, for example, Erickson, *The Road to Berlin*, p.422. He writes "the Courland divisions remained locked up in their peninsula, nothing but a wasted asset."
47. Shtemenko, *The Soviet General Staff*, p.293.
48. Tony Le Tissier, *Zhukov at the Oder: The Decisive Battle for Berlin* (Mechanicsburg, Pennsylvania: Stackpole Books, 2009) p.13.
49. Liddell Hart, *History of the Second World War*, p.647, quoting General Manteuffel
50. Kershaw, *Nemesis*, p. 732 and Speer, *Inside the Third Reich*, pp.414–15 and 423.
51. Trigg, *op. cit.*, p.238 and Cornelius Ryan, *The Last Battle* (London: Collins, 1966) p.311.
52. Andrew Roberts, *The Storm of War: A New History of the Second World War* (New York: Harper Collins Publishers, 2011) p.541.
53. Shtemenko, *The Soviet General Staff*, p.292.

7

SWEDEN AND GERMANY

Germany and Sweden in 1940

Scandinavia was of great importance to Germany both strategically and economically. The strategic importance is rather obvious from looking at a map showing the location of the Scandinavian countries in relation to Germany, the Baltic Sea, the Baltic approaches, and access to the North Atlantic. From Scandinavia, Germany imported both raw materials and finished products that were important to its civilian and war industries. From Norway, Germany acquired aluminum, carbide, fish, and nitroglycerin. Denmark provided the Germans with large amounts of food products. Finland was a source of timber and nickel. Sweden provided high-grade iron ore ideal for making steel, copper, sulfur, and finished products such as ball bearings.

Germany's imports of iron ore from Sweden came mostly from deposits in the Kiruna and Gällivare regions of northern Sweden, with smaller quantities from mines in the country's center. From May to November, the ore from the Kiruna/Gällivare fields reached Germany by sea via the port of Luleå at the northern end of the Gulf of Bothnia. Since this port was normally ice-bound from December to April, in winter the ore was shipped by rail to the ice-free Norwegian port of Narvik.

The Allies believed that stopping ore shipments from Sweden would be an immediate and decisive factor in the war, but this conclusion proved erroneous. The Germans were able to make use of scrap iron, domestic supplies of low-grade ore, and on-hand stockpiling to a much larger degree than thought possible. It was estimated that the Germans imported 22 million tons of iron ore in 1938. About 9.5 million tons came from sources that were no longer available after the outbreak of war. The Allies estimated that another 9 million tons came from Sweden.[1]

The scheduled deliveries to Germany for 1940, as specified in the German–Swedish Trade Agreement, were actually 10 million tons. The Swedes considered it necessary to ship 2–3 million tons of this commitment through Narvik. The Germans were prepared to ship about 3 million of the 10 million tons via rail to the ice-free port of Oxelösund or other ports in southern Sweden, provided arrangements were made for storage during the winter months.[2] While the successful German offensive in the West secured a 14-million ton annual supply of iron ore from the French and Luxembourg mines, Professor Walter Hubatsch claims that the flow of Swedish high-grade ore made the great battles of 1942–44 possible for the Germans.[3] Swedish iron ore was ideal for the production of high-grade steel, since its iron content was twice that of German and French ore. It is therefore quite understandable that Hitler placed access to Swedish iron ore near the top of his priority list.

The port of Narvik and its trans-shipment facilities were thoroughly destroyed six weeks before the Allies captured that town at the end of May 1940. This was a deliberate German decision resulting from a crisis in the German high command after the second naval battle of Narvik, when it became likely that General Dietl and the 3rd Mountain Division might have to withdraw into the mountains along the Swedish border. Hitler ordered extensive destruction of facilities in Narvik and the railroad between Narvik and Sweden. Demolition experts were flown to Narvik to undertake the destruction, which took place in the period April 22–25.[4] The railroad to the border from Narvik was also destroyed when the Germans eventually made that withdrawal.

The devastation reduced the usefulness of Narvik for shipment of iron ore. The German destruction was so thorough that shipments of iron ore could not take place for seven months after the end of hostilities in Norway. The Germans shipped 600,000 tons through Narvik in 1941, about 25 percent of the pre-war level. By 1943 the tonnage had reached 1.8 million. The reason for never reaching the pre-war level had more to do with the very exposed shipping route than with any lingering effects from the destruction of the port facilities. The shipments from southern Swedish ports more than compensated for the reduced volume going through Narvik.

Sweden and the Invasion of Denmark and Norway

Grier writes that "Nazi Germany contemplated attacking Sweden on several occasions throughout the war."[5] I am only aware of one occasion where German thoughts about invading Sweden made it into the planning and preparation phases. Grier's statement might be technically correct since the operative word is "contemplated"—this can mean any thoughts, verbal or written. However, some readers could conclude that Sweden was in constant danger of a German attack and this is not the case. The military in virtually all nations prepare contingency studies and plans for various possible scenarios—that is their job.

In one case, early in the war, the "contemplation" of an invasion made it into the study phase, but was discarded before reaching the planning stage. In the first German study (*Studie Nord*) in preparation for the invasion of Norway in December 1939, a small staff at OKW headed by Colonel Walter Warlimont considered seizing the Swedish mining districts by a landing in Luleå followed by an overland move to the mines. This study was distributed to the service chiefs on December 28, 1939, but Hitler withdrew it on January 23, 1940, and moved the planning for the invasion of Norway to a group in the OKW that became known as the *Krancke* Staff.

The idea to seize the iron ore districts was quickly ruled out, as were proposed threats against Sweden. This dismissal appears to have been at the suggestion of the Seekriegsleitung (SKL; German Naval Staff). It was Warlimont who put an end to any thoughts of action against Sweden when he reviewed a working paper by General Nikolaus Falkenhorst's (the designated commander for the invasion of Norway) staff on February 27, 1940. He may well have been acting on instructions from his superiors, General Jodl and Hitler. The final solution is spelled out in Hitler's directive on March 1, 1940.[6]

The reasons for ruling out any action or threats against Sweden were probably based on a possible unfavorable reaction by the Soviet Union. The German Navy had suggested as the planning proceeded that both the Soviet Union and Sweden should receive assurances that the occupation would only be for the duration of the war and that Germany guaranteed Norway's border.[7] Sweden adopted a policy of strict neutrality at the outset of the Norwegian campaign. Some Norwegian units driven across the border were quickly disarmed and interned. As the campaign progressed and the Germans gained the upper hand, Sweden adopted a more accommodating attitude towards them. When General Dietl's forces, cut off from re-supply, reached the Swedish border, the German government demanded permission from Sweden to send supplies to Dietl's troops through that country. The Swedish government agreed, on April 17, 1940, to permit the transshipment of supplies of "a humanitarian nature."[8] On April 18 Sweden also granted permission for the transit of Red Cross supplies and personnel. The first shipment reached Sweden on April 19 and arrived at the border on April 26. It consisted of 34 railroad cars with 25 tons of medicines and medical equipment, 20 tons of clothing, and 350 tons of provisions. It is estimated that the provisions on the train were sufficient to sustain 4,000 troops for three months. It is very doubtful that Dietl's troops could have held out without these supplies. The train also brought 30 intelligence personnel, apparently disguised as Red Cross workers.[9]

The Germans were also allowed to send personnel to Germany and the first transport consisted of 514 men. These were primarily crews from German merchant ships sunk in Narvik, as well as naval specialists from the sunken destroyers whom the German Navy wanted back in Germany. They were all labeled "shipwrecked sailors." Later in the campaign, when it appeared that the Norwegians would drive the Germans across the Swedish border into internment, the Germans pressured Sweden to enter into an agreement, which was actually an evacuation rather than an internment of Dietl's forces. The Germans requested the Swedish government to provide sufficient railroad transport to move Dietl's forces to Holmesund on the Gulf of Bothnia. The Swedes agreed on the condition that all weapons be left behind in Norway. At Holmesund, Dietl's troops were to embark on ships for Germany. The Swedes held four trains in readiness near the border from the end of May until the end of the Narvik campaign.

Swedish Military Preparedness

At this point it is appropriate to review the strength and readiness of the

Swedish armed forces. The last time the Swedes had been engaged in large-scale hostilities was in 1814, against Napoleon and Norway. There was, as in the other Scandinavian countries, a system of compulsory military service dating back several centuries. The conscripts were, for the most part, hardy individuals used to outdoor life in a severe climate and most had access to and were proficient in the use of firearms. Sweden remained neutral in World War I and after that war the country, like many others, allowed its military preparedness to deteriorate and the introduction of modern equipment lagged. By 1924 the training period for the recruits called to the colors had fallen to four months. The training period and acquisition of modern equipment increased starting in 1936, in the wake of growing international tensions.

At the time of the German invasion of Norway and Denmark the entire Swedish military was placed on alert. The training period for recruits was increased to 450 days. The country was organized into five military districts totaling 35 infantry battalions, four cavalry battalions, and six artillery units of three large batteries each. The units were assigned to 11 regiments. These were in turn often assigned to divisions but most divisions were primarily administrative entities. Regiments were normally the largest maneuver units.

In peacetime, only a cadre was maintained in these units. According to Carl O. Schuster, the normal strength of the peacetime cadre was 79,000. He also places the wartime strength at 270,000 men.[10] There is considerable difference between the figures given by Schuster and those given in Carl-Axel Wangel's 1982 book issued by the Swedish Military Academy through the Military History Publishers.[11] It places the strength of the fully mobilized Swedish Army at 600,000, not counting home guards and other auxiliary units. The explanation is probably that Schuster only included those units which had a standing peacetime cadre. Theoretically, the Swedish Army could be fully mobilized within 72 hours. The army was well equipped, particularly in light infantry weapons, artillery and light anti-tank guns.

By the end of 1941, the order of battle had increased to three corps headquarters and 10 divisional headquarters. Each division normally consisted of three infantry regiments and one artillery regiment. There was also a motorized brigade (cavalry brigade) consisting of three motorized battalions and an armored car squadron. Most of the anti-aircraft weapons were static. These were organized into seven anti-aircraft regiments mostly armed with 75mm and 40mm Bofors guns. There was also an anti-aircraft company assigned to each division, and every regiment and battalion had a platoon each. The anti-aircraft units at division or lower levels were armed with 40mm and 20mm automatic cannons. Two additional motorized brigades, three armored brigades, three bicycle brigades, and four jäger (light infantry) brigades were in the process of being formed in 1941.

The Swedish Air Force was a very professional organization and the number of aircraft in its inventory was not negligible. Its primary operational units consisted of 152 fighters and 114 bombers. The pilots, while well trained, lacked combat experience and the operational performance of their planes did not measure up to the battle-tested German aircraft.

The Swedish Navy was the third largest in the Baltic, after the Soviet and German. While the navy's mission was mainly coastal protection, it did have an offensive capability, primarily through its submarines and modern destroyers. However, the navy viewed its mission as defensive, which included escorting, patrolling, mine-laying, and minesweeping. The ships of the Swedish Navy in late 1941 included 7 aging coastal defense ships, 3 cruisers, 17 destroyers, 23 submarines, 22 torpedo boats, and 40 minesweepers.[12] The Swedish Navy also had an aggressive building program and by the end of the war it had added one cruiser, seven destroyers, eight submarines, 10 minesweepers, and 20 motor torpedo boats.

Overseas purchases of warships did not go as well. The Swedes had ordered three destroyers from Italian yards before the war, but they were not ready until after war broke out. The Swedes planned to sail them home through the German and British blockades. There were no problems with the Germans who even offered to assist in the passage. The British, however, intercepted and impounded the ships, and interned the crews in a Scottish port.[13] The seizure of the warships raised a storm of indignation in Sweden and infuriated Swedish flag officers, some of whom were already considered pro-German. This unwise British action caused lives to be miserable for British agents in Stockholm and its effects lasted to the very end of the war.

A much less grievous incident involving overseas armament purchase took place between the United States and Sweden. Before the outbreak of the war the Swedes had ordered about 300 combat aircraft from the Americans. Only some 60 were delivered before the United States halted the shipments. In order to carry out the air force expansion and modernization program, the Swedish government ended up purchasing 200 aircraft from Italy.[14]

There was a change of command in the German Navy in January 1943 that had a major impact on the naval situation in the Baltic. Both Hitler and Grand Admiral Raeder had been very cautious in the use of the major units of Germany's surface fleet, but for different reasons. Hitler was reluctant to use the capital ships because he wanted to preserve them for the defense of Norway. Raeder, who was also careful in the use of his battleships, was a staunch believer in the importance of the "fleet in being" theory. He believed that the mere existence of the German battleships placed a heavy burden on the British navy and tied up major units that could have been used in other operational areas.[15]

After the lack of success of the surface fleet against the Murmansk convoys in late 1942, Hitler made one of his monumental decisions. Although both Hitler and Raeder are equally to blame for the lack of success, Hitler summoned Raeder on January 6, 1943, and told him he had decided to scrap the surface fleet since it was a needless drain on men and materiel.[16] Raeder offered his resignation and he recommended Dönitz as his successor. Both offers were immediately accepted.

Raeder made one more attempt to convince Hitler of the folly of his decision. He sent Hitler a memorandum on January 15, 1943, where he argued for a balanced fleet in order to present the British with a "fleet in being" threat. He argued that without such a threat the British would be able to turn their whole strength against the U-boats. A respectable surface force would compel the Allies to assign the most modern battleships and aircraft carriers to the North Atlantic, units that they needed in other theaters of the war.[17]

In the end, Hitler did not carry out the wholesale scrapping of the surface fleet. After his anger had subsided, he agreed to keep the battleships *Tirpitz*, *Scharnhorst*, and the heavy cruiser *Lützow* in Norway. Dönitz, although he was a submarine officer and had commanded the U-boat fleet, also saw the foolhardiness of disbanding the whole surface fleet and argued against it. He pointed out, for example, that without sizable surface forces,

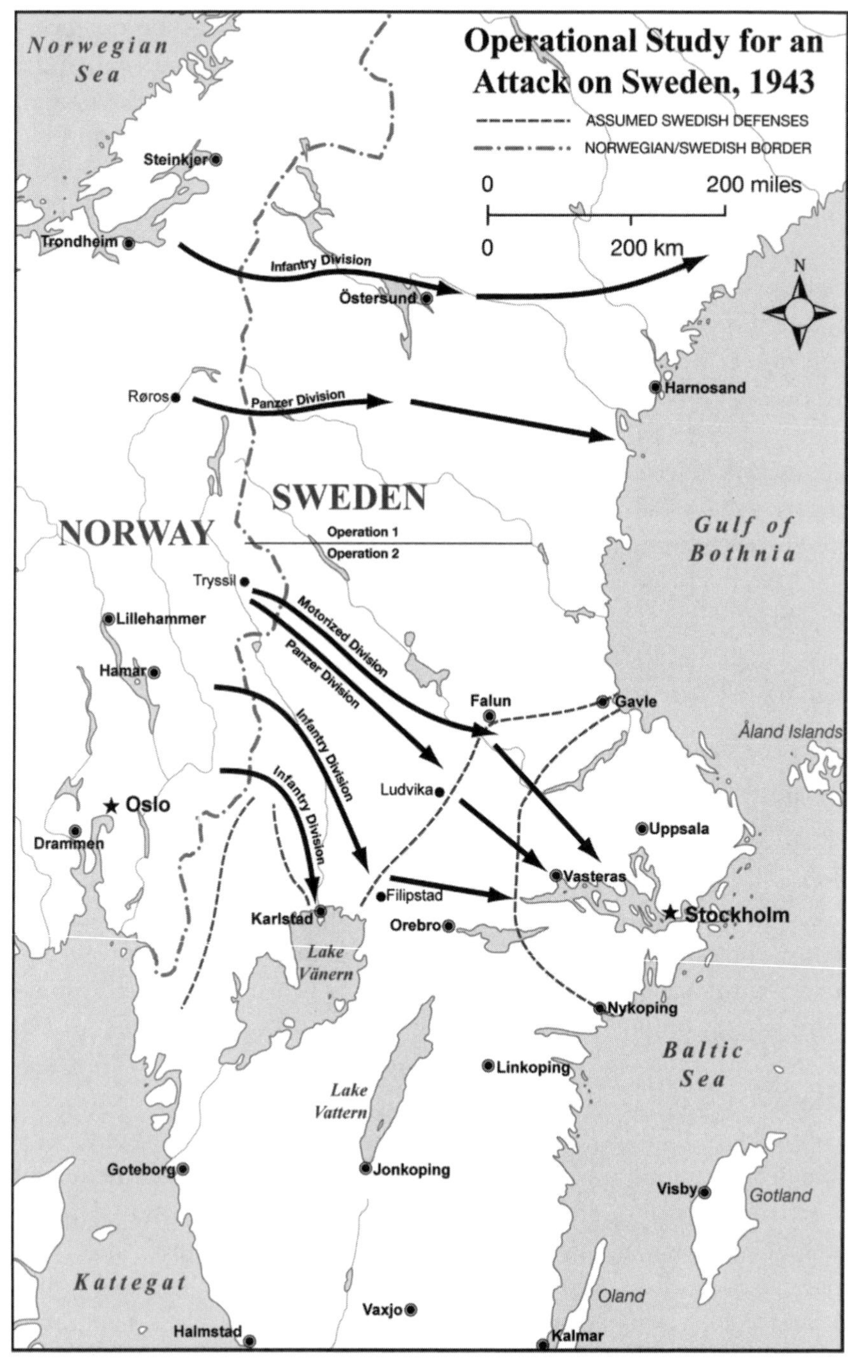
Operational Study for an Attack on Sweden, 1943
ASSUMED SWEDISH DEFENSES
NORWEGIAN/SWEDISH BORDER
0
200 miles
0
200 km
N
Norwegian Sea
Steinkjer
Trondheim
Infantry Division
Östersund
Røros
Panzer Division
Harnosand
SWEDEN
NORWAY
Operation 1
Operation 2
Gulf of Bothnia
Tryssil
Lillehammer
Motorized Division
Panzer Division
Hamar
Infantry Division
Infantry Division
Falun
Gavle
Åland Islands
Ludvika
Oslo
Drammen
Uppsala
Vasteras
Filipstad
Karlstad
Orebro
Stockholm
Lake Vänern
Nykoping
Baltic Sea
Linkoping
Lake Vattern
Goteborg
Jonkoping
Visby
Gotland
Kattegat
Oland
Vaxjo
Halmstad
Kalmar

including heavy ships, the Germans could lose control of the Baltic Sea and he saw those ships as an important tool by which to influence Swedish actions.

Swedish–German Relations 1940–43

Hitler considered Sweden's neutrality in World War II of vital importance to Germany's war effort. Sweden furnished Germany with more than 60 percent of that country's requirements for high-grade iron ore. Air and land transit rights over and through Swedish territory greatly eased Germany's logistics problems in Finland and northern Norway. The Swedish Navy provided escorts for ships carrying iron ore to Germany through its territorial waters.

In the Anglo-Swedish War Trade Agreement it was agreed that Swedish exports to Germany would remain constant at the 1938 level. This meant they had agreed to provide Germany with no more than 10 million tons of iron ore. A German request now asked for an increase in these levels. The Swedes agreed, but the agreement had little practical value since the facilities could only handle the amount agreed to earlier. The Swedes were also very accommodating in allowing German troops to transit Swedish territory between southern and northern Norway. This transit agreement was concluded on July 8, 1940, and a supplement to this agreement on September 14 doubled the allowable transit traffic. These involved for the most part personnel on leave, but occasionally included specialized groups. Wilhelm Carlgren reports that about 1,800 personnel traveled through Sweden each day in October and November and the total had reached 260,000 by the end of the year.[18] Grier writes "From June 1940 until November 1943 Sweden's railroads carried over two million men on leave, more than 700,000 tons of military supplies, and 60,000 wounded (mainly from the front in Finland), many of the wounded on Swedish hospital trains."[19] This is also the number given by Wangel, who adds that nearly 100,000 railroad cars were used.[20] Compare these events to a blank Swedish refusal in 1940 to allow an Allied force to transit northern Sweden on their way to help Finland. However, it is possible that Sweden was aware that the real objective of the Allied expedition was not to help the Finns, but to seize the iron ore mines.

As the Germans marshaled their forces in Finland for the attack on the Soviet Union, the Swedes were also very cooperative. In May 1941 Sweden allowed the 8,000-man strong motorized SS Kampfgruppe Nord to move from Oslo through Sweden to Narvik. The Swedes also permitted the 163rd German Infantry Division to move from Oslo through Sweden to Finland in June 1941.[21]

Relations between Berlin and Stockholm proceeded without any serious problems through 1942. There was no longer any fear in Berlin that Sweden would turn against Germany. Germany was achieving all her goals vis-à-vis Sweden through diplomacy. The same atmosphere existed in Stockholm: the Swedes did not fear a German attack. In view of the fact that the country was surrounded by German forces on all sides, it was critical for Sweden to pursue a frictionless relationship with Germany. Sweden depended on Germany when it came to trade, but also with German allies and the occupied territories.

The major sticking points in relations in this period had to do with the free Swedish press, ships under the control of the Norwegian government in exile that happened to be in Gothenburg harbor, and Swedish naval escort for German ships. The clearly anti-German tone in some of the press led to numerous diplomatic protests from Berlin. It eventually caused the Swedish Foreign Minister to declare that it would be in the nation's best interest for the press to tone down its coverage of political matters. While the tone in the press was indeed tempered, the real feelings remained as before.[22] The 10 Norwegian ships in Gothenburg that were causing problems were, after six months of diplomatic wrangling, allowed to proceed to Great Britain. Only two reached their destination. In all, Sweden tiptoed on a tightrope as far as relations with both Germany and the Allies were concerned.

On July 9, 1941 three large German troop transports hit Swedish mines in Swedish territorial waters near Öland, the second largest Swedish island in the Baltic. The transport sank and 200 German soldiers drowned. This led the Germans to press for Swedish naval escorts through Swedish waters; the request was granted in late July 1941.

Swedish channels remained open to the West and also to the Soviet Union.[23] The United States encouraged Sweden to be prepared to resort to force against any threat against its sovereignty and independence. The Soviets also remained friendly, mostly out of fear that not doing so could drive Sweden into the arms of Germany. Stockholm remained a focal point for diplomatic interaction, as we have seen, when it came to serving as a relay between Moscow and Helsinki.

Admiral Wilhelm Canaris (1887–1945), head of the Abwehr (Department for Foreign Intelligence and Security within the OKW), had created, before the outbreak of war, major branches in countries likely to remain neutral. These were open for business as soon as hostilities began. These well-staffed organizations were established in Spain, Portugal, Switzerland, Sweden, Turkey, and China. The Allied, Soviet, and Japanese intelligence services were equally active in most of these countries. Stockholm was therefore a beehive of espionage, counter-espionage, and double-agent activities. Ladislas Farago writes "As professional neutrals usually are, the country was inundated by them [spies], both belligerents' secret agents and privateers free-lancing for personal profit."[24]

It should be remembered that this was the time that Finnish peace feelers were in full swing—a fact that was well known to the Germans. In the summer of 1943, the Finnish Foreign Minister had informed the United States that Finland would not join the Germans in resisting an invasion of Norway, even if it spilled over into Finland (see Chapter 4). This information was passed through another beehive of espionage activity, Lisbon, Portugal. We don't know if this was known by the German intelligence services.

The state of German–Swedish relations fluctuated with the former's fortunes on the battlefield. It was therefore natural that they reached their high-point early in the war. As the fortunes of war began to shift against the Germans in late 1942, however, the Germans detected a change in Sweden's attitude. In late 1942 and the early months of 1943, Hitler's chronic fear of an invasion of Norway, reinforced by recent events in North Africa, continued unabated. The North African landings appeared to indicate that the Allies were committed to a strategy of attacking on the periphery of Europe, which made Norway a likely next target. Deliberately planted Allied rumors and deception efforts reinforced the German view.

The Swedes had long feared that if the war turned against Germany, they could become a target should the Allies decide to invade Norway. The "rumor mill" was full of stories about a German attack on Sweden in order to eliminate an uncertainty factor in case of an Allied attack against Norway. The Swedes had managed to break the military and diplomatic codes used by Germany soon after the German occupation of Norway. This was made possible by the fact that Germany leased telephone and telegraph lines that passed through Sweden between Oslo and northern Norway. These lines were tapped, as was the line from Berlin to the German Embassy in Stockholm. The cypher code was broken by a Swede named Arne Beurling (1905–86), a professor of mathematics, who also recreated a German encrypting machine through reverse engineering.[25] According to Grier, the Swedes deciphered (2,100km) of telegraph text in 1942 alone.[26] These intercepts continued until mid-1942 when the Germans were tipped off by the Finns. This immediately led the Germans to alter their codes and rely on underwater cables.[27]

In this uncertain and unpredictable environment, Sweden began to take diplomatic and military steps as early as 1942 in case the many rumors of German action against Sweden should come to fruition. The military was ordered to increase its state of readiness. The Swedish king sent a personal message to Hitler and the Swedish government assured both Berlin and Helsinki that the country would defend its neutrality and that it had both the determination and resources to oppose any intervention from the West.

German Invasion Plans and Preparations

Both General Nikolaus von Falkenhorst, the German commander in Norway, and Hitler were deeply concerned about reports from Finnish sources in December 1942 about planned Allied actions against Norway. In addition, the many rumors circulating in Stockholm were passed on by the German attaché system and Abwehr fed them to the OKW, these serving to increase Hitler's paranoia and anxiety. However, both OKW and Falkenhorst discounted the possibility that the Allies intended to occupy Norway since it was viewed as being unrealistic and too costly. Falkenhorst drew the same conclusion about landings in Denmark or in southern and central Norway. He and his command in Norway believed that an attack on the narrow waist of the country between Namsos and Narvik would be the most likely Allied course of action.[28] The distance from the sea to the Swedish border is in some places as short as 19–25 miles (30–40km).

The OKW and the Army of Norway had to consider the possibility that the Allied landing would take place in northern Norway. This was addressed at a planning conference at the OKW in mid-March 1943. It concluded that an Allied landing in northern Norway would only jeopardize the German position in Scandinavia if it were accompanied by a Soviet offensive, a possibility considered unlikely on the rather precarious ground that too much mistrust existed between the Soviet Union and the Western Allies.[29]

A successful landing somewhere at the narrow waist of Norway presented Falkenhorst with a nightmarish scenario. All German forces in northern Norway and Finland would be able to hold out only as long as their pre-positioned supplies lasted. A simultaneous Swedish intervention on the side of the Allies would be catastrophic. The most likely Swedish reaction to an Allied landing in Norway, however, according to reports arriving at the Attaché Branch in Berlin, was that Sweden would adopt a policy of strict neutrality.[30] However, this alone would be exceedingly damaging for Germany, as one had to assume that Sweden would stop all exports to Germany and terminate the transit agreements. This possibility and the fact that the sea lanes along the Norwegian coast would not be usable, led Hitler to decide to increase the levels of pre-positioned supplies in northern Norway and Finland, to an extent where they would be sufficient for one year.

The Germans also sent additional forces to Norway to allow Falkenhorst to form an "operational reserve" (synonym for the forces intended for use against Sweden), which was increased to three divisions by ordering his two corps in southern and central Norway (XXXIII and LXX) to each set aside one division for this purpose. The assumption was that OKW would provide replacements for these divisions. It was decided on February 5, 1943, that these additional forces would be in the form of six fortress battalions and a mountain division.[31] Five days later Lieutenant General Rudolf Bamler (1896–1972), Falkenhorst's Chief of Staff, issued orders for the XXXIII Corps to release an additional division for the operational reserve as soon as the 14th Luftwaffe Field Division promised by OKW arrived in Norway. That Hitler and the OKW were willing to commit the equivalent of three divisions to Norway at the time of Stalingrad and the subsequent Soviet winter offensive demonstrates better than anything their concern for the northern flank.

On February 10, General Bamler selected an officer to lead the planning effort in case action against Sweden became necessary. The officer selected was Lieutenant General Adolf von Schell (1893–1967), the commander of the 25th Panzer Division in Norway. The appointment order came with some specific guidance.[32] It was presumed that Schell would be the commander of the three-division force being assembled, which included his own Panzer division. Schell was directed to send one division across northern Sweden towards the Gulf of Bothnia to serve as a blocking force designed to keep Swedish forces in the north from interfering with the main operation. The main drive into Sweden would come from southern Norway, with the mission of capturing Stockholm and airfields in southern Sweden.

In view of the situation on other fronts, the plan to give the Army of Norway a mountain division was scrapped, but the 14th Luftwaffe Field Division arrived as promised. With its arrival the Army of Norway had 12 divisions, including one poorly trained and badly equipped armored division.[33] Schell was told to assume that the Allies had crossed into Sweden and had captured airfields in the southern part of the country. It was also to be assumed that the Swedes would resist any violations of their territory.

OKW soon realized that the mission given to Schell was unrealistic in view of the forces he would have available. He was tasked to invade a relatively large country with three infantry divisions and one armored division, the latter being in poor shape. Falkenhorst had no further forces to spare for the operation in view of Hitler's orders for an absolute defense of the long Norwegian coast following recent British/Norwegian commando raids (Lofoten and Vågsøy). To cope with the problem of inadequate forces, General Jodl directed the Army of Norway and the Twentieth Mountain Army to come up with a coordinated study for the defense of the whole Scandinavian area, but to do so in a way that avoided "even the appearance of encroaching on Swedish sovereignty." These were verbal instructions given on March 16, 1943, but Hitler quickly ordered that there be no follow-up written instructions. On this subject Ziemke writes:

> Both Hitler and Jodl were obviously anxious to avoid offering Sweden any provocation at that time, especially since militarily they were not in a position to accept the consequences; but it was

> quickly demonstrated that the latter condition was one which Hitler, at least, did not intend to tolerate indefinitely.[34]

It soon became apparent that there were differences between Hitler and Jodl. Falkenhorst had requested additional fortress battalions in lieu of the mountain division that was not coming. OKW turned down this request only to find out a few days later (March 13, 1943) that Hitler had ordered six more fortress battalions to Norway and had asked OKH whether it would be possible after all to send a mountain division from the Eastern Front. He also ordered the 25th Panzer Division brought up to full strength and issued heavy assault weapons.[35]

This was the situation when the Chief of Staff, Twentieth Mountain Army (General Hermann Hölter, 1900–89) and Chief of Operations, Army of Norway (Colonel Bernhard von Lossberg[36]) arrived in Germany on March 16, 1943, for a planned conference on the situation in Scandinavia, referenced in Chapter 3.[37] Hölter reported that there was not much the Twentieth Mountain Army could do to help the Army of Norway in case of an Allied invasion. A suggestion by Jodl that one division be withdrawn from one of the two German corps in central Finland was quickly rejected by Dietl, the commander of the Twentieth Mountain Army. OKW announced that a "rebuilt Stalingrad division"—295th Infantry Division—would be sent to Norway.[38]

On March 23, OKW informed Falkenhorst that an additional regiment would be added to the 295th Infantry Division, plus eight fortress battalions, an increase from the six mentioned earlier. Falkenhorst attached five of these battalions to the 295th and the other three were used to create reserves. The 295th would be stationed in the Trondheim area, where it would relieve the 181st Infantry Division, which would become part of the "operational reserve." The 25th Panzer Division was receiving modern tanks and assault guns and being brought up to full strength. This was to be completed before the end of June.

Schell and his staff were meanwhile busy carrying out the Army of Norway's task of preparing plans for an invasion of Sweden. It was referred to as *Studie Schweden* and was completed and submitted to the Army of Norway on April 6.[39] The plan's assumptions estimated that the Germans would encounter 9–12 Swedish division-size units distributed in three groupings. One was near Östersund in north-central Sweden. The second group was positioned around the capital, Stockholm, and the third northwest of Lake Väner.

Surprisingly, the intelligence on the Swedish forces was rather poor. In the Fourth Military District, bordering Finland and northern Norway, the Swedes had one infantry regiment and five separate battalions. In the Second Military District in north-central Sweden, there was only one separate battalion. The bulk of the Swedish forces were along the Norwegian border east of Oslo. They also covered Stockholm. In that district there were three infantry divisions, two infantry battalions, and one tank brigade. In the southern part of the country (District Three) there was one infantry division, one infantry brigade, one infantry regiment, and two separate battalions. There were also two infantry battalions on the island of Gotland.[40]

The Germans knew they would face formidable terrain that favored the defense. The west–east river valleys come off the mountain range (Kölen Mountains) dividing the Scandinavian Peninsula and serve as a watershed. Steep valleys restricted north–south movements and therefore maneuverability. The tactics that Schell settled on were based on swift movements and they appear almost reckless. The Germans were hoping that relentless pressure by leapfrogging the lead combined-arms elements as was done in Norway in 1940 would work. The Germans also put much emphasis on the fact that they would face an enemy not accustomed to war. Schell wrote, "It can be expected that the enemy, unaccustomed to battle and, in any case, not credited with a high degree of enthusiasm for combat, will not be able to hold against this method of operation with heavy and armored weapons, particularly, if it is possible—as planned—to appear where least expected."[41]

Schell prepared two options in accordance with his directive from the Army of Norway. In an oversimplified form, Option 1 consisted in one drive from the Trondheim area with one infantry division directed at Östersund. The 25th Panzer Division would attack from the Røros area on the southern flank of the infantry division. It was considered relatively easy to continue this option to the Gulf of Bothnia after Östersund was captured. While this option could reach the Gulf of Bothnia, it was only a partial solution, as the Swedish forces in the north and those in the south would be left unmolested.

The second option was more comprehensive and involved additional forces. Schell proposed a northern drive consisting of a motorized division and a Panzer division through the river valleys east of Trysil near the Swedish border. By adopting these routes two of the Swedish defense lines would be flanked and the first organized defensive line expected to be encountered was the outer defense perimeter of Stockholm. In the south, two infantry divisions would cross the border east of the Oslo area. There were two lines of Swedish defenses in this area: one along the border and the other at the northern tip of Lake Väner. It was hoped to avoid both these defensive lines, which meant that the first line to be encountered would be the outer defenses of the capital. This operation called for several small parachute and amphibious landings.

The Germans recognized that the Swedes might pull back their forces in the vicinity of Lake Väner and assemble up to seven divisions for a counterattack against the Germans approaching from the north. Schell concluded that such an operation by the Swedes "required quick decisions, great daring, lightning execution, and great flexibility in the high and intermediate leadership, which are not expected of the Swedes."[42] Option 2 was, like Option 1, very risky and based on a low opinion of the Swedish military.

In adopting the tactics used in their invasion of Norway in 1940, the Germans appear to have forgotten the two key ingredients to German success in southern and central Norway: surprise and the quick capture or destruction of the mobilization centers and supply depots. These ingredients threw Norwegian attempts to mobilize into chaos, except for northern Norway, and there the Germans soon faced a desperate situation that was only salvaged by their attack in the West.[43] None of the two ingredients for success could be counted on in their plan for Sweden. The massing of forces in Norway near the Swedish border would make both strategic and tactical surprise impossible and there appears to have been no effort to neutralize the Swedish mobilization and supply organizations. Once fully mobilized, the Swedish order of battle was also impressive. It would have consisted of nine infantry divisions, three ski brigades, five artillery regiments, four mountain artillery battalions, three engineer battalions, five anti-aircraft regiments, four tank regiments, and four mountain artillery battalions. It was therefore important to disrupt the mobilization by carrying out a speedy operation.

The German air and naval offensives against the Murmansk convoys had marked the Luftwaffe's high-water mark in Norway with respect to operational strength. Since then, the Luftwaffe strength in Norway had been seriously weakened by transfers to other fronts. In the summer of 1943 it consisted of 70 fighters and ground-support aircraft and 50 bombers. These were expected to carry out their normal missions on the Norwegian coast as well as support the attack on Sweden. It was difficult, if not impossible, with these scarce resources to carry out the precision ground-support operations that had characterized the 1940 invasion of Norway. Without air superiority it would be problematic to prevent the movement of Swedish reserves to counter the drives that Schell envisioned.

Colonel Lossberg, the Operations Officer of the Army of Norway, reviewed the Schell plan and quickly decided that a combination of the two options would be required to hold out a prospect for success.[44] However, it was still far from certain that the forces would be available to combine the two options. After abandoning a suggestion to trade three divisions from the Eastern Front with three divisions in Norway, the Germans were left with Hitler's decision to create three new divisions for Falkenhorst's operational reserve. Two of these were to be static divisions, one to be formed in Germany by July 1, and one to be formed in Norway ready by August 1 with cadre from existing divisions in Norway and recruits from Germany. This, according to OKW plans, would free two infantry divisions for the operational reserve. Hitler also decided to create another Panzer division for Norway by September 15, 1943, using elements from the Eastern Front.

Falkenhorst announced that he would use the two static divisions to free the 214th and 269th Infantry Divisions. The six-division operational reserve thus created would be positioned in such a way that it could reinforce the coastal region in case of an Allied attack and also be available for use in the planned operations against Sweden.[45] One regiment would also be positioned near Narvik as a reserve. Falkenhorst requested two corps headquarters from Germany to control the six divisions.

The German Navy saw the Swedish Navy as a significant threat that could be contained only if its units were trapped in port at the start of hostilities. If it were successful in doing so, the German Navy anticipated no serious problems in carrying out its part of the operation. The Germans planned to trap the Swedish naval units by mining the entrance to the harbors the day before the attack, much as they and the Finns had done in bottling up the Soviet Baltic Fleet in 1941. However, the two situations were vastly different. The Swedish Navy was located in multiple harbors, while the Soviet Baltic Fleet was located in one place, Kronstadt, with a long and narrow passage to the open sea.

To accomplish its mission, the German Navy planned to reinforce the Baltic Training Fleet with destroyers and minelayers. They counted on the fleet's four cruisers and one World War I battleship to deal with any Swedish units that might put to sea, despite the minefields or units already on patrol in the Baltic. Swedish naval units at sea were expected to inflict losses on German shipping.

The German Navy, in their wishful thinking, hoped to capture intact most of the Swedish destroyers, submarines, torpedo boats, and 40 minesweepers if the land operations progressed as anticipated. Here again they misunderstood their own success in Norway in 1940, which led to the capture of more than half of the Norwegian fleet. The element of surprise that led to the success in Norway could not be counted on in the case of Sweden. The Swedish fleet, particularly the modern destroyers, torpedo boats, and submarines would be a welcomed addition to the German Navy, but the Swedish cruisers and five coastal defense ships were considered too outdated to be of any value.

While the German Navy requested only a two-month notice, it sounded some notes of caution about the wisdom of the whole operation. If it did not go as smoothly as hoped, Germany risked the loss of its submarine training area and the paralysis of the submarine fleet and heavy shipping losses in the Baltic. A protracted operation could also disrupt supply shipments to Finland, the loss of Swedish iron ore, and an end to transit across Swedish territory. The German Navy also worried that a protracted operation could result in the intervention of American and British air forces. As late as May 23, 1943, the SKL worried about the attitude of Finland to a German attack on Sweden. This was no doubt intended for Hitler's eyes, as it dealt with the epicenter of his many concerns in the Baltic. He was desperately trying to keep Finland in the war and would be sensitive to anything that jeopardized his efforts.

The German Navy also worried that a simple pre-emptive strike on

Sweden could create the very circumstances Germany hoped to avoid: an Allied landing in Scandinavia. The SKL pointed out that timing was not ideal, as the German Foreign Ministry was about to open critical negotiations with Sweden on trade and transit. The final conclusion by SKL was that the capture of Leningrad and the elimination of the Soviet Baltic Fleet should be preconditions for any move against Sweden.[46]

Falkenhorst informed his subordinate on June 21 that he intended to conduct large-scale maneuvers in the fall after all promised forces had reached the theater. Some of the units arrived on schedule, but one infantry division and one Panzer division had not arrived. The greatest transformation was regarding the 25th Panzer Division, which had become a full-strength division with 21,000 men assigned.[47] These numbers are misleading, however. The 25th Panzer Division personnel consisted of green troops equipped with captured foreign equipment. The other divisions were in a similar condition. The personnel were old, they lacked the means to maneuver, and the usual élan and tactical proficiency were simply not there.

The rapid deterioration of the German positions in other theaters began to cast a dark cloud over the planned operations against Sweden. The failure of the offensive against the Kursk salient doomed any hopes that Leningrad would be taken. The situation in Russia was complemented by deterioration of the German status in the Mediterranean and increased worries about Allied landings in France or the Balkans. Matters were also worsening in Swedish–German relations in general. The Nazi leadership was furious at the Swedish assistance in the evacuation of Jews from Denmark. The Germans planned to arrest and deport all the Jews in Denmark and this became known to the Danish resistance in September 1943; an exodus of Jews from Denmark to Sweden followed. About 8,000 were received by the Swedes and given asylum. About 500 were arrested by the Germans and sent to concentration camps. Norwegian Jews were also crossing the border to Sweden and given asylum.

Influenced by the weakening German military situation and pressure from the Western Allies, Sweden notified Germany on June 29, 1943 that the troop transit agreement would not be renewed. On August 5 that year Sweden decided that all transit was to end before October. The German plans for action against Sweden were also beginning to collapse. By the end of July 1943 the OKW informed the Army of Norway that the infantry division it was waiting on would not be available. Falkenhorst was also told that the additional Panzer division would not arrive by September as planned.

It was already an unaffordable luxury for Germany to keep 25 divisions tied up in Norway and Finland so as to be ready for an "in case" scenario. It appears that Hitler had begun to recognize this reality. In August he ordered the 25th Panzer Division to the French coast. This transfer was followed by that of the 181st Infantry Division to the Balkans. These transfers caused the fall maneuvers to be scaled back, aimed primarily at potential Allied landings in central Norway. With only two divisions, instead of the hoped-for six in the reserve formations, any move against Sweden was ruled out by both Falkenhorst and Bamler. Though the Army of Norway was directed to continue studies on how to counter a change in Sweden's stance, invasion was no longer a practical solution. Dealing with Sweden would have to wait until a future time, a time that never came.

Deteriorating Relations

The last two years of the war were marked by a rapid shift in Swedish policy. By 1944 the Swedes had concluded that Germany would lose the war. This realization and increasing pressure from the Western Allies were the primary reasons for this policy change, which began with the refusal to renew the transit agreements in late summer of 1943. In August of that year the Swedes announced that Swedish ships bound for German harbors would no longer be insured. Since Swedish ships had carried 40–50 percent of the export to Germany, this action was tantamount to refusing to allow Swedish ships to carry cargo to Germany and it put the Germans in a precarious position. At about the same time, the Swedes refused the passage of German ships through its territorial waters and on September 27, they closed their Baltic ports to foreign ships. The Germans could still import via the dangerous Narvik route or through ports in southwest Sweden, but the export of iron ore and ball bearings saw an immediate drop of more than 30 percent. The trade agreement with Germany was eventually cancelled. In order not to give the Swedes an excuse to go over to the Allies, the SKL issued a directive on September 29 that all violations of Swedish territorial waters were to be avoided.[48]

Sweden had become increasingly involved in the Finnish–Soviet negotiations for an armistice. In the fall of 1943 and spring of 1944, the Swedes repeatedly urged the Finns to reach an accommodation with their historical enemy, a move that undermined German policy. The Germans were aware of these actions, but there was not much they could do for fear that doing anything would be counterproductive.

From 1943 onward the Swedes undertook to train and arm Norwegians and Danes in Sweden. Such activity drew protests from Germany, and Sweden found it necessary to refer to the activity as the training of police troops. More than 50,000 Norwegians had fled to Sweden and by the end of the war 15,000 fully trained and armed Norwegians were organized into ten battalions, which entered Norway on May 8, 1945. The number of Danes who had fled to Sweden was much smaller and the trained personnel were organized into a brigade of 3,600 men, who entered Denmark on May 5, 1945.

In the last year of World War II, German relations with Sweden were of course driven by Hitler's views, but the German Navy had a large input in what happened. At times there was a dichotomy in their views—Hitler did not want to do anything that jeopardized relations with Sweden, while the German Navy at times took a more aggressive stance. Within the German Navy, the SKL was very cautious while the operational commanders in the Baltic often clamored for some action against Sweden. Hitler was upset by the drift in Swedish policy away from Germany and continued to worry about Swedish intervention in the war. Dönitz worried about the loss of the submarine training areas. These were already in jeopardy as a result of Finland's withdrawal from the war and heavy aerial mining of the training areas by the British. Soviet submarines were operating in the Baltic Sea as of October 1944. Admiral Hubert Schmundt (1888–1984) and later Admiral Oskar Kummetz (1891–1980),[49] the German naval commanders in the Baltic, were very suspicious of the Swedes and took a more aggressive stance than Dönitz and the SKL.

There are no indications in the records that Sweden harbored any aggressive designs with respect to Germany. Those actions most often mentioned were purely contingency plans aimed at warding off German aggression or encroachments on Swedish interests. Swedish plans in 1943 to launch attacks in the direction of Oslo and the Norwegian waist between Trondheim and Narvik were counterattack plans in case of a German invasion.[50]

Frequent Swedish aerial and naval reconnaissance off the coast of the Baltic States were intelligence-gathering operations directed as much against Soviet activities as they were against the Germans. Yet they led to several encounters that resulted in the loss of at least two Swedish aircraft and two fishing boats. These activities, as far as can be determined, took place in international waters, except possibly the sinking of the fishing vessels. These confrontations ceased after the Swedes defended themselves and Dönitz, Ribbentrop, and Hitler intervened to halt provocative actions. Eventually, the Swedes curtailed their activities and the SKL directed that even in the restricted war zone in the eastern Baltic, commanders were to make sure that no Swedish ships were sunk.

Swedish activities in the Gulf of Bothnia also have a simple explanation. The Åland Islands, between Sweden and Finland in the northern Baltic, were demilitarized in accordance with an international treaty in 1921. Because of fear that Germany or the Soviet Union would occupy them in case of war, the Finnish and Swedish governments had agreed in the late 1930s that Finland should, with Swedish assistance as a co-guarantor of the islands, embark on their partial remilitarization. This was approved by the signers of the 1921 agreement and by the League of Nations.[51] Germany considered occupying these islands in 1944 under the operation code-named *Tanne West*, noted above. The objective of the operation was to secure the sea routes from ports in the Gulf of Bothnia to Germany. The Finns had a relatively strong garrison on the Åland Islands that would no doubt resist a German attack. Furthermore, such an operation would be sure to draw strong reaction from Sweden as co-guarantor to the status of the islands. Finally, forces could only be spared by taking a division from the German army in Denmark, something that was considered too risky in view of perceived Allied threats against the German northern theater of operations. Because the plan presented both problems and risks, Hitler cancelled it on September 3, 1944.

Strong German naval units continued to visit the northern Baltic. The Swedish Navy and air force carried out frequent reconnaissance around the islands, possibly at the urging of the Finns. The Swedish Navy had contingency plans for dealing with German actions against the Åland

Islands but, again, they were strictly defensive in nature.

With respect to Courland and Hitler's oft-mentioned reason for holding this peninsula—to influence Swedish actions—there was no factual foundation for Hitler's concern and he must have known this to be true. Grier is right when he observes that "Sweden's reaction to Germany's defense of Courland was not quite what Hitler claimed."[52] He points out that at the very time Army Group North took up its position in the Courland Peninsula, Sweden ordered a decrease in military readiness. The Swedes had by now concluded that there was practically no danger of a German attack and they paid scant attention to the Courland pocket. Robert Payne is on the mark when he writes that Hitler confounded his generals "often by giving reasons for a course of action that were not the real reasons."[53]

NOTES

1. William Norton Medlicott, *The Economic Blockade* (London: HMSO 1952-59), Vol. 1, Chapter 4, Section 6.
2. *Fuehrer Conferences on Matters Dealing With the German Navy 1940*, Memorandum by the War Economy and Armament Division of the OKW, dated February 22, 1940, translated and printed by the Office of Naval Intelligence, Navy Department, Washington, D.C. (1947) volume 1, pp.18–19.
3. Lunde, *Hitler's Pre-Emptive War*, p.550.
4. Lossberg, *op. cit.*, p.70 and Lunde, *Hitler's Pre-Emptive War*, pp.283–85.
5. Grier, *op. cit.*, p.157.
6. Trevor-Roper, *op. cit.*, pp.61–64.
7. Lunde, *Hitler's Pre-Emptive War*, pp.15, 59, 62, and 550.
8. Oluf Sundell, *9. April* (Stockholm: Sohlmans, 1949) p.227.
9. German Third Mountain Division, *Kriegstagebuch*, 04261130. These and later specialists were mostly camouflaged military personnel. A message from Group XXI (Nr. 298 dated May 22, 1940. at 1900 hours reads: "40 machine-gun and mortar specialists are leaving Berlin for Narvik via Sweden at 1000 hours on May 23. A further 80 specialists will follow in about 3 days. Appropriate attire will be worn for the purpose of concealment."
10. Carl O. Schuster, "What if? German Plans to Invade Sweden in World War II," in *Command Magazine*, Issue 9 (1991) p.51.
11. Carl-Axel Wangel, *Sveriges Militära Beredskap 1939–1945* (Köping: Militärhistoriska förlag, Militärhögskolan, 1982).
12. Wangel, *op. cit.*, pp.322–25 and Schuster, *op. cit.*, p.51.
13. Ladislas Farago, *The Game of the Foxes: The Untold Story of German Espionage in*

the United States and Great Britain During World War II (New York: David McKay Company, Inc., 1972), p.524.

14. Wangel, *op. cit.*, pp.338–51.
15. Ziemke, *The Northern Theater of Operations*, p.238.
16. Hitler's initial decision called for the decommissioning of all ships larger than destroyers.
17. Raeder as cited in Chris Mann and Christer Jorgensen, *Hitler's Arctic War: The German Campaigns in Norway–Finland, and the USSR, 1940–1945* (Hersham: Ian Allan Publishing, 2002) pp.139 and 141.
18. Carlgren, *op. cit.*, p.84.
19. Grier, *op. cit.*, p.154.
20. Wangel, *op. cit.*, p.498.
21. Lunde, *Finland's War of Choice,* p.76.
22. Carlgren, *op. cit.*, pp.84–85.
23. Farago, *op. cit.*, p.526 gives an example of Sweden feeding intelligence to the Allies. On May 20, 1941, the Swedish cruiser *Gotland* spotted the German battleship *Bismarck* and the heavy cruiser *Prinz Eugen*, escorted by three destroyers, northbound in the Kattegat. This information was passed to the Norwegian naval attaché who in turn provided the information to the British. This allowed the British to assume correctly that the ships sighted were going to break into the North Atlantic and take the necessary actions that led to *Bismarck*'s sinking at the end of the month.
24. Farago, *op. cit.*, pp.512 and 521. Farago devotes three fascinating chapters to the espionage activities in Sweden (pp.511–56).
25. This same professor also managed to decipher 10,400 messages to and from the Russian Baltic Fleet.
26. Grier, *op. cit.*, p.250, note 24 and Carlgren, *op. cit.*, p.106.
27. Grier, *op. cit.*, p.157.
28. Army High Command, Norway (AOK Norwegen) Ia, Nr. 773/43 and views of the Chief of Staff, AOK Norwegen found in Ia 15/43, dated March 21, 1943.
29. Lunde, *Finland's War of Choice*, pp.247–48.
30. Schuster, *op. cit.*, p.48.
31. Ziemke, *The German Northern Theater of Operations*, p.253.
32. AOK Norwegen, Ia, Nr. 3/43, instructions for the Commanding Officer, 25th Panzer Division on February 10, 1943.
33. Ziemke, *The German Northern Theater of Operation*, p. 255, and note 39.
34. *Ibid*, p.255 and the OKW *Kriegstagebuch* dated March 3, 1943, as well as Walter Warlimont's testimony on the OKW War Diary at the International Military Tribunal.
35. *OKW Kriegstagebuch*, March 13, 1943.
36. This is the same officer who figured prominently in the planning for Operation *Barbarossa* (see Chapter 2).
37. Lunde, *Finland's War of Choice*, pp.247–48.
38. OKW *Kriegstagebuch*, March 16, 1943.

39. Army of Norway *Kriegstagebuch, Studie Schweden* by Commanding General, 25th Panzer Division, dated March 31, 1943.
40. Carlgren, *op. cit.*, p.238.
41. Ziemke, *The German Northern Theater of Operations*, p. 258.
42. *Ibid*, p.260.
43. Lunde, *Hitler's Pre-Emptive War*, especially pp.218–48.
44. Army of Norway *Kriegstagebuch*, Review of Studie Sweden, dated April 12, 1943
45. According to the Army of Norway *Kriegstagebuch* entries dated May 5 and 14, 1943. and Ziemke, *German Northern Theater of Operations*, p.261, the two Panzer divisions and the 214th Division were to be stationed west and southwest of Oslo, in the Sarpsborg–Halden area. The 269th Infantry Division would be north of Oslo, in the Lillehammer area, while the 181st Infantry Division would be positioned northeast of Dombås. The 196th Division would be stationed north of Trondheim with one regiment at Steinkjer and one at Bodø.
46. Ziemke, *The German Northern Theater of Operations*, pp.261–62.
47. *Ibid*, p.262.
48. Grier, *op. cit.*, p. 162.
49. Admiral Huber Schmundt had commanded the naval task force against Oslo in April 1940. It was the most unsuccessful of the six naval task forces and he was severely criticized for approaching the Norwegian forts in a single file with the flagship leading and at a slow speed. The result was the loss of the most modern warship in the German Navy, the heavy cruiser *Blücher* and more than 1,000 soldiers and sailors. Admiral Oskar Kummetz commanded the failed Operation *Regenbogen* (Rainbow) against Convoy JW51B in December 1942 that led to Großadmiral Raeder's dismissal and Hitler's decision to scrap the surface fleet. The reasons these officers survived and were promoted must have been political and ideological.
50. Grier, *op. cit.*, p.159.
51. Lunde, *Finland's War of Choice*, p.10 and p.329.
52. Grier, *op. cit.*, p.165.
53. Payne, *op. cit.*, p.435.

8

New German Submarines and Their Training Areas

The German Submarine Situation in 1943

The German submarine fleet that Karl Dönitz assumed command of in January 1939 was actually a neglected part of the German Navy.[1] It consisted of only 57 boats and less than half could be considered modern. Early in the war, Dönitz argued for attacks against merchant shipping as the best strategy for his submarines, but his superiors Raeder and Hitler preferred attacks against British warships. Their position soon changed because of the difficulties of such attacks.

Primarily due to Dönitz' efforts, there was a dramatic increase in the size of the submarine fleet, to where it numbered about 250 in January 1942 and more than 400 a year later. The increase in the size of the submarine fleet was accompanied by a spectacular increase in their success against merchant shipping. The most successful years for Dönitz' submarines were 1942 and the early part of 1943, and this was basically due to US entry into the war. The submarines enjoyed great success off the US East Coast and in the Caribbean, because US ships were lacking in anti-submarine protection. However, extraordinary results were also achieved in the Atlantic. The climax in the battle for the Atlantic was reached in the spring of 1943. The Allies lost more than 500,000 tons of merchant shipping in the Atlantic in March 1943. Yet the tide was turning as total losses to Allied shipping in the North Atlantic dropped drastically from a high of 1,066 ships in 1942 to 285 ships in 1943.[2] When one compares the successes achieved in these two years with German submarine losses we are confronted with a stark difference: The Germans lost 86 submarines in 1942 but in 1943 the losses had risen to 243 vessels.[3] Grier writes that "Rarely has a period of victory been so closely followed by one of utter defeat."[4]

There were numerous reasons for this drastic turn in the fortunes of the German submarines. The Allies had expended enormous resources on the development of effective countermeasures to the submarine threat. An important intelligence break came in May 1941 when the British captured a German submarine with a complete Enigma code machine with instructions on its use. This intelligence bonanza allowed the Allies to read the German submarine radio traffic and take countermeasures. The Germans continued to believe that their code was unbreakable and the only change they made was to introduce a fourth rotor into their Enigma machines in January 1942, but this was instituted as a "product improvement" and not as a result of any knowledge that the enemy had broken the code. Max Hastings writes that this refinement nevertheless defied the code-breakers throughout 1942.[5]

While the ability to read submarine messages was probably the most important factor in the turn of events, it was accompanied by other important developments. These must be viewed against the German failure to strive for technological improvements in their submarines, as long as the German Navy was enjoying great success at sea. In late 1942 and 1943 the Allies had begun to provide protection for their convoys in the form of escort carriers. It meant that the convoys now had air cover, either short-range or long-range, from their departure point to their destination. Radar, the creation of anti-submarine protective groups, and the installation of high-frequency direction finding equipment (HF/DF) also played important roles in the turning of the tide. The German countermeasures focused on the air threat and the Allied use of radar, basically ignoring the danger posed by HF/DF.[6]

When submarine losses continued to mount, reaching 38 in May 1943, Dönitz ordered his boats to leave the North Atlantic. With the withdrawal of the submarines from the Atlantic, there was a danger that the German Navy would be just a bystander to events for the rest of the war. In his memoirs Dönitz describes his dilemma as follows: "In June 1943 I was faced with the most difficult decision of the whole war. I had to make up my mind whether to withdraw the boats from all areas and call off the U-boat war, or to let them continue operations in some suitable modified form, regardless of the enemy's superiority."[7] It was not in the nature of such an ambitious officer as Dönitz basically to give up on a role for his navy, so his difficult deliberations probably had more to do with how he could overcome the obstacles and thereby retain his influence with Hitler. Dönitz therefore did not despair and quickly regained his optimism, as reflected in his many briefings of Hitler, which are referenced below. This newfound optimism is also displayed in a statement he made on January 20, 1944:

> The enemy has succeeded in gaining the advantage in defence. The day will come when I shall offer Churchill a first-rate submarine war. The submarine weapon has not been broken by the setbacks of 1943. On the contrary, it has become stronger. In 1944, which will be a successful but a hard year, we shall smash Britain's supply [line] with a new submarine weapon.[8]

While new U-boats were being developed Dönitz decided to put his conventional submarines back in operation. He reasoned that if the Allies did not face a submarine threat, they would stop the convoy system and start sending single ships across the Atlantic. The Germans calculated that this would save the Allies about 33 percent in transport requirements. The redeployment of submarines in 1944 relied on operations by two or three rather than the former "wolf pack" method, and their area of deployment was limited.[9]

It appears that Dönitz kept Hitler well informed about the submarine losses, starting in April 1943. Instead of showing any pessimism, Dönitz argued for an increase in submarine construction from 25 per month to 30 per month.[10] Hitler agreed. In the same month as he withdrew his submarines from the Atlantic, Dönitz received Hitler's approval again to increase submarine production, this time to 40 per month. He also requested that Speer, as Reich Minister of Armaments and War Production, take over all naval construction. Hitler agreed on May 31, 1943.

Dönitz' goal in placing naval construction under Speer may have been to achieve a higher priority. While German war production priorities are difficult to determine accurately—they were often shifting due to Hitler's vacillations and constant rivalries within the Nazi hierarchy—to have Speer involved could only be a plus for the navy. The rocket program is a good illustration. On June 10, 1943, in one of his pep-talks to his military leaders, Hitler stated that the Germans had only to hold out and that London would be leveled to the ground and Britain forced to surrender. He set October 20, 1943, as the start date for massive rocket attacks.[11] Churchill, quoting Speer, states that each V-2 required about as many man-hours as six fighters and 1,500 skilled workers were transferred from the anti-aircraft and artillery production to support the V-2 program.[12] In late July Hitler settled on a monthly production of 900. Speer calls this whole notion absurd. Because of technical difficulties, the V-2 was not ready until September 1944 and then was militarily a dismal failure—in the words of Speer "nothing but a mistaken investment."[13] In retrospect, he deplores that he had not insisted on the continued development of the surface-to-air missiles that were much closer to becoming operational in large numbers.

In August 1944, in one of his erratic moods, Hitler ordered the production of fighter planes stopped. This was at the same time as he ordered 2,000 fighter aircraft to support operations on the Western Front. General Adolf Galland (1912–96), commander of the Luftwaffe's fighters, was very upset and asked Speer to accompany him to see Hitler to argue against the decision. Hitler was unmovable and he berated his visitors. Speer writes that this was the first command by Hitler that he disobeyed by ordering fighter production to proceed as planned.[14]

Speer and his associates brought aircraft production to its highest level of the war in the fall of 1944. Despite this amazing accomplishment, Hitler had to do with less than 900 combat aircraft for the Ardennes Offensive.[15] The problems were lack of fuel and shortages of trained and experienced pilots. About one-quarter of the allotted aircraft were lost in a massive New Year's Day attack on Allied airfields and installations.

The constant shift in priorities threw the whole apparatus into chaos. Hitler could recite an unbelievable array of statistics on military output, but he appears to have lacked the requisite knowledge of the fields of science and production. Robert Waite observes correctly that Hitler used his incredible memory for detail both as a crutch and as a weapon against those who disagreed with him.[16] Germany's war economy was therefore hampered by divided authority and responsibility. The inertia this created was further reinforced by traditional resistance to centralization of priorities, and Hitler's preference for the "divide and rule" approach. For example, Göring was responsible for the aircraft industry, Walter Funk (1890–1960) for the civilian economy under the Economics Ministry, General Georg Thomas (1890–1946) for military procurement under the OKW, and Speer for the Ministry of Armaments.

German economic leaders such as Speer tried to convince Hitler of the need for full centralized control of the allocation of resources. Mark Harrison at the Department of Economics at the University of Warwick writes:

> Ultimately, however, they were unable to secure it; in particular, Speer could not extend his influence over German labour, under the protection of Nazi traditionalists like [Fritz] Sauckel (the protégé Of Hitler's personal secretary, Bormann) of the Reich Labour Office. At the height of Germany's economic mobilization the principle of divided responsibilities meant that her economy remained full of untouched reserves of industrial capacity, of female labour, of Himmler's SS resources.[17]

Speer produced amazing results after his appointment in 1943 as Reich Minister of Armaments and War Production. However, while the new organization overcame some of the decentralization, problems of divided authority, split responsibility, and particularly cronyism continued to hamper German war production.

Grand Admiral Dönitz

Throughout the period 1943 to the end of the war, Hitler repeatedly stressed the importance of having a safe area for submarine training, and cited that as one of the many reasons for holding on to the Baltic coast. This coincided with the period during which the German Navy's submarine fleet was undergoing a major transformation, and Grier offers this as "the most likely reason why Hitler chose to defend Courland and other bridgeheads along the Baltic" and that the decision concerned "the Atlantic Ocean more than the Eastern Front."[18]

While Grier may be right, such a decision was not rational. The Soviets could easily cut their way to the Baltic coast west of Courland. Such is in fact what happened. It would put their air force within striking distance of the German submarine training areas and quickly bring the harbors along the coast within range. Furthermore, the eastern Baltic was already lost when Finland withdrew from the war, Soviet submarines and torpedo boats were exiting the Gulf of Finland, and Soviet forces had reached the Bay of Riga.

Dönitz' memoirs are strangely silent on the policy aspects of this subject and on his close relations with Hitler. He devotes considerable space to technical aspects of the submarine program and to the obstacles, but little to his own views on one of the cardinal reasons given by Hitler for desperately trying to hold on to the coastal area of the Baltic. There is one exception which takes the form of a self-serving excuse and needs to be quoted in its entirety:

> In these activities the supply and evacuation of the Army in Courland became something of special importance. On July 9, 1944, I had given Hitler my opinion on the effect that a Russian breakthrough to the coast of Courland would have on the situation at sea in the Baltic, and, as far as the German Army in Courland was concerned, at numerous subsequent conferences I had confined myself solely to the technical problems of its supply and evacuation. I had not expressed any views on any other aspect of the situation.
>
> Before the conference at Fuehrer Headquarters on March 17, 1945, General Guderian, the Chief of the General Staff, told me that Hitler's unwelcome decision to hold Courland had been taken partly on naval considerations. I replied that I was convinced that Hitler's decision had not been influenced in any way by the situation at sea and that if he, Guderian, had any doubts on the subject, I felt that the matter should be cleared up at once. That same day Guderian gave his appreciation of the situation on the eastern front. I told Hitler that, from the Navy's point of view, "the holding of West Prussia was still, as it always had been, of primary importance and that, from the point of view of the situation at sea, the defence of Courland was of no importance. The carrying of

> supplies to Courland was nothing but a burden to the Navy."
>
> Hitler thereupon explained his reasons for not giving up Courland. These were based entirely upon the exigencies of the situation on land.[19]

Grier is obviously on the mark when he concludes that Dönitz' biography is not trustworthy.[20] Those who wrote the foreword and prologue to Dönitz' memoirs appear to go out of their way to describe the grand admiral as non-political and even unaware of the persecution of the Jews.[21] Despite claims to the contrary, Dönitz became a member of the Nazi party in early 1944. Those who rose to high rank towards the end of the war such as Ferdinand Schörner, Lothar Rendulic, and to a lesser extent Heinz Guderian, had one thing in common: they had proven themselves to be loyal supporters of Hitler and his ideology and Dönitz was cut from the same cloth.[22]

Dönitz' views on Jews are rather well documented. He admitted at the Nuremberg trial that 12,000 concentration camp inmates worked in the navy yards and that he had personally visited two camps. Under questioning by Sir David Maxwell-Fyfe, a statement made by Dönitz in a speech on Heroes' Day, March 12, 1944 was read back to him. Dönitz did not deny making this statement:

> What would have become of our country today if the Fuehrer had not united us under National Socialism? Split parties, beset with the spreading poison of Jewry, and vulnerable to it because we lacked the defense of our present uncompromising ideology, we would long since have succumbed under the burden of this war and delivered ourselves up to the enemy who would have mercilessly destroyed us.[23]

A book edited by Alan E. Steinweis and Daniel E. Rogers provides additional evidence of Dönitz' ideological leanings. On one occasion he blamed Swedish action in closing its territorial waters on that country's fear of "international Jewish capital," and in 1944 he stated "I would rather eat dirt than see my grandchildren grow up in the filthy, poisonous atmosphere of Jewry."[24]

Albert Speer as Minister of Armaments and War Production worked closely with Dönitz. Speer admitted his guilt at the Nuremberg trials and was sentenced to 20 years' imprisonment. Despite their cooperation in the submarine program, it appears that Dönitz opposed Speer's efforts at the end of the war to thwart Hitler's scorched-earth policy. A book which appeared in 1976 tried to rehabilitate Dönitz, and the contributors included a number of senior officers in the United States and the United Kingdom.[25] According to Albert Speer, Dönitz' admiration for Hitler appears to have continued long after World War II ended.[26]

Dönitz died in December 1980 and was buried on January 6, 1981. He had lived out his life in a small town in Schleswig-Holstein on the pension of a naval captain, since the West German government had ruled that all subsequent promotions were due to Hitler. Although the German government refused to accord him military honors and prohibited military personnel in attendance from wearing uniforms, a number of German and British naval officers disobeyed the order.[27]

Whatever opinion one has about Dönitz and the Nuremberg Military Tribunal, it is important to keep both his military background and relationship to Hitler in mind when considering his actions in the period 1943–45. He was a submariner, deeply interested in the activities of that service. He frequently called his deployed submarine captains for reports and opinions. In so doing, he may have unwittingly contributed to submarine losses due to Allied HF/DF capabilities. Statements that the training of submarines and their crews was possible only in the eastern and central Baltic may have been true in 1943 and the first half of 1944, but not later that year or in 1945. There may therefore be a smidgen of truth in Dönitz' statement that he had not argued for the retention of the Courland Peninsula after July 9, 1944.

The New Submarines

The new submarines being developed by Germany in the period 1942–45 are well covered in military literature, both in books and on the internet and therefore not detailed herein.[28] Grier's book on this subject is exceptionally well researched, comprehensive, and balanced. Many of the other books tend to show a service bias: seeing the trees but not the forest.

The improvements in submarines to the point where they would be capable of contesting the Allies focused on alterations to existing submarines and the development of two new types. The alteration was to outfit existing submarines with snorkels. This was not a German, but a Dutch invention outfitted on their submarines. The snorkel allowed the submarine to travel long distances without surfacing as long as they periodically came up to periscope depth for fresh air and recharging the batteries.

The first new submarines to become operational were the Type XXIII. They were small coastal submarines designed to replace existing coastal submarines and operate in the shallow waters of the North Sea, Irish Sea, Mediterranean, and Black Sea. They could remain submerged, fully or at periscope depth, almost all the time and they were faster than the submarines they were replacing. The XXIIIs carried a crew of 14, were 114ft (35m) long, weighed about 250 tons and were able to cruise underwater at 12.5 knots for one hour. Their maximum diving depth was 330ft (100m). A major disadvantage of the Type XXIIIs was that they carried only two forward torpedoes and when these were used the submarine had to return to base to reload, since they had to be reloaded externally. The Type XXIII could be transported by rail, but considerable disassembly was required.[29]

The Type XXI submarines integrated the same technology as the Type XXIIIs. They were intended for the high seas, had a crew of 57, were 237ft (72m) long, and had a displacement of 1,620 tons. Their streamline hulls allowed for high underwater speed and shorter diving time. The large hull provided greatly increased battery capacity, approximately triple that of existing submarines. They could maintain a submerged speed of 17.5 knots for 90 minutes and more than 12 knots for a period of 10 hours before recharging batteries using the snorkel. However, they remained vulnerable to Allied aircraft when snorkeling because it was often possible to see the underwater shape of the submarine, despite the fact that the snorkel itself was difficult to spot. The vastly increased submerged speed not only allowed them to outrun many surface ships, but also gave them the ability to close quickly on a target (existing submarines had to surface to make quick approaches to a target). XXIs had a long underwater range (c. 340 nautical miles/640km at 5 knots), itself a great improvement in safety. They carried six bow torpedo tubes and, because of the hydraulic reloading system, they were capable of firing 18 torpedoes in less than 20 minutes. Their diving depth was 376ft (115m).

There were also numerous other technological improvements for which information is available in a large number of books. The vessels produced were truly revolutionary submarines and may well have dealt a heavy blow to the Allied trans-Atlantic traffic if they had become available in time and in sufficient quantities. Designs based on the Type XXI were adopted by both the Western Allies and the Soviets after the war.

Hitler's military experience as a soldier in the List Regiment on the Western Front in World War I was, as we have seen, instrumental in shaping his views in World War II. His own claim is that these were the most formative years of his life.[30] It appears that he served honorably and was awarded the Iron Cross, both Second and First Class as well as the black Wound Badge; it was unusual for a soldier with the rank of Gefreiter (corporal) to be awarded the Iron Cross, First Class. Hitler was a messenger and lived at the regimental headquarters, and some have hinted that his proximity to the officers of the regiment may have helped in obtaining this decoration.[31]

Based on his background and the fact that Germany was a continental power, it was natural for Hitler to be more concerned with the operations of his army than with those of his air force and navy. He also felt let down by the promises made by those services (i.e. the Battle of Britain and the loss of capital ships). On the other hand, it was primarily the army that had carried out the attempt on his life in July 1944.

After the army and air force suffered severe reverses in 1942 and 1943, Hitler may have concluded that it was necessary to look elsewhere to reverse his fortunes. When Dönitz, full of enthusiasm, briefed Hitler on the new submarines and their potential in July 1943, he found an attentive listener. Dönitz' presentation was music to Hitler's ears and a change from the dreary and depressive reports he received from the other services. He wanted to know when the first of these submarines would be ready. Dönitz answered that the current estimates of November 1944 would be too late and he requested Speer, who was present, to speed up production. Hitler ordered Speer to give the construction of these submarines top priority.[32]

Submarine Production

In the fall of 1943, Dönitz ordered 152 Type XXI and 140 Type XXIII submarines. Speer examined the plans and he promised the first Type XXI would be ready in April 1944. Speer determined that the need for early availability of the submarines ruled out the luxury of making a prototype. This later resulted in a number of problems. Speer had established a Central Board for Ship Construction with representatives from both the navy and the Armaments Ministry. He selected Otto Merker (1899–1986), a man from the automobile industry to head the board.[33] To reduce the construction time, Merker proposed a modular approach. Naval engineers estimated that this would reduce construction time from about 22 months to 5–9 months. It would also halve the time submarines were in slips, greatly reducing the time they would be vulnerable to Allied bombing. Merker's decision on modular construction may have been influenced by the American building of Liberty Ships.

A great number of industrial sites were involved in this mammoth project. Each hull consisted of eight prefabricated sections with final assembly at the shipyards. Some of these sections weighed as much as 150 tons and were too heavy for the rail system. Consequently, they were shipped via rivers and canals to the final assembly yards in Danzig, Bremen, and Hamburg. The Germans planned eventually to transfer all assembly operations to a gigantic bomb-hardened assembly plant at the Valentin submarine pens in the small port of Farge downriver from Bremen. Work on this enormous facility began in early 1943.[34] The plant was nearly complete in March 1945 when it was severely damaged in an Allied air raid using bunker-buster bombs.[35] It was still not completed when the war ended.

Although Dönitz had expected 152 XXIs and 140 XXIIIs to be completed by the end of October 1944, the completion schedule could not be followed for a variety of reasons as detailed below. Only 118 Type XXI were completed by the end of the war and only four of these were ready for combat.[36] Only 59 Type XXIIIs of the 140 planned for were ready by the end of the war and only six put to sea, the first on 29 January 1945 and the last on 4 May. None was sunk while engaged in operations.[37]

Production Obstacles

There are those who claim that the new boats should have been given a higher priority in armament production. They forget the fact that Hitler was caught in a "Catch 22" situation. If he reduced the priority accorded the Luftwaffe, the facilities needed for submarine construction and the synthetic oil refineries would have been destroyed earlier than was the case. If he reduced the priority for the army, replacements for the hard-pressed units in both the East and West would quickly slow down, as would equipment for the new divisions that were being formed. Lowering the priorities for the other two services could only lead to undesirable situations and a shortening of the war. Professor Grier provides some interesting and telling figures in this regard. He notes that the steel required for the Type XXI submarines "would have provided Guderian 5,100 additional tanks" and that another 'miracle weapon' program, the V-2 rockets "devoured resources equivalent to 24,000 combat aircraft." He concludes that "the German war effort certainly would have benefited more from five thousand tanks than from Dönitz' 'miracle weapon.'"[38]

A possible solution to the problem was to withdraw units that were ordered to defend the "fortified places" to shorter defensive lines. The wisdom of some decisions can only be judged retrospectively. This was not the case with allowing large forces to be voluntarily encircled or besieged without realistic prospects for relief or re-supply. History tells us that this is a virtually certain prescription for disaster. The new submarine program, on the other hand, cannot be judged realistically except in retrospect.

The lack of prototypes for the new submarines and the fact that many companies involved in the modular construction had little experience in shipbuilding caused severe problems. Much time was wasted because the modular sections did not interlock properly because specific tolerances were exceeded. Additional delays were caused by the long training time required for crews. Most sources note that the normal submarine training time was about three months, but the new types, because of their advanced technology and design complexity, required around six months. The Allies had also started—on August 7, 1944—heavy aerial mining of the Bay of Danzig, now the primary German training area.[39] The mining forced the Germans to move their training to the less suitable Bay of Lübeck. A number of new submarines that were near the completion of trials and ready to head to Norway for stationing were lost in the Bay of Lübeck, probably victims of mines. The loss statistics of Claes-Göran Wetterholm undoubtedly include those lost in routine training accidents.[40]

Allied bombing of production and assembly facilities became an increasing problem for German submarine output. Except for the mining operations in the Baltic, the Allies did not make a concerted effort to damage and destroy the German submarine facilities until January 1945. This objective was simply not on the priority list of the strategic air offensive. Instead, the priorities of the Allied heavy bomber forces were:

- Synthetic oil facilities
- Transportation network
- Tank and mechanized transport production facilities.

The British Admiralty was aware, however, that the Germans were developing new submarines. Intelligence was collected not only through an analysis of Enigma deciphers but by reconnaissance flights over German harbors. By mid-December the National Intelligence Division had come up with a rather accurate estimate and status of the new German submarine production. They estimated that 95 Type XXIs were under construction or in various stages of preparation and that 35 had already been commissioned. The Enigma deciphering even allowed the British to conclude that the commanders appointed to skipper these submarines were experienced and capable.[41]

From their information on the German submarine program, the Allies were less worried about the existing submarines being fitted with snorkel and the Type XXIII than they were about the ocean-going Type XXI. The Allies felt that they could handle the threat from the snorkel and Type XXIII submarines by using existing anti-submarine warfare assets to the maximum. However, they felt that the Type XXI could seriously impede transport across the Atlantic and threaten landing operations if those submarines were deployed in sufficient numbers. Only a dramatic increase in anti-submarine warfare assets could counter this possibility. The alarming intelligence reports caused the Admiralty to urge a heavy bombing campaign against submarine production facilities and slips.

The Royal Air Force, which was somewhat skeptical about the navy's intelligence, concluded that an aerial campaign of the kind that was suggested by the Admiralty had to be on such a large scale that it would constitute a serious detraction from existing priorities. They noted that German armored forces and the Luftwaffe were seriously constrained by lack of fuel and that any relaxation on existing priorities would lead to the resurgence of the Luftwaffe and allow the Germans to increase their operations vastly on all fronts. The German coal and oil supplies had, by January 1945, been cut to a fraction of what was needed to prosecute the war on two fronts. Therefore, they argued, there should be no shift in priorities until it was shown that the naval commands could no longer cope with the threat.

In the end, the Admiralty convinced the Combined Chiefs of Staff in mid-December 1944 that it was necessary to take the requested action as long as it did not imperil existing priorities. Heavy Allied bombers were ordered to carry out secondary strikes against submarine facilities. Below is a listing of major raids carried out against the submarine facilities and a summary of their results:[42]

- 18/19 December 1944—a "target of opportunity" raid by 227 Lancaster bombers dropped 817 tons of bombs on Gdynia, a port on the west side of Danzig Bay. The bombs sunk two submarine depot ships, a torpedo boat, and five merchant ships. An oil refinery ship, the World War I battleship *Schleswig Holstein*, and a Type XXI—about to undertake the final training exercise in the Gulf of Danzig—were heavily damaged.
- The first attack by the US Eighth Air Force was carried out on December 31, 1944, when 324 bombers attacked Hamburg, dropping 740 tons of bombs. The Germans shot down 24 aircraft. The raid resulted in the destruction of four Type XXI submarines while seriously damaging two others. A large depot ship and several other vessels were also destroyed.
- An attack on the canals through which pre-fabricated sections were brought to the assembly yards was carried out on January 1, 1945, resulting in the Dortmund–Ems and Mittelland Canals being put out of service until February 6.
- A very successful raid was carried out by the Eighth Air Force against the submarine assembly yard at Hamburg on January 17. The results of the 360 tons of bombs dropped were impressive. Three commissioned Type XXI were destroyed and nine others were seriously damaged. Five merchant ships were also sunk and three damaged. The US lost three aircraft.

- Precision bombing by small groups of Mosquitoes, each carrying a 4,000lb bomb, was carried out against a Type XXI yard in Bremen. These attacks were carried out nightly from February 17 until the end of the month. The most successful attack was carried out on February 21/22. Two Type XXIs were damaged and the launch of three others blocked by debris.
- Eighth Air Force carried out a 198-aircraft raid on the yards at Bremen on February 24. While only one Type XXI was sunk, two floating cranes and the crane used for preparing the submarine were badly damaged.
- An unusually heavy attack by 407 bombers of the Eighth Air Force was carried out on March 11 against the Bremen yard. This attack was so damaging that it virtually shut down the yard.
- A damaging raid on the canal system in February again made it unusable. Another raid on the canal system on March 3-4 damaged it beyond repair.
- Three devastating raids were carried out against the facilities in Hamburg—two by the Royal Air Force and three by the Eighth Air Force. The facilities were virtually brought to a standstill. Eleven older submarines were sunk and five Type XXI were damaged beyond repair. A new destroyer and 15 other ships were also sunk.
- Two destructive attacks were carried out in late March on the gigantic submarine pen at Farge, near Bremen. One raid was carried out by the Royal Air Force while the other was delivered by the Eighth Air Force. The damage delayed construction.
- Heavy raids were carried out by the Eighth Air Force in April 1945 on the port facilities at Kiel. A total of 1,184 aircraft dropped 3,138 tons of bombs. Three older submarines, two liners, and 10 other ships were sunk.
- The British were also busy over Kiel. On the night of April 8–9, 427 bombers dropped 1,503 tons of bombs. Five commissioned Type XXI submarines and five merchant vessels were sunk. Nightly raids by Mosquitoes were carried out from 21 to 27 April.

- Kiel was attacked again on the night of 14–15 April by 467 British bombers. Seven older and two Type XXI submarines were sunk in the British raids and the facilities were practically destroyed in the combined raids.

Raids not directly linked to the air campaign against the new submarine facilities were also damaging. For example, the bombing of factories in Hanover and Hagen destroyed the production plants for batteries. The only other plant producing batteries for the submarines was at Posen and it was captured by the Soviets in January 1945. The Soviet advance also stopped all work at the submarine assembly yard at Danzig.[43] Churchill writes that the Soviet capture of Danzig, one of the three principal submarine bases, was a great relief to the British Admiralty. He observed that the resumption of the submarine war on the scale envisioned was clearly impossible.[44]

The production of the smaller Type XXIII was not nearly as affected by Allied bombing as the Type XXI. Only five of these boats were destroyed by bombing. There were two reasons for this lesser damage. First, the assembly site in Hamburg was sheltered in hardened concrete bunkers. Second, the other assembly point in Kiel was not heavily damaged by bombing. However, the output of these boats dropped off because the supply parts dried up. The production dropped from nine boats each month in 1944 to four in February 1945.[45]

Dönitz, with his single-minded focus on the submarine war, was probably one of the very few among the senior German leaders who still believed in early 1945 that the war could be turned around. He was repeatedly forced to explain to Hitler why the 1943 production schedule was continually falling behind. In these "excuse" sessions he always maintained that the turning of the tide was just around the corner, when he knew that was not the case. Hitler would not have tolerated this from his generals, but Dönitz had apparently ingratiated himself to Hitler in such a way that it was tolerated.[46] His optimistic approach to a person who faced disasters on all fronts may be one explanation. Their ideological compatibility was undoubtedly also important. Raeder, Dönitz' predecessor, met with Hitler infrequently, but Dönitz became practically a fixture at Hitler's briefings and conferences.

Dönitz had focused his entire naval strategy during the last two years of the war on the deployment of the new submarines. While the Germans came up with a design that profoundly influenced future submarine designs, their immense efforts did not help them turn the tide in World War II. The most promising new boats—Type XXIs—never launched a single torpedo at an enemy.

NOTES

1. Dönitz spent most of his career in the submarine service. In World War I he served in the surface fleet for a while and in the 1920s he was involved with torpedo boats. In the 1930s he commanded a training cruiser, the *Emden*, for a short period.
2. Various sources give differing data on Allied shipping losses. See, for example, Terry Huges and John Costello, *The Battle of the Atlantic* (New York: Dial Press, 1977); John Terraine, *Business in Great Waters: The U-Boat Wars, 1916–1945* (London: Leo Cooper, 1989); Nathan Miller, *War at Sea: A Naval History of World War II* (New York, Scribner, 1995); and Clay Blair, *Hitler's U-Boat War: The Hunted, 1942–1945* (New York: Random House, 1998).
3. http://uboat.net/fates.
4. Grier, *op. cit.*, p.168.
5. Max Hastings, *Winston's War: Churchill, 1940-1945* (New York: Alfred A. Knopf, 2010) p.206. This may have been a contributing factor to the large Allied losses in 1942 and early 1943.
6. Dönitz, *op. cit.*, Jürgen Rohwer's Afterword, p.494.
7. Dönitz, *op. cit.*, p.406.
8. Winston S. Churchill, *Closing the Ring* (New York: Bantam Books, 1962) p.14
9. Dönitz, *op. cit.*, pp.406–09.
10. The figure of an average of 25 new submarines per month had not been reached.
11. Speer's decision not to brief Hitler in detail about the potential of atomic weapons was no doubt influenced by his experience with a man who was quickly excited about a program that promised victory and his demands for immediate results. The scientists had briefed Speer that the development of atomic weapons would take at least three years, something that Hitler would not have accepted.
12. Churchill, *Closing the Ring*, p.197.
13. Speer, *Inside the Third Reich*, p.365.
14. *Ibid*, pp.407–09.
15. Erickson, *The Road to Berlin*, p.449.
16. Robert G. L. Waite, *The Psychopathic God Adolf Hitler* (New York: New American Library, 1978) p.503.

17. Mark Harrison, "Resource mobilization for World War II: The U.S.A., U.K., U.S.S.R. and Germany, 1938–1945" in *Economic History Review* (1988) pp.171–92.
18. Grier, *op. cit.*, p.167.
19. Dönitz, *op. cit.*, pp.399–400.
20. Grier, *op. cit.,* p.xx.
21. Dönitz, *op. cit.* Toland, in his introduction appears to support Admiral Chester W. Nimitz' claim that Dönitz was not an ardent Nazi or even a member of the Nazi Party.
22. Dönitz was found guilty at the Nuremberg Trial of planning and waging aggressive war and violations of the law of war. He was sentenced to 10 years in prison. Some of the misconceptions about the admiral may stem from the alleged letters written to him by over 100 senior Allied officers expressing their disappointment at the fairness of his trial and sentence.
23. *Nuremberg Trial Proceedings*, volume 13, May 10, 1946, p.392, Document Number 28978-PS.
24. Alan E. Steinweis and Daniel E. Rogers, *The Impact of Nazism: New Perspectives on the Third Reich and its Legacy* (Lincoln, Nebraska: University of Nebraska Press, 2003). The book is a compilation of essays and the one dealing with Dönitz is written by David Grier.
25. Henry Strutz and Harold Keith Thompson (eds), *Doenitz at Nuremberg, a Reappraisal: War Crimes and the Military Profession* (New York: Amber Publishing Corporation, 1976).
26. See various entries in Speer's *Spandau Diaries*.
27. En.wikipedia.org/wiki/Karl_Dönitz.
28. The new submarines were referred to by the Germans as *Elektroboote* (electric or electro boats) because of their large electric motors.
29. Grier, *op. cit.*, p.172.
30. Weber, *op. cit.,* provides an interesting view of Hitler's service as a soldier. See, for example, pp.288–314 and 340–47.
31. See for example Alan Bullock, *Hitler: A Study in Tyranny* (London: Penguin Books, 1962) p.52.
32. Grier, *op. cit.*, p.172.
33. *Ibid*, pp.172–7.3
34. About 12,000 concentration camp inmates, prisoners of war, and other forced labor took part in the construction of this immense facility.
35. Stephen Flowers, *Barnes Wallis' Bombs: Tallboy, Dambuster & Grand Slam* (Gloucestershire: Tempus Publishers, 2004) pp.350–51.
36. Adam Tooze, *The Wages of Destruction*: *The Making and Breaking of the Nazi Economy* (London: Penguin Books, 2006) pp.617–19.
37. The figures given by Tooze are almost identical to those given by V. E. Tarrant, *The Last Year of the Kriegsmarine: May 1944-May 1945* (London: Arms & Armour Press,

1996) p.183. Tarrant, for example, writes that only 116 Type XXI were completed.

38. Grier, *op. cit.*, p.182 and note 58 quoting various sources.
39. While the concerted effort to mine the training area began in August 1944, the SKL noted, according to Grier, *op. cit.*, p.181, repeated instances beginning as early as April 1944, such that the submarine training areas and shipping lanes in the Baltic had to be closed because of the mine threat.
40. Claes-Göran Wetterholm, *Dödens Hav—Östersjöen 1945* (Stockholm: Prisma Bokförlag, 2002).
41. Tarrant, *op. cit.,* p.183.
42. These figures are based on Tarrant, *op. cit.*, pp.183–89.
43. Churchill, at the Yalta Conference in February 1945, had requested that the Soviets capture Danzig as quickly as possible since it was one of the three assembly facilities for the Type XXIs. Danzig was captured by the Soviets in March 1945.
44. Churchill, *Triumph and Tragedy*, p.462.
45. Tarrant, *op. cit.*, pp.188–89.
46. An example of Dönitz' groveling behavior is the fact that he insisted on launching the first Type XXI submarine on April 19, 1944, which happened to be the day before Hitler's birthday. The results were predictable. Grier reports that there were still openings in the hull that had to be patched with wood and the submarine had to be immediately returned to dry dock and was not commissioned until July 28, 1944.

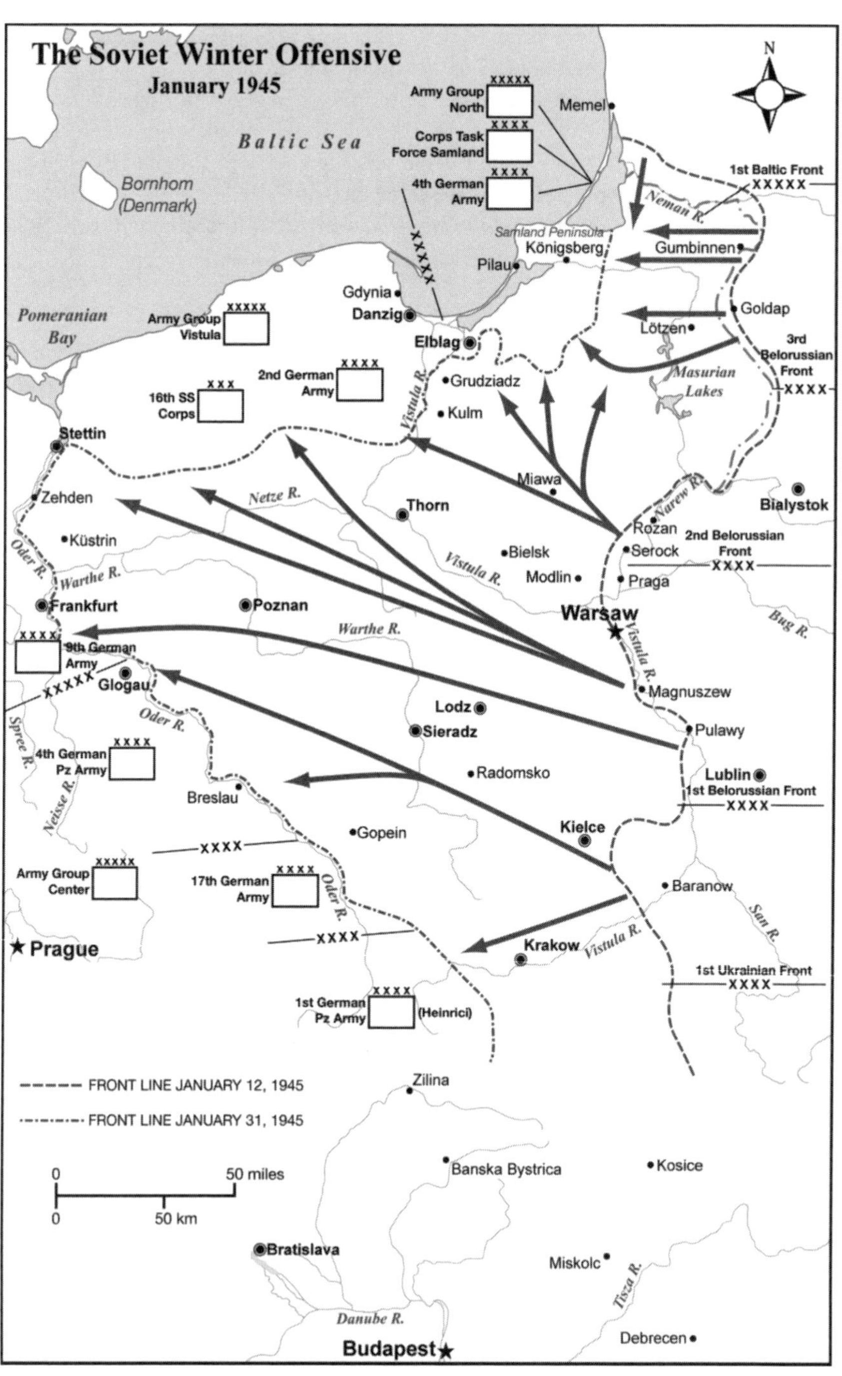
The Soviet Winter Offensive
January 1945
Baltic Sea
Bornhom (Denmark)
Army Group North
Corps Task Force Samland
4th German Army
Memel
1st Baltic Front
Neman R.
Samland Peninsula
Königsberg
Gumbinnen
Pilau
Gdynia
Danzig
Goldap
Lötzen
Pomeranian Bay
Army Group Vistula
Elblag
3rd Belorussian Front
2nd German Army
Grudziadz
Masurian Lakes
16th SS Corps
Kulm
Vistula R.
Stettin
Miawa
Zehden
Netze R.
Thorn
Narew R.
Bialystok
Rozan
2nd Belorussian Front
Küstrin
Bielsk
Serock
Oder R.
Warthe R.
Vistula R.
Modlin
Praga
Frankfurt
Poznan
Warsaw
Bug R.
Warthe R.
9th German Army
Glogau
Magnuszew
Lodz
Oder R.
Sieradz
Pulawy
Spree R.
4th German Pz Army
Radomsko
Lublin
1st Belorussian Front
Breslau
Neisse R.
Gopein
Kielce
Army Group Center
17th German Army
Oder R.
Baranow
San R.
Prague
Krakow
Vistula R.
1st Ukrainian Front
1st German Pz Army
(Heinrici)
FRONT LINE JANUARY 12, 1945
FRONT LINE JANUARY 31, 1945
Zilina
0
50 miles
0
50 km
Banska Bystrica
Kosice
Bratislava
Miskolc
Tisza R.
Danube R.
Budapest
Debrecen

9

Overview of the Soviet Winter Offensive

The Situation in the East

The area between the Baltic and the Carpathians had been relatively quiet since the end of Operation *Bagration* late in the summer of 1944. The key word here is "relatively" since, as we saw in Chapter 6, bitter fighting continued in Army Group North's area culminating in its withdrawal to the Courland Peninsula. Another pocket was formed at Memel as the Soviets cut their way to the Baltic coast both north and south of the city. It was this Soviet drive that fully isolated Army Group North.

At the end of 1944 we find the Soviet armies positioned along the Vistula River to its great bend and then north along the Narew River. They held several bridgeheads across each—at Serock and Rozan on the Narew and at Pulawy, Magnuszev, and Baranow on the Vistula. The Soviets had an extremely impressive array of forces confronting the Germans on the Eastern Front in January 1945. Soviet field strength had grown to 6,500,000 men, and they were about to hurl around 500 rifle divisions in 55 mixed armies and six tank armies at the Germans. No less than 13,000 tanks and 15,000 aircraft were ready to roll. The First Belorussian and First Ukrainian Fronts alone consisted of 163 infantry divisions. In addition the Germans were outnumbered 17 to 1 in the air.[1]

The Second and Third Belorussian Fronts in the north with 12 armies faced Army Group Center's three armies. Their superiority was even more ominous on the First Belorussian and First Ukrainian Fronts opposite Army Group A.[2] There the Soviets had 2,200,000 troops, 6,400 tanks and self-propelled assault guns, and 46,000 indirect-fire weapons. Against these two fronts Army Group A's Seventeenth, Fourth Panzer, and Ninth Armies could muster only 400,000 troops, 1,150 tanks, and 4,100 indirect-fire weapons.[3] The air situation in the center of the front was nearly as lopsided. About 1,875 German planes of all types faced more than 10,000 Soviet aircraft.[4]

Operation *Bagration* had suffered logistically in its closing days. The Soviets intended to avoid a similar situation in their next offensive. By January they had completed the most massive logistical buildup of the war. The two fronts—First Belorussian and First Ukrainian—received 132,000 carloads of supplies. That was more than received by all four fronts before *Bagration*. Nine million rounds for indirect-fire weapons were made available to the two fronts as an initial issue along with 30 million gallons of gasoline and diesel fuel.[5]

OKH's Eastern Intelligence Branch issued its estimate of Soviet intentions and capabilities in December 1944. It concluded that the main Soviet effort would be delivered against Army Group A by the First Belorussian and First Ukrainian Fronts. In an important revision in January 1945, the OKH concluded that the expected offensive against Army Group Center had the lower Vistula area as its objective while the drive against Army Group A could go as far as Berlin. The OKH expected the offensive to begin in the middle of January.[6]

General Heinz Guderian, the OKH Chief of Staff, was very uneasy about the situation in the East. He visited Hitler at the *Adlerhorst* (temporary Führer headquarters in the Taunus Mountains) on Christmas Eve 1944 to plead for a change in strategy. Guderian wanted Hitler to call off the Ardennes offensive and move all forces that could be spared to the Eastern Front. His pleas were in vain, however. Hitler called the estimated build-up of Soviet forces in the East "the greatest bluff since Genghis Khan" and refused to call off the operations in the West. He also refused to withdraw units from Norway or from the Courland pocket.[7] Hitler demanded that the person responsible for the report, General Gehlen, be fired. Guderian refused and Hitler, who had other things on his mind, apparently forgot.

In early August 1944, General Jodl had suggested that the extensive occupied territories were a drain on Germany's resources and he proposed a withdrawal from Finland, northern Norway, northern Italy, and most of the Balkans. The proposal called for the establishment of more defensible positions along the Tisa and Sava Rivers and the southern foothills of the Alps. This shift would shorten defensive lines and release a large number of divisions. At first Hitler adamantly refused, but then on August 20 he relented to the extent of directing Albert Speer to give an appraisal of the raw materials situation after such a withdrawal. Before the appraisal was completed, Hitler again changed his mind and did not show the slightest interest in any voluntary withdrawals. Speer notes that by now Hitler's moods had become totally unpredictable.[8] Without giving Guderian any hint at their Christmas 1944 meeting about what he was about to do, Hitler transferred the headquarters of the IV SS-Panzer Corps along with two Panzergrenadier divisions to Army Group South for a relief operation against Budapest.[9]

Guderian had good reasons to feel gloomy. He was particularly concerned about Army Group A, commanded by General Joseph Harpe (1887–1968). Since the transfer of the Ninth Army to this army group in November 1944, it occupied a long front stretching from the northern border of Hungary to the confluence of the Vistula and Narew. This long front was defended—from south to north—by First Panzer Army, the Seventeenth Army, Fourth Panzer Army, and the Ninth Army. It was a thinly held front, amounting to little more than a string of strongpoints with hardly any depth.

Army Group Center under General Georg-Hans Reinhardt was responsible for covering the approaches to East Prussia and Danzig. At the beginning of December 1944, this army group was in better shape than all others. Its three armies—Third Panzer, Fourth, and Second—had 33 infantry divisions and 12 Panzer or Panzergrenadier divisions to defend a 360-mile (575km) front. This situation changed radically by the end of the year. Five Panzer divisions and two cavalry brigades were stripped away for transfer to other fronts and another Panzer division was taken away in early January.

Guderian visited the Eastern Front in early January. Army Group A's briefing in Krakow on January 8 was pessimistic, but realistic. It estimated that the Soviets would be able to cover the distance from the Vistula to Silesia in six days. Guderian tentatively approved a plan involving an adjustment of the front around the Baranow bridgehead that would have shortened the line and made units available as reserves. The plan involved organizing the front into two sectors, referred to as the *Hauptkampflinie* and the *Grosskampflinie*. The *Hauptkampflinie* is perhaps best described in English as the frontline or line of contact. The second sector was called the *Grosskampflinie* or main battle line. This line was located about 5 miles (8km) behind the front, in the case of the Fourth Panzer Army. Here was a tactical concept sometimes used by the Germans during and since World War I. By withdrawing most forces from the frontline to the main battle line a day or so before the expected onslaught, it was hoped that the heavy enemy artillery preparation would hit the relatively empty frontline trenches. General Gotthard Heinrici (1886–1971), known as a defensive expert, had practiced this tactic with considerable success on the Eastern Front. He also used it in the battle for Seelow Heights on the Oder in 1945.

In this case the withdrawal to the main battle line would also straighten and shorten the front between the Fourth Panzer Army and the Ninth Army, making it more difficult for the Soviets to conduct encirclements. Army Group Center also requested permission to withdraw to a line on the East Prussian frontier, a move that would shorten its lines and make reserves available.

Guderian reported to Hitler at the Adlerhorst on January 9. His main purposes were to seek approval for the proposal made by Army Group Center to withdraw and to argue for reinforcements from the Western Front to go to Army Groups A and Center rather than to Hungary to protect the oil fields. Hitler refused all of Guderian's requests and recommendations, including the adjustment Guderian had tentatively approved for Army Group A.[10]

Hitler's refusal to even allow a minor tactical adjustment to Army Group A's frontline shows how utterly irrational Hitler's behavior had become by this stage of the war. For Guderian even to feel that he needed Hitler's permission for this action speaks volumes about the total subordination of the famous German General Staff.

Soviet Plans

While Guderian and OKH were gloomy about the future, the Soviets were full of optimism. The Stavka plans amounted to a quick operation to end the war. It was to be executed in two phases. The first phase, expected to last 15 days, involved a drive to the Oder and Lower Vistula. The main drive out of their bridgeheads on the Upper Vistula would be executed by the First Belorussian Front under Marshal Georgi K. Zhukov and the First Ukrainian Front under Marshal Ivan S. Konev (1897–1973).

The First Ukrainian Front was to break out of the Baranow bridgehead and head west to Radom. Its right-flank units were to assist the First Belorussian Front in destroying the Germans in the area between Radomsko and Kielce. The drive would continue to Krakow and the industrial region of Upper Silesia before ending along the Oder. The First Belorussian Front was to break out of the Pulawy and Magnuszev bridgeheads. The front's right flank would encircle Warsaw while the main force would continue towards the city of Lodz in the south and Kutno west of Warsaw on the road to Poznan. The drive was to continue via Poznan to the Oder in the vicinity of Küstrin and Frankfurt am Oder.

The Second Belorussian Front under General Rokossovsky was to break out of the Serock and Rozan bridgeheads on the Narew north of the Vistula bend. Its mission was to drive northwestward to the Baltic and clear the lower Vistula area. General Polkovnik Chernyakovsky's Third Belorussian Front was to drive west from its positions east of the Masurian Lakes toward Königsberg. It was hoped that it would be able to encircle the Fourth German Army under General Friedrich Hossbach (1894–1980) in the lake area. The Fourth German Army was tasked with the defense of the East Prussian frontier.

While the main Russian forces were driving towards the Oder and the Lower Vistula, the Baltic Fronts were busy along the coast. In addition to keeping the Germans under pressure in the Courland Peninsula and around Memel, the First Baltic Front, on the right of the Third Belorussian Front, was driving along the Bay of Courland in the direction of Königsberg.

The Soviet plan did not call for a pause along the Oder. They expected the German defenses to crumble and their armies to be shattered in the initial phase. The First Belorussian and First Ukrainian Fronts were to continue the drive to Berlin and then to the Elbe River (possibly even the Rhine). This part of the operation was expected to take about 30 days.[11]

The State of the Wehrmacht

Some observers have pointed out that things looked better for the Germans at the beginning of 1945 than they had in September 1944. The Soviets had not made any substantial gains north of the Carpathians. Army Group South had almost regained its balance after being virtually destroyed in August 1944. The Germans were close to completing their withdrawals from Greece and Albania and the Western Allies were stopped at the Gothic Line in Italy. The Ardennes offensive had not succeeded in its strategic objective, but it had upset the Allied schedule and delayed their advance into the heart of Germany.

However, these improvements were illusions. Germany's ability to hold its fronts had been on a downward spiral, and in the next few months that spiral would spin out of control. The first element in this collapse was the lack of trained manpower to keep the space/force ratio from worsening.

By October 1944 German strength on the Eastern Front had fallen to fewer than 1,800,000 men, and about 150,000 of these were Russian auxiliaries. This constituted a drop in strength of about 400,000 since June 1944.[12] The replacements arriving in the period September 1 to December 31, 1944, went primarily to create new units, which resulted in an illusory increase in units but a glaring discrepancy between authorized strength and present for duty strength in existing formations. The Germans "fixed" part of this problem by simply reducing the 1944 table of organization by 700,000 spaces. The fact that a cumulative shortfall of 800,000 unfilled spaces still existed after the change to the table of organization is a telling illustration of the manpower problem. Self-delusion was carried to great lengths. Artillery units of brigade size were designated "corps" and groupings of one or two battalions of armor and infantry were designated "brigades."

In the months following Operation *Bagration*, a number of unorthodox measures were taken to cope with the falling strength. Goebbels was ordered to come up with 1 million men through the Nazi Party machinery. By the end of the year he had achieved 50 percent of that goal through new recruits and inter-service transfers. In October 1944, Hitler activated the *Volkssturm* (home guard) composed of men between the ages of 16 and 60 who were otherwise exempt from the draft. About 200,000 men from military schools and training centers were organized into *Gneisenau* and *Blücher* battlegroups. The units thus formed failed to live up to their impressive names.

The number of replacements between August and December 1944 was slightly larger (1,569,000) than the losses sustained by the army (1,457,000) for the period June–November. What these units had in common was poor training, poor leadership, and inadequate numbers. General Manteuffel's written observations on the state of the troops along the Vistula front in January 1945 are worth repeating:

> We now had to pay for our tardiness in retiring from the great salient [Ardennes] which in any case was bound to be lost in the end . . . our troops were more tired even than we had expected, and were no longer capable, either physically or mentally, of coping with a tough, well-equipped and well-fed enemy. Replacements received in January were inadequate both in quality and quantity, being mostly older men or of a low medical category and ill-trained as well.[13]

The Germans were also suffering in the materiel field. While production of fighter aircraft, tanks, and assault guns reached new heights in late 1944, due to Speer's efforts, that output could not be sustained because of the heavy bombing of the Ruhr.[14] What was even more alarming was the fact that the Western Allies were closing in on the Ruhr and the Soviets would soon overrun Upper Silesia, where many production plants had been moved to avoid the strategic bombing. The most glaring deficiency was in oil production, where there had been a catastrophic decline. Despite great efforts to change to synthetic oil, overall output had fallen because synthetic oil facilities were at the top of the Allied strategic bombing priorities. The Romanian fields were lost and the hold on the Hungarian fields was tenuous.

Hitler continued his insistence on not making voluntary withdrawals and holding so-called "fortified places" bypassed by the Soviets. While holding some communications centers made military sense because they complicated Soviet supply operations, the vastly increased mobility of the

Soviet military machine reduced the importance of communication hubs. Tens of thousands of troops were uselessly sacrificed trying to hold places that had little military significance.

During the offensive, Army Group North and Army Group Center were isolated—in Courland, East Prussia, and East Pomerania. While some units were evacuated, those that remained encircled represented a terrible waste of manpower at a time when those many hundreds of thousands of troops were needed further west. Army group and army headquarters had become mere mechanical instruments for transmitting the Führer's increasingly irrational will. This alarming tendency began much earlier and represented a great change from the first two years of the war.

German military leaders were taught to expect the unexpected on the battlefield and were instructed to deviate from plans in order to achieve their goals. It was a cornerstone of German military doctrine that leaders were expected to make quick decisions and equally quick executions. Part of that doctrine was that higher German echelons kept their intervention in operations of subordinate units to a minimum. These principles go far back in Prussian history and are referred as *Auftragstaktik* (task tactics) and *Selbständigkeit der Unterführer* (independence of subordinates). They were immortalized by Friedrich Wilhelm von Seydlitz' reply when Frederick the Great repeatedly attempted to get Seydlitz and his cavalry to attack the unbroken Russian infantry line at the battle of Zorndorf in 1758: "Tell His Majesty that my head will be at his disposal after the battle, but that as long as the battle lasts I intend to use it in his service."[15]

Muth, who claims that the German and Prussian officer corps had "the greatest culture of disobedience—with maybe the exception of the French," continued: "The stories and events that kept alive the virtue requiring an officer—even in war—to disobey an order 'when justified by honor and circumstances' were corporate cultural knowledge within the Prussian and German officer corps."[16] In the pages that followed the quote, Muth gives examples that contradict the popular view that a Prussian officer had a robot-like obedience to his superiors. He relates that Frederick the Great, who was furious about the looting of his Charlottenburg Castle, ordered Oberst Johann F. A. von der Marwitz to even the score by looting the castle of one of his opponents, the Elector of Saxony. Marwitz, commanding one of the crack Prussian regiments, refused and immediately resigned.[17]

The culture described by Muth was severely diluted by the immense expansion of the German armed forces and the Nazi ideology. Nevertheless, there are examples from the early part of World War II which illustrate that this concept was alive and well in some quarters.[18] Yet this had all changed by 1942–43, and Robert M. Citino argues persuasively that new communications technologies, a key to mobile operations, contributed to the demise of the earlier doctrine, as mentioned in Chapter 5. Improved communications allowed higher commanders, especially Hitler who distrusted his generals, to intervene in operational matters. This tendency reached ridiculous levels in January 1945. Incensed at the withdrawal from Warsaw, Hitler, in order to maintain absolute control over decisions at the front, ordered that special radio teams be stationed at army and corps headquarters. The commanders were responsible to report all important events through this new radio channel and to make situation reports four times a day of all the facts that might be necessary for decision-making by the highest leadership.[19]

The constant shifting or relief of commanders, which had reached a point of grave disruption during Operation *Bagration*, continued on an accelerated pace in 1945. The quality of senior commanders also deteriorated as loyalty to Hitler became the only real prerequisite. Two loyal disciplinarians—Generals Ferdinand Schörner and Lothar Rendulic—are typical examples. Hitler's quest for loyalty reached a ludicrous level when he appointed the amateur Heinrich Himmler to command Army Group Vistula.

The continuous shift in commanders may have been part of Hitler's control mechanism. Commanders who were in their positions for short periods of time did not have a chance to become thoroughly familiar with their units, their subordinates, and their new sectors. Hitler—with his fascination for irrelevant details—could therefore easily demonstrate that he had a better understanding of the situation in a particular sector than a newly appointed commander.

Soviet Assaults

On January 12, 1945, the Eastern Front exploded as Konev's First Ukrainian Front, with nine armies at its disposal, launched its offensive out of the Baranow bridgehead, followed a few days later by the other fronts to its right. For all their forewarning of the offensive, the Germans were caught in a tactical surprise. The weather was overcast and foggy and the Germans had expected the Soviets to wait for better weather so they could fully utilize their immense air superiority.

The Soviet infantry attack began late in the morning of January 12 after a devastating artillery bombardment. The German frontline positions were overwhelmed. By noon on the first day, the Soviet infantry had opened gaps that allowed tank forces to pass through. By 1700 hours the Soviets had advanced some 12 miles (20km). The XLVIII German Panzer Corps' divisions were destroyed. The reserve corps—XXIV Panzer Corps—was ordered to counterattack but its two divisions near the Baranow bridgehead were overwhelmed before they could get out of their assembly areas.[20]

The German troops paid a heavy price for Hitler's refusal to allow Guderian to make the tactical adjustment to the front he had recommended on January 9, which would have allowed the German armored reserves to be stationed outside the reach of Soviet artillery. The Germans estimated that the bombardment cost them 60 percent of their own artillery and the personnel loss was a staggering 25 percent.[21] The three divisions of XLVIII Panzer Corps were overwhelmed and destroyed. The same fate befell XXIV Panzer Corps, the designated counterattack force. The Fourth Soviet Tank Army turned north on January 13 while the Fifty-Second and Third Guards Tank Armies pushed directly west. Before nightfall Soviet spearheads had reached the Nida River where a 43-mile (70km) gap provided a clear route to Upper Silesia and the Oder. The remnants of XXIV Panzer Corps went into positions around Kielce.

Because the Soviet offensive was staggered, General Smilo von Lüttwitz'(1895–1980) Ninth Army on Army Group A's left flank, had two days warning before the First Belorussian Front attacked from the Pulawy and Magnuszev bridgeheads on January 14. It did not help much. Both frontline corps were badly cut up and lost half their strength before the day was over. The Soviets had linked their bridgeheads west of the Vistula River by nightfall on January 15 and established a solid 310-mile (500km) front, which was rapidly moving west and north.

The entry in the OKH war diary for January 15 paints an unusually stark picture of the situation in the East:

> The Russians have achieved their breakthrough. It is feared that within two days they will have reached the Upper Silesian border. The forces of Army Group are hopelessly inadequate . . . the divisions moved from the West by the Führer on the 13th will not arrive before the 19th, which will be too late.[22]

On January 15 the right flank of the First Belorussian Front, the Forty-Seventh Army, broke through the German lines north of Warsaw on the boundary between Army Groups A and Center. On the same day, three armies from the First Ukrainian Front drove the remnants of XXIV Panzer Corps out of Kielce.

The Third Belorussian Front under Chernyakovsky opened the offensive against Army Group Center on January 13 with an attack on Third Panzer Army north of Gumbinnen. This was followed on January 14 with an attack by the Second Belorussian Front under Rokossovsky out of the bridgeheads at Serock and Rozan against the Second German Army. Both Third Panzer Army and Second Army withstood the Russian onslaught for two days and sealed all penetrations. It was not the Soviets who changed this promising beginning for Army Group Center, but Hitler. As Rokossovsky was attacking out of his bridgeheads on the Narew, Hitler ordered Panzer Corps *Grossdeutschland* and its two Panzer divisions in Army Group Center transferred to Army Group A.

The weather during the opening of the offensive was characterized by fog, and this had prevented the Soviets from fully exploiting their massive tank and air superiorities. The weather began clearing in the north on January 15 and the Third Panzer Army was forced back to keep its front from falling apart. The weather also cleared in the Second Army area on January 16 and the main force of the Second Belorussian Front—five armies and an assortment of tank and mechanized corps—broke through from the Rozan bridgehead and headed northwestward for the mouth of the Vistula.

Since the Third Belorussian Front had failed to make a substantial breakthrough against the Third Panzer Army, it switched its main forces northward opposite the Fourth German Army for another try. In view of what was happening in the Army Group A and Second Army areas, this was the time to pull Fourth Army and Third Panzer Army back from their exposed positions. Such a withdrawal would prevent encirclement, shorten the front, and provide reserves. General Reinhardt proposed such a withdrawal on January 16 but Hitler refused.[23] The most he was willing to do was transfer two divisions from the Fourth Army to shore up the Second Army against Rokossovsky's drive. As usual, this compromise band-aid solution left things worse than they were. The Fourth Army was weakened and, if left in its positions, was an invitation to encirclement. The two divisions made practically no difference for the Second Army.

German Leadership Chaos

Belatedly, on January 13, Hitler ordered two infantry divisions transferred to the Eastern Front from the West, though the OKH did not expect them to arrive before January 19. The following day, as we have seen, before anyone had a firm idea of how the offensive would develop, he ordered Panzer Corps *Grossdeutschland* and its two Panzer divisions transferred from Army Group Center to Army Group A. Next day he also ordered Army Group South to send two Panzer divisions to Army Group A.

While some have credited Guderian with convincing Hitler to take these steps, they appear to have been made by Hitler on his own volition, particularly the transfer of Panzer Corps *Grossdeutschland*. A report by General Guderian on January 14 may have contributed to igniting the law of unintended consequences, similar to the action Hitler took when Generalfeldmarschall Küchler relayed an optimistic report by General Lindemann (see Chapter 4).[24] Guderian had said that it looked like Army Group Center might be able to prevent a breakthrough from Narew to East Prussia. That may have been all that was required for Hitler to order the transfer of Panzer Corps *Grossdeutschland* and two divisions to Army Group A. The transfer hurt Army Group Center and did little to assist Army Group A. Within days of the transfer Army Group Center's front broke and the Soviets were on their way to pinning it against the Baltic coast, since Hitler would not allow a retreat to the Vistula.[25]

It is unlikely that Guderian agreed to the transfer since he had argued (on January 14 and 15) that the Eastern Front would succumb without sizable and timely reinforcements from the West and a halt to Army Group South's offensive so that its armored divisions could be provided to Army Group A. However, Hitler refused to provide additional divisions from the West or to stop Army Group South's offensive.

With the Ardennes Offensive at an end, Hitler moved his headquarters from Adlerhorst to Berlin in the evening of January 15. In his absence the OKH issued a directive allowing Army Group A some operational latitude in the area of the Vistula bend, including permission to evacuate Warsaw. Hitler became incensed when he discovered that it was too late to countermand the directive, as it was already being executed. He had the three senior officers of the OKH's Operations Branch arrested and relieved General Harpe, the army group commander. General Schörner was appointed to take Harpe's job.[26]

What followed was a dizzying shifting of commanders in the middle of a decisive battle. General Rendulic was brought down from Norway to replace Schörner as commander of Army Group North. Rendulic's appointment was short-lived; Army Group North was renamed Army Group Courland on January 26, and the following day—after 12 days in command—Rendulic was sent to command the new Army Group North (formerly Army Group Center). General Heinrich von Vietinghoff (1887–1952) assumed command of Army Group Courland on January 27, but on March 10 he was sent to command in Italy and Rendulic again assumed command of Army Group Courland. These officers hardly had time to unpack, much less become familiar with their commands.

Upon Hitler's arrival in Berlin on the evening of January 15, Hitler told Guderian, to the latter's dismay, that he was moving the Sixth SS-Panzer Army's two corps from the Western Front to Army Group South instead of to Army Groups A or Center.[27] Army Group South was the same organization that had just been ordered to release two Panzer divisions to Army Group A.

Soviet Pursuit

By January 17, the Soviets were into the pursuit phase of their offensive nearly everywhere. Zhukov's leading tanks and infantry had advanced 60 miles (100km) from their start lines. The entire Soviet operation showed dash in exploiting success, dismissal of whatever counterattacks the Germans could muster, and an increased disregard for open flanks that began at the end of Operation *Bagration*. The remnants of XXIV Panzer Corps between Konev and Zhukov's drives was thrown back to the Pilica River. Konev's spearheads crossed that river and moved against Radomsko and Czestochowa. Stavka ordered both Zhukov and Konev to accelerate their drive to the Oder, and Konev to use his second echelon to take Krakow and the Upper Silesia industrial area.

One of the first acts of the energetic but sometimes brutal General Schörner was to relieve the commander of the Ninth Army, General von Lüttwitz. It can be safely assumed that the relief was carried out at Hitler's bidding, as he was fuming at the failure of the Ninth Army to hold Warsaw. General Theodor Busse (1897–1986) was appointed to command the Ninth Army. Schörner also began to send optimistic reports to Hitler. He said that he would be able to defend Upper Silesia when he received the two promised Panzer divisions from Army Group South and gave the Seventeenth Army the mission of defending Silesia. He further assured Hitler that the Soviet drive toward Poznan in the gap between the Fourth Panzer Army and Ninth Army could be sealed with generation of new forces. He did not explain where these forces would come from.

The dispositions and orders Schörner gave to the Fourth Panzer and Ninth Armies reveal that he was either engaged in wishful thinking or that he did not fully grasp the situation in his new command. He ordered the Fourth Panzer Army to stop the Soviet drive toward Breslau at a point west of Czestochowa. The Soviets were already in Czestochowa, and the Fourth Panzer lacked the forces to carry out the mission, since XXIV Panzer Corps had become separated from the army's left flank. The army was in fact reduced to the remnants of two divisions and a couple of brigades. Schörner also ordered the Ninth Army to hold between Lodz and the Vistula and to launch a counterattack to the south. The objective was to close the gap between the Ninth Army and the Fourth Panzer Army.

The Soviet pursuit was so overwhelming and swift that all plans were overcome by events. Both Zhukov and Konev's tank columns were advancing at a rate of 25–31 miles (40–50km) a day and the infantry at 19 miles (30km). Zhukov's forces bypassed Lodz and headed for Poznan. Konev's forces were heading to Breslau, throwing the Fourth Panzer Army back to the German border, while some of his infantry armies turned south to Upper Silesia.

Ninth Army (XL Panzer Corps and Panzer Corps *Grossdeutschland*) was trying to hold a line south of Lodz long enough for XXIV Panzer Corps to cross the Pilica River. Contact between Panzer Corps *Grossdeutschland* and XXIV Panzer Corps was established along the Warte River on

January 22, but they were both driven westward in the relentless Soviet offensive.

Along with them on the roads was a mass of refugees fleeing in terror from the Soviets, who were beginning to exact revenge on civilians. The slaughter of civilians on the Eastern Front by both sides was on a scale that has no equal in modern history. The callous and inhuman behavior of the Nazis toward foreign civilians in the East is well known, but now they applied it to their own citizens. Although everyone knew that a storm was brewing after the Soviets reached the Upper Vistula in August 1944, no plans were made to evacuate the millions who would be caught in that inferno. The provincial Gauleiters did nothing to save the civilians in their area—they were forbidden to do so. Thus when the Soviet winter offensive started it caused millions of German refugees to flee for their lives, taking only what they could carry into terrible winter conditions. It was a miserable human tragedy of gigantic proportions.

A wide gap had developed between the Seventeenth German Army screening the industrial region of Upper Silesia and the Fourth Panzer Army, which had been driven back to the Oder. The Third Guards Tank Army had reached Namslau in Silesia. Konev turned this army south on January 21 along the Oder River behind the left flank of the Seventeenth Army. His armies closed on the Oder along a 224-mile (360km) stretch between Kosel and Glogau between January 21 and 24. The Soviets crossed the river in several places, while the Fourth Panzer Army was left holding bridgeheads on its east bank on both sides of Breslau. Schörner's orders for the Fourth Panzer Army to counterattack the Soviet bridgeheads on the west bank could not be executed.

The Third Guards Tank Army of the First Ukrainian Front coming into Silesia from the northwest appears to have deliberately left an escape route open at the southern end of the Silesian pocket. If so, it was probably a sanctioned action to avoid heavy fighting that would have destroyed much of the industrial region. The Soviet plan was to capture this area as intact as possible. The German Seventeenth Army, with Schörner's permission, withdrew through this opening between January 28 and 30.[28] In the north, the Soviets had managed to make breakthroughs in the sectors of the Second German Army and the Third Panzer Army. This created the possibility that the Fourth German Army would be encircled. Requests from General Reinhardt, commander of Army Group Center, to move the Fourth Army out of mortal danger were refused. There was a distinct possibility that both the Fourth Army and the Third Panzer Army would be encircled in the interior, about 125 miles (200km) from the coast. This would doom the two organizations, since they would not be able to receive re-supply. Hitler finally relented to let the Fourth Army retire a short distance, but insisted that the area around the Masurian Lakes be held.

On January 23, the Second Belorussian Front cut its way to the Baltic coast near Elbing, thereby isolating Army Group Center. The Fourth Army, under General Hossbach, withdrew from Lötzen on January 24 without permission. He intended to take the whole army on a breakout to the west on January 26, and establish a new line from Friedland to Wartenburg. Reinhardt requested Guderian's support, but it was refused. Both Hossbach and Reinhardt were relieved within two hours after making the withdrawal decision. Rendulic, as brutal and loyal to Hitler as Schörner, was appointed to command the army group that was now designated Army Group North. His orders from Hitler were to hold Königsberg and what was left of East Prussia.[29]

In the end, Third Panzer Army was pressed into the Samland Peninsula while the Fourth Army held a narrow corridor to Königsberg. The Second Army had been transferred to Army Group Vistula, a new army group in the north created on January 23. This was considered necessary to fill the gap that had developed between Army Group Center and Army Group A, brought about by the First Belorussian Front bypassing Poznan on January 25 and heading directly for the Oder as the Second Belorussian Front turned north along the Lower Vistula. Guderian had argued for bringing in General Weichs from Army Group F in the Balkans to take over Army Group Vistula, but Hitler gave the command to Heinrich Himmler. Hitler ordered Himmler to close the gap between the two army groups—A and Center—to cover Danzig and Poznan, and to maintain a corridor to East Prussia.[30]

Some of the tasks given Army Group Vistula were already overcome by events. Poznan was bypassed. The Soviets were about to reach the Baltic at the mouth of the Vistula, thereby isolating Army Group Center in East Prussia and severing the corridor that Hitler wanted kept open. For no apparent reason, as noted above, the Germans resorted to a massive re-designation and re-shuffling of units on January 26 and 27. Army Group North was designated Army Group Courland while Army Group Center became Army Group North. Army Group A became Army Group Center. The new Army Group Center lost the Ninth Army to Army Group Vistula. Himmler thus ended up commanding a front with many bends and twists from the mouth of the Vistula in the north to Glogau on the Oder, where it tied into the new Army Group Center.

To defend this long front, Army Group Vistula had an assortment of units, many of them untried. It had two SS divisions, one Latvian SS division, Volkssturm units, and remnants of the Ninth Army. Two major units of the Ninth Army—XXIV Panzer Corps and Panzer Corps *Grossdeutschland*—were now part of the new Army Group Center. Two divisions were encircled in Torun (Thorn) and a similar size force was encircled at Poznan. It made some sense to try to hold Poznan as it was the major transportation hub east of the Oder.[31]

The First Belorussian Front reached the Oder north of Küstrin on January 31 and by February 3 it had closed up to the river from Zehden south of Stettin to its left boundary. While the Germans still held bridgeheads east of the river, the Soviets held bridgeheads north of Küstrin and south of Frankfurt am Oder. The Germans were bringing in a motley assortment of reinforcements to shore up the fronts in Pomerania, West Prussia, and along the Oder. These included the so-called *Gneisenau* and *Blücher* battlegroups, Volkssturm units, and navy and Luftwaffe personnel organized into infantry units. After having adamantly refused to withdraw the troops in Courland and East Prussia before they were surrounded, Hitler now allowed some of these units to be brought out by air and sea. On January 17 he ordered one Panzer and two infantry divisions out of Courland. A further two-division draw-down was ordered on January 22. These five divisions joined Army Group Vistula.

In less than three weeks, the Soviets had completed one of the most spectacular advances of the war, almost 310 miles (500km). At Küstrin, Zhukov's front was only 40 miles (65km) from Berlin and there were no obvious reasons for not carrying out the second phase of the offensive—seizing Berlin and moving to the Elbe. The daily Soviet losses in the offensive were about 20 percent less than in Operation *Bagration*.[32] The front commanders—Zhukov and Konev—reported to Stalin on January 26 that they would be ready to continue to Berlin after a stop of a few days (3–6) to replenish supplies and reorganize.

The space/force ratio advantage that should have swung decisively in Germany's favor and allowed it to form a tight front along the Oder/Neisse and elsewhere did not materialize because of the lengthy fronts the Germans were forced to defend as a result of Hitler's adamant refusal to make any meaningful withdrawals. This will be discussed in more detail in the next chapter.

NOTES

1. Erickson, *The Road to Berlin*, pp.429 and 447. See also Guderian, *Panzer Leader*, p.391 for the number of divisions in each of the fronts hurled at Army Groups A and Center.
2. In September 1944 Army Group North Ukraine was re-designated Army Group A and Army Group South Ukraine became Army Group South.
3. Ziemke, *Stalingrad to Berlin*, p. 417, quoting Soviet sources. Fritz, *op. cit.*, p.441 gives a slightly different figure for Army Group A.
4. British Air Ministry, *op. cit.*, p.386. Again, Fritz' figures are somewhat different. He reports that Army Group A and Army Group Center had only 300 fighters on January 10, 1945, and these faced 10,500 aircraft. He does note that these two army groups were reinforced with 300 fighters and 700 ground-attack aircraft on the eve of the Soviet offensive.
5. Ziemke, *Stalingrad to Berlin*, p.420.
6. *Ibid*, p.416 and notes 22 and 23 quoting OKH Eastern Intelligence Branch summaries 4404/44 and 81/45.
7. Guderian reports in his memoirs on the many times he attempted to convince Hitler to withdraw from Courland as Chief of Staff of the OKH—see, for example, Guderian, *Panzer Leader*, p.372 and pp.412–13. His last attempt was at a stormy meeting with Hitler in early February 1945, at which time he asked for Dönitz' support but apparently that was not forthcoming.
8. Speer, *Inside the Third Reich*, pp.405–06.
9. Heinz Guderian, *Erinnerungen eines Soldaten* (Heidelberg: K. Wowinckel, 1951) pp.345–49.
10. *Ibid*, p.351.
11. General Sergei M. Shtemenko as cited by Ziemke, *Stalingrad to Berlin*, p.419.
12. These 1,800,000 troops broke down roughly as follows: 421,000 in Army Group North; 695,000 in Army Group Center; 458,000 in Army Group A; and 217,000 in Army Group South. This does not include the approximately 200,000 in the

Twentieth Mountain Army, withdrawing from Finland to Norway and the roughly 300,000 troops in Norway since Finland and Norway were OKW (Armed Forces High Command) theaters of operation.

13. Max Hastings, *Armageddon: The Battle for Germany, 1944–1945* (New York: Alfred A. Knopf, 2004) p.244.
14. British Air Ministry, *op. cit.*, p.309.
15. Görlitz, *History of the German General Staff*, p.4 and Muth, *op. cit.*, pp.169–70.
16. Muth, *op. cit.*, p.168.
17. *Ibid*, p.170 and Waldemar Erfurth, *Die Geschichte des deutschen Generalstabes von 1918 bis 1945* (Göttingen: Verlag Musterschmidt, 1957) p.151. Von Marwitz was later recalled to active duty and promoted to Generalmajor. The inscription on his gravestone, still located near the battlefield of Fehrbellin reads: "He saw Frederick's heroic times and fought with him in all his wars. He chose disgrace when obedience brought no honor."
18. See, for example, Valentin Feurstein, *Irrvege der Plicht 1938–1945* (München: Verlag Welsermühl, 1963) p. 75 and Lunde, Hitler's *Pre-Emptive War*, p.388 and pp.528–30.
19. Führer order number 00688/45 as quoted in Ziemke, *Stalingrad to Berlin*, p.423, note 48.
20. Ziemke, *Stalingrad to Berlin*, p. 421.
21. Hastings, *Armageddon*, p. 244. See also Guderian, *Panzer Leader*, p. 390.
22. OKH War Diary entry for January 15, 1945 as translated in Hastings, *Armageddon*, p.246.
23. Ziemke, *Stalingrad to Berlin*, p.429.
24. Message from General Guderian to Hitler on January 15, 1945, in the OKH Operations Divison's files (Nr. 450 010/45), as quoted in Ziemke, *Stalingrad to Berlin*, p.429 and note 65.
25. Fritz, *op. cit.*, p.444; Tony Le Tissier, *Zukov at the Oder*, p.31; Guderian, *Panzer Leader*, pp.391–92; and Ziemke, *Stalingrad to Berlin*, p.422.
26. Ziemke, *Stalingrad to Berlin*, p.422.
27. Guderian, *Erinnerungen*, p.357.
28. It was not unusual for Hitler to tolerate actions by his very loyal followers such as Model, Dönitz, Schörner, and Rendulic that he would not have tolerated from others.
29. Ziemke, *Stalingrad to Berlin*, p. 432.
30. *Ibid*, p.42.5
31. A German garrison of about 12,000 troops continued to defend Poznan after it was encircled. The city fell to the Soviets on February 23, 1945.
32. Bellamy, *op. cit.*, p.645.

10
The Fate of the Enclaves

The Failed **Sonnenwende** *(Solstice) Operation*

General Guderian had planned a counterstroke against Marshal Zhukov since the end of January 1945. It was intended to be a two-pronged offensive, with one drive from Stargard in East Pomerania and another one from the Glogau–Kottbus area.[1] Stargard is located east of Stettin and southwest of Kolberg. Guderian argued that the Sixth SS-Panzer Army, commanded by General Josef (Sepp) Dietrich (1892–1966), consisting of five Panzer divisions, should form the southern prong. Sepp Dietrich's Panzer army had taken part in the Ardennes Offensive, and Hitler refused to divert this army from its scheduled move to Hungary.

Guderian writes that in his arguments with Hitler about Operation *Sonnenwende* in the early days of February, he "considered a prompt evacuation of the Balkans, Italy, Norway, and particularly Courland" a necessary precondition for successfully defending Germany's borders. Hitler immediately turned down his withdrawal proposals and the meeting became exceedingly acrimonious. Guderian told Hitler "You must believe me when I say it is not just pig-headiness on my part that makes me keep on proposing the evacuation of Courland. I can see no other way left to us of accumulating reserves, and without reserves we cannot hope to defend the capital. I assure you I am acting solely in Germany's interests."[2] This caused a violent outburst from Hitler and things became so heated between the two that Göring finally pulled Guderian into an adjoining room to calm him down.

Hitler's decision not to allow the Sixth SS-Panzer Army to be diverted from its transfer to Hungary reduced Guderian's offensive to a southward attack from the Stargard area behind the Soviet Oder front. Guderian planned to attack on a 30-mile (50km) wide front and demanded speed for a deep thrust. In what can only be described as a remarkable feat at this point of the war, Guderian managed to scrape together from other sectors of the Eastern Front, and from the West, two corps headquarters and ten divisions, seven of those Panzer divisions.

Problems plagued the operation from the start. Guderian did not want any of the divisions employed prematurely, but Himmler had difficulties holding the staging area and eventually committed several of the new divisions to other tasks. Guderian wanted an early date for the counterattack, but Himmler dragged his feet. It came to a stormy showdown with Hitler on February 13 where Guderian demanded that the Deputy Chief of Staff of the Army, General Walter Wenck (1900–82), receive a special mandate to command the offensive.[3] In another compromise decision, Hitler agreed to Guderian's proposal for Wenck to command the operation under Himmler, but the specific responsibilities of each were not spelled out. After a quick inspection trip, Wenck discovered that most of the forces for the counterattack were not ready and decided to launch the offensive piecemeal, starting with a one-division attack against Arnswalde where a small German garrison was encircled.[4]

The one-division attack by the 11th SS-Panzergrenadier Division *Nordland* from the Eleventh SS-Panzer Army was launched on February 15. Catching the Soviets by surprise, the troops captured the town of Arnswalde. This initial success convinced Himmler to commence the whole operation on February 16. That day, however, was wasted in probing attacks and the offensive was irretrievably stuck before it got started. General Wenck was severely injured in an automobile accident on his way to brief Hitler. The German tanks were confined to roads because of rain and mud and the badly executed operation ended on February 18.

Soviet Pause

The Soviet delay in executing the second phase of the winter offensive from February to April 1945 has been a subject of much controversy among both military professionals and military historians. Some disagree with the decision, arguing that the Soviets had a chance of securing Berlin much quicker and with much lower losses in February. Others argue that the dangers on the flanks could have resulted in a successful German counter-attack and further prolonged the war.

While the *Sonnenwende* operation caused very little damage to the Soviets, there are those who believe that it may have brought the Germans an unexpected dividend with profound consequences. A mood of caution seemed to have taken hold of Stavka as it delayed the planned advance on Berlin and the Elbe without a pause along the Oder/Neisse. It seems odd that an organization which had shown little fear of exposed flanks since the beginning of Operation *Bagration* should suddenly be gripped by fear. Instead of continuing the westward drive across the Oder/Neisse the Soviets shifted their focus to clearing operations in Pomerania and Silesia. Stalin's alleged resentment at Zhukov's hero status may also have played a role.

Zhukov relates the telephone conversation he had with Stalin on January 25 which led to the pause. Stalin asked what his future plans were. At that time Zhukov stated that he was ready to continue on to Berlin without a pause and he did not think the German forces in Pomerania posed any serious threat. Stalin allegedly told him that he could not do that because a 100-mile (160km) gap (an exaggeration) had developed between Zhukov's right flank and the left flank of the Second Belorussian Front. He also noted that Marshal Ivan Konev, who commanded the First Ukrainian Front, would be busy mopping up in his area and would therefore not be ready to protect Zhukov's left flank. Stalin said the pause would last 10–15 days.

Nowhere has the debate over the wisdom of the pause been more heated than among some of the Soviet military leaders of the winter offensive. In his book *The End of the Third Reich*,[5] Marshal Vasily Chuikov (1900–82) levels heavy criticism at the decision to pause along the Oder. In his own book, Zhukov takes issue with his fellow marshal by defending the decision. In Zhukov's rebuttal to Chuikov's criticism, the threat from Pomerania that he had minimized in his earlier conversation with Stalin suddenly grows dramatically—to over 40 divisions.[6] In a commentary note on the same page, Harrison Salisbury writes "Actually, in offering so many reasons against the immediate drive to Berlin and in emphasizing the risks, Zhukov is contradicting his own specific proposals to Stalin in late January and early February when he wanted permission to go directly into the attack." In a comment on the following page Salisbury notes that this was the period leading up to the Yalta Conference and refers to a claim by Shtemenko that "there is substantial reason to believe that Stalin had some geopolitical considerations in mind in pausing before the final smash at Berlin."

Zhukov also refers to postwar statements by Keitel and Guderian that they were preparing a major offensive operation out of Pomerania against the right flank of the First Belorussian Front.[7] I have found no reference that either the OKW or the OKH were seriously contemplating such a move, particularly in the wake of the failed *Sonnenwende* operation. And, in the real world, the Germans were not capable of a serious counterstroke at this time because their forces were spread wide along the Baltic coast in defensive battles and because they lacked the necessary fuel. Hitler even refused a request on February 17 to allow Second Army, now part of Army Group Vistula, to make a limited westward withdrawal to tie securely into the left flank of the Eleventh Panzer Army.[8] By this request Guderian hoped to keep a corridor open to East Prussia, a link that was in danger because of German weaknesses in the center of Army Group Vistula.

On February 17 Stavka ordered Zhukov, commanding the First Belorussian Front, to send major portions of his front to the north to assist the Second Belorussian Front, commanded by Rokossovsky, in cleaning out its left flank in East Pomerania. This was not as much of a shift in emphasis as some have suggested. It was always the mission of the First Belorussian Front to clear the Oder delta in the Stettin area.

Some writers have credited the fiasco-ridden *Sonnenwende* operation, the German Samland attack, and the German attack against the Hron bridgehead in Hungary with changing Soviet plans.[9] The timeline fails to support this conclusion. While the *Sonnenwende* operation actually began on February 16, that in Samland did not start until February 19, and at Hron on February 17. It is therefore doubtful that these German operations influenced Stavka to modify offensive plans, a modification that actually appears to have been made before those dates (see below). Furthermore, it is not likely that the carefully calculating Stavka would have made a split-second decision to change the nature of operations considering all of the massive logistic implications that would have entailed. It is more likely that it had been under consideration for several days. Zhukov's book, quoted above, indicates that the pause decision was transmitted to him on January 25, but we don't know how long it had been in the works. The OKH intelligence service (FHO) had reported on February 13 that the Soviets were likely to postpone their attack on Berlin while they cleared their flanks in East Pomerania and Silesia.[10] All these rule out any influence on the Stavka decision by the *Sonnenwende* operation or events in Samland and Hungary.

At the beginning of the winter offensive on January 12, the Soviets had good reason to be in a hurry. Since Hitler had cancelled the Ardennes Offensive on January 3, the Soviets no doubt expected the Western Allies to resume a rapid drive into the heart of Germany. However, the Allies spent January and February recapturing lost ground and in heavy fighting west of the Rhine. Consequently the Soviets may have concluded that there was no longer a reason to hurry.

The military situation on the Western Front changed radically in March. The Western Allies had closed on the Rhine River and established bridgeheads on its east bank: the Twelfth Army Group in early March at Remagen and the Twenty-First Army Group about two weeks later. The drive to encircle the Ruhr industrial region was in full swing. This changed the military situation and immediately energized the Soviets. It is therefore very plausible that the contrasting lack of urgency in February was due to the fact that the Allied armies were not in motion. However, the continued strength displayed by the German Army may also have played a role in the decision to pause. The combined losses admitted to by the First Ukrainian and First Belorussian Fronts in their drive from the Vistula to the Oder amounted to about 193,000 casualties. The Germans reported 77,000 killed, 334,000 wounded, and 192,000 missing for a total of 603,000 casualties in January and February.[11] Despite these losses the German strength on the Eastern Front—about 2 million—was slightly higher than at the start of the Soviet winter offensive, although almost 600,000 of these were bottled up in Courland and other coastal enclaves.[12] The quality of the troops is an entirely different matter, as the best troops were those cut off from the main front. An early thaw caused problems for the Soviet supply operations, as had German possession of two communications centers in their rear, Poznan and Breslau. These were major road and railroad hubs, and as long as they were in German hands they hampered Soviet logistic flows. While Poznan fell on February 23, Breslau held out until May 6.

The space/force ratio was also working against the Soviets. The maneuver room for their armies became restricted as they moved west against ever shrinking German fronts. The Soviets had two fronts on the Oder/Neisse and Lower Vistula and there was hardly maneuver room for any more. The Germans benefited from the shortened fronts—it was about 250 miles (400km) from the Baltic to the left flank of the First Ukrainian Front near the Slovakian border. However, Hitler's refusal to make sensible withdrawals along the Baltic coast added almost 310 miles (500km) to this front.[13] It will always remain a fertile ground for speculation what impact a withdrawal of the German forces isolated along the Baltic coast would have had on the Soviet offensive into Germany.[14]

Guderian gives the following order of battle in early February 1945. There were 22 divisions in Army Group Courland, including two Panzer divisions. Army Group North in the area around Königsberg consisted of 19 infantry and five Panzer divisions. There were also remnants of several more divisions. Army Group Vistula, in the area between the Vistula and the mouth of the Oder, had 25 infantry and eight Panzer divisions.[15] Some of these divisions were mauled and understrength, but were a far cry better than the motley units—poorly trained and under-equipped—scraped together to defend the Oder and Neisse Rivers, with the exception of a few veteran divisions that we find there. When units encircled in interior pockets are counted, nearly 100 divisions could have been saved for the defense of the Reich by withdrawing but here, too, the time was running out.

The Soviets expected the Germans to mount a determined defense of Berlin, so a hasty and ill-prepared advance could result in embarrassing problems. All these factors undoubtedly played into the Stavka decision to delay the original second phase of their offensive and turn their attention to the flanks. In the interim the Soviets were able to occupy significant parts of Austria in the Vienna Offensive.

The Second Belorussian Front under Rokossovsky, Third Belorussian Front under Chernyakovsky, and the First Baltic Front under Bagramyan were already facing north opposite the German enclaves along the Baltic coast. The Second Belorussian Front's mission had always been to drive northwestward and clean out the Lower Vistula area in the vicinity of

Danzig. The objective of the Third Belorussian Front had been Königsberg. The First Belorussian Front under Zhukov had the mission of driving to the Oder from Guben in the south to the vicinity of Stettin in the north. Zhukov ended up at the end of February holding an L-shaped front with his forces facing both north and west. Between Guben and Schwedt it faced west, but from Schwedt to south of Bublitz it faced north. The forces facing west were opposed by Army Group Vistula, primarily the Ninth German Army. No major redeployments were therefore required in order to have the three Belorussian fronts launch operations against the German forces holding the Baltic coast from Stettin in the west to Königsberg in the east.

The Courland and Memel Pockets

The battles for the enclaves had begun long before the Soviet decision to pause along the Oder/Neisse. The Soviets had basically decided to ignore the Courland Pocket, since no special provisions were made regarding it in their plans for the winter offensive. The Courland Group of Soviet Forces kept on periodically hammering away at the enclave. Two of the six epic battles for the slowly shrinking Courland Pocket took place during the winter offensive. It appears that the later Soviet efforts against the pocket were designed to eat away the supplies the Germans were receiving by sea, thereby assuring that the troops in the pocket presented no offensive threat.

The fifth battle for Courland began on February 27 and ended on March 13. In its wake General von Vietinghoff, the commander of Army Group Courland, reported that his forces probably would not be able to withstand a major attack in the future. Vietinghoff's report resulted in his transfer to Italy and he was replaced by a Hitler loyalist, Rendulic. The sixth and last battle began on March 17 and ended on April 3.[16]

The German forces in Courland still comprised two armies (Sixteenth and Eighteenth) with eight corps and 21 divisions.[17] Guderian, with tepid support from Dönitz, tried again to convince Hitler to withdraw from Courland. Dönitz confirmed that by marshaling all the navy's transport assets, a withdrawal by sea was possible and could be carried out over a period of nine days.[18] In turning down this last request Hitler came up with new reasons that no longer involved his Swedish bogeymen or the submarine training areas. He maintained that the losses in such a withdrawal would be prohibitive and a large number of Soviet units would no longer be tied down.[19]

The port of Memel to the southeast of the Courland Pocket had remained besieged since the First Baltic Front split the Third Panzer Army in October 1944, forcing XXVIII Corps of that army into a beachhead. The corps was isolated except for a tenuous connection to the south over what is referred to as the Curonian Spit.[20] Two of the three divisions in the pocket were evacuated by sea due to heavy losses and replaced in the same way with another division. The success of the Soviet East Prussian Offensive to the south made the pocket untenable and it was abandoned by XXVIII Corps on January 27, 1945. The corps withdrew to the Samland Peninsula via the Curonian Spit. The Soviets took control of Memel on January 28, 1945, after eliminating the German rearguard.

The Königsberg, Samland, and Heiligenbeil Pockets

Soviet actions against the East Prussian/East Pomeranian coastal strip had actually started well before February 17. These battles are commonly referred to as the East Pomeranian Offensive and the East Prussian Offensive. They were actually parts or extensions of the original Soviet winter offensive. The East Pomeranian Offensive that took place in both Pomerania[21] and West Prussia lasted officially from February 10 to April 4, 1945 and will be discussed later in this chapter.

The fighting in East Prussia had been going on since January 1945. Soviet spearheads reached the shore of the Vistula Lagoon on the Baltic coast on January 25, cutting off the German forces in East Prussia from the rest of Germany. This forced the Germans to supply the surrounded forces by sea. As mentioned in the previous chapter, Hitler renamed three army groups on January 25, 1945. Army Group North became Army Group Courland; Army Group Center (the army group surrounded on that day in East Prussia) became Army Group North and Army Group A became Army Group Center.

By late January 1945, the Third Belorussian Front had surrounded Königsberg, for a time severing the tenuous connection to the Samland peninsula and the port of Pillau. The Third Panzer Army was trapped in Königsberg along with 200,000 civilians.[22] Food was in short supply and the civilians were forced to decide whether to remain in the city and starve, cross the lines and submit themselves to the mercy of the Soviets, or attempt the difficult and hazardous route to a port where they could board ships to the West. About 2,000 per day chose to cross the frozen Frisches Haff to Pillau in the hope of being evacuated by sea. In an action that was not exactly a profile in courage, Erich Koch (1896–1986), the Nazi Gauleiter of East Prussia, whose place was in Königsberg, decided to stay in the relative safety of Pillau after he returned from a trip to Berlin. When that place became unsafe he simply disappeared.

The First Baltic Front under the command of Bagramyan had orders to cooperate with the Third Belorussian Front in clearing East Prussia. The Soviets managed to sever the narrow connection between Königsberg and the German troops in Samland, a connection the Germans had desperately tried to keep open. The First Baltic Front had forced the remnants of the Army Detachment (Armeeabteilung) Samland into the Samland Peninsula. Chernyakovsky, the commander of the Third Belorussian Front, was killed in the fighting and Marshal Aleksandr Vasilevsky (1895–1977) took command. With the appointment of Vasilevsky, the First Baltic Front was attached to his command on February 22 and renamed as the Samland Front.[23]

The Soviets had planned an attack on the Germans forces in the Samland Peninsula for February 21, but in a move that caught the Soviets by surprise the Germans attacked on February 19 to reopen the connection between Samland and Königsberg. In a coordinated effort, forces from the Third Panzer Army in Königsberg and the Fourth Army in Samland attacked the Soviet forces that had severed the corridor that linked Königsberg to the Samland Peninsula. The German attack was successful and the corridor from Königsberg to the Samland Peninsula was reopened.[24] The period leading up to the re-opening of the land bridge to the Samland Peninsula is often referred to as the First Siege of Königsberg.

By the third week in February, the Soviets had compressed the German forces in East Prussia through continuous attacks into basically three pockets. One was around the city of Königsberg, one on the Samland Peninsula,[25] and one on the coast of Frisches Haff, normally referred to as the Heiligenbeil Pocket. It was not an easy task for the Soviets to take Königsberg. There were five German divisions at nearly full strength in the city—approximately 130,000 troops. The city was also well fortified in three concentric rings with 15 forts built in the late 1800s. These forts were interconnected by a series of underground tunnels. Counterattacks by German troops on the Samland Peninsula could also be expected.

The attack on Königsberg began on April 6, 1945. Two Soviet armies—the Thirty-Ninth and Forty-Third—attacked from the north while the Eleventh Guards Army attacked from the south. The skies were dominated by the Red Air Force, which carried out precision bombing against the defenders.

The fighting was especially vicious, and the house-to-house combat took a heavy toll on both sides. In the evening of April 7, General Otto Lasch (1893–1971), the commander of German forces in the city, sent a message to Hitler's headquarters explaining that further resistance was pointless and asked for permission to surrender. Hitler's answer was to defend the city to the last man.

On April 8, the Eleventh Guards Army crossed the Pregel River and established a bridgehead. They advanced northward and linked up with the Soviet troops approaching from the north. Königsberg was again cut off from the German troops on the Samland Peninsula (Army Detachment Samland) after an attempt by German troops to break out of Königsberg failed. On April 9 the German defenders in Königsberg began to be overwhelmed, and any semblance of a coordinated defense ended. General Lasch realized that further resistance was pointless and on his own initiative he notified the Soviets that he was prepared to surrender. The surrender became final just before midnight on April 9.

Approximately 80 percent of the city was destroyed, first by British bombing in August 1944 and then by Soviet shelling and street fighting. According to Soviet figures, the Germans lost 42,000 killed and 92,000 captured. Their own losses were placed at 60,000.

German defense efforts on the Samland Peninsula were largely focused on the port of Pillau, the main evacuation point for casualties and East Prussian civilians. Throughout the siege of Königsberg, Samland had been defended by Army Detachment Samland under the command of General Hans Gollnick (1892–1970). The remnants of Second and Fourth Armies, which were destroyed in encirclements at Danzig and Heiligenbeil (see below), were combined into the Army of East Prussia (Armee Ostpreussen). The mission of this new organization, of which Gollnick's forces became part, was to defend the Samland Peninsula, the Vistula Delta, and the Hel Peninsula.

The offensive against Army Detachment Samland was conducted by the Samland Front under Bagramyan. The Soviet forces involved in the attack consisted of the Fifth and the Thirty-Ninth Armies with the Eleventh Army in reserve. At the start of the attack Bagramyan called on the Germans to surrender, but he received no reply.

The Soviet attack began on April 13 and most of the defenders were scattered in the assault. One Volksgrenadier division was overwhelmed at the town of Rauschen on the northwestern part of the peninsula. A regular infantry division that had been withdrawn from Memel, along with a heavy armor detachment in the north of the peninsula, was driven into the town of Palmicken where it was destroyed. Soviet forces broke through near the city of Fischhausen, which is located at the northern shore of the Frisches Haff, directly west of Königsberg and northeast of Pillau. The German 5th Panzer and 28th Jäger Divisions were driven out of Fischhausen and cornered on the Peyse Peninsula, across Frisches Haff from Pillau. There they were overwhelmed, as there were no places to which they could retire.[26]

The German defenses on Samland Peninsula were pushed back towards Pillau. Despite a stubborn defense the town was captured by the Eleventh Guards Army on April 25. Remnants of the German IX Corps withdrew to the Frische Nehrung, which is basically a narrow sandbar on the northern side of the Frische Haff. While some managed to escape to the Danish island of Bornholm, the rest remained on the Frische Nehrung to the end of the war. The Soviets claimed that the Germans suffered 80,000 casualties during the operations on the Samland Peninsula.

The Fourth German Army had withdrawn toward Elbing at the northern end of Frisches Haff after it withdrew from Lötzen on January 23. Through appalling winter weather, the Fourth Army's withdrawal was accompanied by thousands of civilians fleeing from the Soviets. The army hoped to make it to Elbing, which was still held by German forces from the Second Army, but they found their path blocked by Soviet forces. The Germans launched an attack on January 26 and lead elements of one division managed to reach Elbing, where it linked up with the 7th Panzer Division from the Second Army. This success was short-lived. The Soviets regrouped and drove the Germans back in four days of hard fighting. The

Fourth Army and some units from the Second Army found themselves encircled in the Heiligenbeil and Braunsberg area with their backs to the Frisches Haff. The Fourth Army Commander, General Hossbach was relieved on January 29 and his place taken by General Friedrich-Wilhelm Müller (1897–1947).[27]

The day after Müller assumed command he was ordered to cease all breakout attempts.[28] There were thousands of civilians in the pocket, desperate to escape. This book cannot in any way deal adequately with the unimaginable suffering of the civilian refugees, who were fleeing to the West to escape the brutal retribution exacted by the Soviets for the atrocities committed by the Germans in Russia. While it would take volumes to come close to doing justice to this tragic and horrendous aspect of the war, a few words about the magnitude of the problem are in order.

Many millions were fleeing ahead of the advancing Soviet armies in appalling winter conditions with only those possessions they could carry. Since the Soviet armies were located along the Oder/Neisse, most refugees opted to flee towards the coast in the hope of getting on a refugee ship that would bring them to relative safety in the West. The roads were clogged with these wretched individuals seeking safety, and their presence became a significant factor in military operations.

The Nazis had forbidden all evacuation until it was too late to do so in an orderly manner. No plans had been put in place and there was a devastating shortage of food and fuel. Tens of thousands of these refugees died from frost, exhaustion, or from being killed by the Soviets. The throngs of fleeing civilians—old people, women, children, and the sick—go a long way to explaining the fierce resistance offered by the German troops in the defense of the embarkation ports. The stellar role of the German Navy in the evacuation effort is addressed later in this chapter.

The Soviets attempted to break through the perimeter of the Heiligenbeil Pocket in early February, but their efforts failed. The defenders were given effective naval gunfire support by ships such as the heavy cruisers *Admiral Scheer* and *Lützow*, firing at almost maximum range from the Baltic Sea.[29] Since the German troops in East Prussia had no reasonable hopes of halting the Soviet onslaught or even of surviving, their fierce resistance can only be explained by a sense of duty, self-preservation, and a desperate effort to keep the evacuation routes open for civilian refugees. The able-bodied among the refugees were drafted into Volkssturm units to bolster the defense.

The Soviets undertook a determined operation to eliminate the pocket on March 13. It took over two weeks of bitter fighting before the Heiligenbeil Pocket was overwhelmed on 29 March. Two elite divisions were evacuated by sea during the fighting, and the remnants of the Fourth Army withdrew to the Kahlholzer Peninsula or were scattered into small pockets along the coast, at some points digging in on the beaches. The last evacuation from Kahlholz and Galga took place on March 29 in an operation where the 562nd Volksgrenadier Division sacrificed itself as a rearguard. While accurate figures on casualties may never be known, the Soviets claim that German casualties were 93,000 dead and 46,448 prisoners.

The East Pomeranian Offensive

The primary mission of the Second Belorussian Front—under Konstantin Rokossovsky—was to protect the right flank of the Soviet drive into Germany, in other words the right flank of Zhukov's First Belorussian Front. In doing so he was expected to drive toward Pomerania and Danzig. It appears that Rokossovsky's orders were further refined during the offensive to a push directly north to the town of Elbing.[30]

Stalin appears to have worried about the German forces in Pomerania—resulting in Stavka's decision to place the three right flank armies of Rokossovsky's Second Belorussian Front under the control of the Third Belorussian Front. Rokossovsky, who was reinforced by an army from Stavkva's reserve, was directed to concentrate his efforts on clearing the Baltic coastline in West Prussia and Pomerania from Danzig to Stettin.[31]

In a drive to Köslin, the Second Belorussian Front split the Second German Army from the Third Panzer Army,[32] pushing the latter behind the Lower Oder near Stettin on March 19. General Walter Weiss'(1890–1967) Second Army was eventually driven into an enclave along the Bay of Danzig. The town of Grudziadz on the Vistula was surrounded and its one-division garrison surrendered in March. After a Soviet breakthrough at Köslin on March 2, Second Army found itself completely cut off from the rest of its Army Group.

On March 1, Zhukov put the right flank of his First Belorussian Front —one shock army, two guard tank armies, and the First Polish Army—in motion towards the north. This drive cut off the left wing of the Third Panzer Army after General Erhard Raus (1889–1956) was denied permission to withdraw. The right flank of the Third Panzer Army withdrew in the direction of Stettin.[33] Rokossovsky opened another phase of his offensive on March 6, capturing Elbing on March 10. Weiss, who had warned that Elbing could not be held, was relieved of his command by Hitler on March 9 and replaced by General Dietrich von Saucken (1892–1980) who was born in nearby Fischhausen. When he reported to Hitler on March 12, he was told that he would be under the command of the Gauleiter of Danzig. Saucken, an ultra-conservative Prussian with strong anti-Nazi feelings, reportedly slammed his hand on the map table and stated, "I have no intention of placing myself under the orders of a Gauleiter." To everyone's surprise Hitler acquiesced and told him to keep the command to himself.[34]

After the fall of Elbing, the Second Army withdrew in disarray into Danzig and Gdynia, where they were besieged by the Second Belorussian Front. The Soviets managed to split the German defenses on March 22; Gdynia fell on March 26 and Danzig on March 28. The remnants of the Second German Army withdrew to the Vistula delta northeast of the city and from there they were evacuated to the Hel Peninsula.[35] According to Soviet information, the Germans lost 39,000 soldiers killed and 10,000 captured in the fighting at Danzig.

Kolberg is a sizeable seaport on the Pomeranian coast that the Germans planned to use to supply enclaves along the Baltic coast. The city was full of refugees from Pomerania, and it was surrounded by elements of the First Belorussian Front on March 4. The defenders were a motley mixture of Volkssturm, elements of the Third Panzer Army, and French and Latvian Waffen-SS. Most of the troops were from Army Group Vistula.

The first units to attempt to take Kolberg were Soviet forces from the First Belorussian Front. They managed to penetrate the city on March 4, but were repulsed by the defenders after some stiff fighting. The nearby city of Köslin fell to the Soviets on the same day and it was planned to use forces freed by the capture of Köslin as reinforcements for a new attack on Kolberg. Instead, the Soviets decided to turn the operation over to the First Polish Army, part of the First Belorussian Front. The Polish troops taking part in the operation eventually numbered more than 28,000. The first Polish assault on the city failed as the Germans desperately tried to hold on to cover evacuations that were in progress. The Germans abandoned most of the city on March 17, leaving behind a force of 2,000 as a rearguard. More than 80 percent of the city was destroyed in the heavy fighting. Most of the inhabitants and about 70,000 refugees from surrounding areas, as well as 40,000 German soldiers, were evacuated by German naval forces by sea to Swinemünde. Polish casualties were over 4,000.

Operation Hannibal

Hannibal was the name given to the German naval operation involving the evacuation by sea of German troops and civilians from Courland, East Prussia, and the Pomeranian ports from mid-January to May 1945. Dönitz ordered Admiral Kummetz, as Naval High Commander, Baltic, and Admiral Konrad Engelhardt, head of the navy's shipping department, to plan and execute the evacuation or rescue operation. The order to start the evacuations was issued on January 23, 1945. Dönitz states in his memoirs that his aim had been to evacuate as many people as possible away from the Soviets.[36]

Hannibal turned into one of the largest emergency sea evacuations in history. Over a period of 15 weeks, somewhere between 494 and 1,080 merchant vessels of all types, including fishing boats and other craft, and Germany's largest remaining naval units, would transport between 800,000 and 900,000 refugees and 350,000 soldiers across the Baltic Sea to Germany and German-occupied Denmark.[37] This was more than three times the number of people evacuated at Dunkirk.[38] The operation had to run a gauntlet of British aerial-laid mines and Soviet aircraft, small naval units, and submarines operating in the Baltic. This resulted in some dramatic losses, some of which are highlighted below.

The liners *Wilhelm Gustloff*, *Hansa*, and the whaling factory ship *Walter Rau* left Gdynia on January 30, 1945, bound for Kiel. The *Hansa* was forced to return to port with mechanical trouble, but *Gustloff*, with more than 10,000 civilians and military personnel aboard, continued. The ship was torpedoed and sunk by the Soviet submarine *S-13* off the Pomeranian coast—the estimated 9,400 fatalities made this the worst single ship maritime disaster in history. Those on the *Walter Rau* eventually made it to safe harbor. The *Steuben* sailed from Pillau on February 9 with between 3,000 and 4,000 on board, mostly military personnel, heading for Swinemünde. It was also sunk by *S-13*, just after midnight on the day of departure. There were only 300 survivors. On February 22 the *Göttingen* sailed from Courland, carrying 5,000 soldiers. It was torpedoed in the morning of February 23 with the loss of 3,000.[39]

There were successes, however. In early March, a task force composed of the heavy cruiser *Admiral Scheer* accompanied by three destroyers and the *T-36* torpedo boat, covered a German bridgehead near Wollin. During this operation, small naval craft managed to evacuate over 75,000 soldiers and civilians who had been isolated in the area. They were taken to larger warships and other transports lying offshore. While a number of these transports were sunk, large liners such as the *Deutschland* managed to break through carrying up to 11,000 soldiers and civilians each. During the night of April 4/5, a flotilla of small boats and landing craft evacuated over 30,000 soldiers and civilians from the Oxhöfter Kämpe and took them to the Hel Peninsula. It is estimated that nearly 265,000 individuals were evacuated from the Danzig area to the Hel Peninsula during the month of April.

On April 15, another large convoy consisting of four liners and other transports left the Hel Peninsula with more than 20,000 soldiers and civilians. This movement brought new tragedies. On April 16, the *Goya* was torpedoed and sunk by the Soviet submarine *L-3*, with the loss of more than 6,000 lives; 183 survived. Yet from May 1 to May 8, more than 150,000 people were evacuated from the Hel Peninsula's beaches. At 2100 hours on May 8, 1945, the last day of the war, a convoy consisting of 92 large and small vessels left the city of Libau with 18,000 soldiers and civilians. While several hundred of those who had boarded small ships were captured by Soviet motor torpedo boats, evacuations to the west continued for at least a week after all such movements were prohibited by the terms of the German surrender.

In addition to the *Goya*, *Gustloff*, *Steuben*, and *Göttingen*, 157 other merchant vessels were lost during the 15-week duration of Operation *Hannibal* (January 23–May 8, 1945).[40] Nevertheless, it was one of the most successful evacuations in history and saved the lives of untold numbers of civilians. It was successful due to the professionalism and sense of duty of the soldiers who protected the evacuation points, and the civilian and naval crews of the ships who risked all in making repeated journeys. While the loss in lives was high, the civilians were prepared to take the risks to reach safety further west.

Safety in war is a very relative term and this was also true for north Germany in 1945. The primary ports receiving the refugees—Warnemünde, Swinemünde, and Sassnitz—were completely overcrowded. The Chief of Staff of the Soviet Air Force, Marshal Sergei Khudiakov (1902–50), made an urgent request for the Western Allies to bomb Swinemünde in order to disrupt the supply operations for German forces further east. The mission was given to the US Eighth Air Force, which sent 677 bombers escorted by around 450 fighters to strike the town. Pritt Buttar reports that an estimated 23,000 Germans died in the raid, almost all refugees from the east.[41] Many refugees were left behind in ports and on the beaches and suffered the consequences of the mind-boggling lack of empathy on the part of Hitler and the Nazi civilian hierarchy.

NOTES

1. Guderian, *Panzer Leader*, p.406.
2. *Ibid*, p.412.
3. *Ibid*, pp.413–15.
4. Ziemke, *Stalingrad to Berlin*, p.447.
5. Vasily Ivanovich Chuikov, *The End of the Third Reich*, translated from the Russian by Ruth Kisch with an introduction by Alistair Horne (London: Panther Publishers, 1969).
6. Georgi K. Zhukov, *Marshal Zhukov's Greatest Battles*, translated by Theodore Shabad with an introduction and explanatory comments by Harrison E. Salisbury (New York: Pocket Books, a division of Simon & Schuster, 1970) p.250.
7. *Ibid*, p.249.
8. This was not a Panzer army at all, but was scraped together from various elements by Himmler, including remnants of the Third Panzer Army, remnants from the Ninth Army, and other assorted units. The order of battle looked impressive on paper, with 13 divisions assigned, but, as pointed out by Antony Beevor, *op. cit.*, p.89, it was stretching reality to even call it a corps.
9. Guderian does not mention anything about the possible effects of the *Sonnenwende* operation on the Soviets but Ziemke, *Stalingrad to Berlin*, p.448, believes that it had "an impact on the Soviet side altogether out of proportion to the befuddlement that had surrounded the operation since its inception."

10. Christopher Duffy, *Red Storm on the Reich: The Soviet March on Germany 1945* (Edison, New Jersey: Castle Books, 2002) p.186.
11. Hastings, *Armageddon*, p.260.
12. This may be a low figure. Robert Jackson, *Battle of the Baltic: The Wars 1918–1945* (South Yorkshire: Pen & Sword Books Limited, 2007) p.180, writes that as of late February 1945, around 560,000 troops were bottled up in Courland and East Prussia alone.
13. The direct distance from Stettin to the port of Windau on the Courland Peninsula is 256 miles (412km).
14. Guderian, *Panzer Leader*, p.411 lists the following forces in Courland and the other enclaves as of early February, not counting those in Army Group Vistula's area that were facing south: the Courland Army Group had 20 infantry and two Panzer divisions; the new Army Group North was composed of 19 infantry and five Panzer divisions.
15. Guderian, *Panzer Leader*, p.411.
16. Ziemke, *Stalingrad to Berlin*, pp.464 and 470.
17. Franz Kurowski, *Bridgehead Kurland: The Six Epic Battles of Heeresgruppe Kurland*, translated by Fred Steinhardt (Winnipgeg, Manitoba: J. J. Fedorowicz Publishing, Inc., 2002) p.201.
18. *Ibid*, p.203. This may be an erroneous figure since Dönitz still maintained that 90 days would be required and Kurowski may have confused the statement he attributes to Dönitz to a study made by Army Group Courland at about the same time.
19. *Fuehrer Conferences on Matters Dealing with the German Navy* (1945) p.85.
20. The Curonian Spit is the name given to a narrow 60-mile (98km) stretch of sand dunes separating the Curonian Lagoon from the Baltic Sea and it runs from the port of Klaipeda in the north to the Samland Peninsula in the south.
21. Pomerania stretched along the south shore of the Baltic Sea roughly from the Recknitz River near Stralsund in the west to the mouth of the Vistula River near Danzig in the east. East Prussia stretched from Danzig in the west to Memel in the east.
22. Beevor, *op. cit.*, p.50.
23. Duffy, *op. cit.*, p.203.
24. Beevor, *op. cit.*, p.88.
25. The Germans still held a narrow land connection to the adjacent German pocket on the Samland Peninsula.
26. Duffy, *op. cit.*, p.219.
27. General Müller was considered one of the more brutal German generals in WWII. As a result of his actions in Crete he was given the nickname "butcher of Crete." He was captured after the war, tried by a Greek military court, convicted of war crimes, and executed in 1947.
28. Duffy, *op. cit.*, p.173.
29. *Ibid*, p.204.
30. *Ibid*, p.170.

31. Ziemke, *Stalingrad to Berlin*, p.440.
32. The Third Panzer Army had been trashed earlier, particularly by General Bagramyan's First Baltic Front drive to Memel in October 1944. That is why part of this army was involved in the fighting in East Prussia while part of it was found in Pomerania.
33. Duffy, *op. cit.*, p.188.
34. Beevor, *op. cit.*, p.120.
35. Duffy, *op. cit.*, pp.223–25.
36. Dönitz, *op. cit.*, p.434.
37. Andreas Kossert, *Damals in Ostpreussen* (München: Deutsche Verlags-Anstalt, 2008) p.160.
38. Dönitz, *op. cit.*, p.434 writes that more than 2 million soldiers and civilians were brought to safety. It is possible that Dönitz' figures include evacuees prior to the start of Operation *Hannibal.*
39. Kurowski, *op. cit.*, p.202.
40. Unless otherwise noted, the evacuation statistics are mostly from Kossert, *Damals in Ostpreussen*, cited above.
41. Pritt Buttar, *Battleground Prussia: The Assault on Germany's Eastern Front 1944–45* (Oxford: Osprey Publishing, 2010), p.235.

Conclusion

A number of reasons put forth by Hitler for his wave-breaker concept in the Baltic were given in the introduction. They were addressed at various points in the book and it is now time to summarize the findings and arrive at conclusions about their usefulness and validity. Many can be likened to a drowning man grasping for straws to stay afloat.

Geographic and Economic Reasons

The fear of a Finnish withdrawal from the war is a recurring theme in Hitler's reasoning, particularly in the early stages of the withdrawal. However, this possibility had been a reality since the German debacle at Stalingrad in the winter of 1943, if not earlier. The subsequent flirtations between Finland and the Soviet Union were well known to the Germans, primarily through their liaison with Marshal Mannerheim's headquarters, but also through the German network of informers in Stockholm. The evidence that Finland might leave the war was real and planned for by the Germans and resulted in a directive to the Twentieth Mountain Army and the Army of Norway (Directive 50) issued over Hitler's signature in September 1943.

By this time, the military situation for the Germans had not improved since the winter of 1942/43, and the peace feelers and proposals had increased in frequency and scope. While the Finns were influenced by what happened in the Leningrad area and the Baltic States, they focused on the forest, not the trees. For by the summer of 1943 the Germans were in retreat in virtually all areas of operations—the Eastern Front and in the

Mediterranean, and the tide of war had also turned against the Japanese in the Pacific. The Finns reached the conclusion that Germany and Japan could not win the war and, within that context, it made little difference if the Germans held on to a strip of the Baltic coast while suffering massive defeats in other areas.

Mannerheim was surprised by the 1944 Soviet offensive against his country. He assumed that Stalin would opt to leave Finland alone and allow its fate to be determined in a general settlement after the war. For Finland it was now imperative to make peace with the Soviets as long as that peace left the country as an independent nation. The Finns also needed time to make arrangements to replace the grain shipments they had received from the Germans and this was finally accomplished through an agreement with the Swedes.

Hitler was well aware of the sentiments in Finland and the policy that country had adopted. Nevertheless, he continued to cling to the slimmest of hopes that the Soviet terms to Finland would be unacceptable, despite Mannerheim's message to the Germans that the country could not endure another bloodletting like the one suffered in the Soviet offensive in June–July 1944. Such hopes are no foundation for a policy. Finland was lost because of German misfortunes on all fronts and that country's conclusion that Germany would be defeated. Clinging to the Narva front or Courland under that scenario was therefore of little consequence to the Finns, as long as German armies were ground to pieces on other fronts. It was a serious mistake by Hitler to think that Finland was more influenced by events in the Baltic than by their overall assessment that the industrial might of the West combined with the seemingly endless human resources of the East would prevail. In short, they had a better grasp of reality than Hitler.

The possible entrapment of the Twentieth Mountain Army in Finland is of course totally linked to Finnish actions. This was realized in Directive 50, issued in September 1943. The fate of that army was directly linked to a speedy withdrawal into northern Norway. The risk of entrapment was not as much connected to Finland's withdrawal from the war as it was to Hitler's foot dragging because of his next fear—the loss of Finnish nickel.

Hitler's bogus worry that the end of Finnish nickel shipments would lead to a collapse of the German war industry was put to rest by Albert Speer, his armament and war industry czar, in 1944. Speer said that there was sufficient nickel on hand to last well into 1946 and that the lack of chrome and oil would bring war production to an end long before the stockpile of nickel was exhausted.

The breakout of the Soviet Baltic Fleet was another factor tied to the situation in Finland. The Gulf of Finland was open to the Baltic Sea as soon as the Soviets and the Finns cleared the minefields. For reasons explained elsewhere in this book, the Soviets decided not to sortie with their heavy naval units. Submarines and torpedo boats, however, made an appearance from October 1944. These posed a threat to German shipping in the Baltic as well as to the German submarine training areas and their re-supply and evacuation efforts for the enclaves.

A justification for holding on to the Panther Line and the Narva front often given by Hitler was the protection of the Latvian shale oil fields. We have seen that this oil had little impact on Germany's overall oil requirements. The fact that some of this oil was used by the German Navy may be another reason why that service was eager to defend as far forward as possible. However, it was certainly not something that a rational mind would conclude warranted the sacrifice of hundreds of thousands of Germany's best troops. By this stage of the war, the reliance was on the Romanian oil, domestic oil, and increasingly on synthetic fuel.

Swedish intervention in the war was a subject raised repeatedly by Hitler. The Swedes had no intention of entering World War II. This fact must have been known to Hitler because of the constant flow of information from the Abwehr's elaborate network of informants in Sweden, including members of the Swedish Navy, the one service in that country that was decidedly pro-German. Whether or not the Germans held the Courland Peninsula was of no interest to Sweden, despite Hitler's claims to the contrary.

The loss of transit rights through Sweden, and the end of iron ore and finished products importation, transpired despite Germany's clinging to the Baltic coast. Like Finland, Sweden had concluded that Germany would lose the war and they adjusted their policies accordingly. There was always the danger that Sweden would actively side with the Allies in case they invaded Norway. I have found no evidence that Sweden intended to intervene unless they were prompted to do so by actions of German forces in Norway. The stationing of large forces in Norway had become a drain on

German resources, but Hitler repeatedly refused to consider a drawdown or withdrawal from the one operations area that had early in the war attested to his "military genius." In fact, Hitler went to the other extreme in January 1945 by sending a ski brigade to reinforce the troops in Norway.[1]

The threat to the submarine training area was a recurring theme in Hitler's reasoning for holding on to the Baltic coast. Yet that reason had also lost much of its validity before the creation of the Courland and Memel enclaves in October 1944. Soviet submarines were about to start prowling the Baltic, and the training areas were increasingly coming within the reach of Soviet aircraft. In addition, the Royal Air Force had begun a campaign to heavily mine the shipping lanes in the Baltic, including the submarine training areas. This effort was launched in August 1944.

The advent of the new submarines was delayed, not because of the lack of training areas, but because of production problems and eventually —starting in December 1944—by a heavy Allied bombing campaign against the submarine assembly facilities and factories making essential parts for those submarines. Dönitz repeatedly misled Hitler by assuring him that mass activation of the new submarines was just around the corner. This led to a fallacious belief that this service would turn the tide of war. An entry in the diary of Joseph Goebbels, the Reich Minister of Propaganda, probably reflected Hitler's beliefs based on misleading information from Dönitz. The entry on March 8, 1945 reads: "Our sole great hope at the present lies in the U-boat war."[2]

Conceptual Reasons

Hitler's assumption that holding "fortified places," including enclaves along the Baltic coast, would frustrate the Soviet advance into Germany because it required more forces to encircle and eliminate such places than it did to defend them was proven increasingly wrong as the war progressed. It was a false economy of force argument.

Hitler based his concept on a military situation that had changed dramatically, a fact he failed to see or ignored. Significant increase in Soviet mobility, loss of German air parity, growing fuel shortages reaching catastrophic dimensions, an ever-growing disparity in field strength, and a momentous decline in the quality of German troops doomed the wave-breaker concept. Hitler's earlier success in keeping the Demyansk Salient and

Kholm Pocket supplied undoubtedly contributed to his views of the usefulness of "fortified places" and the wave-breaker concept, and he failed to realize that in 1942 it took all the resources the Luftwaffe could muster at a time when air parity still existed. The "fortress" and "wave-breaker" concepts used by Hitler also caused the forces in the "fortresses" and enclaves to be lost for the defense of the Oder/Neisse line. This undoubtedly brought the inevitable end to a faster fruition, as did the rather meaningless Ardennes Offensive, with its objectives totally out of Germany's reach.

Strategy

We now come to the use of the term "strategy" to describe Hitler's adoption of the wave-breaker concept in the Baltic. The use of that term gives the concept more military legitimacy than it deserves. The operations that are described in this book falling under the wave-breaker concept cannot legitimately be termed a strategy, since they fail to meet the basic criteria of that rudimentary tool of the military profession (clearly defined and reasonably obtainable objectives, adequate resources, and logical strategic concepts).

It is noted in Chapter 1 that Hitler was no lightweight when it came to political and military strategy before the invasion of the Soviet Union. He was not a mere visionary or adventurer. Hitler was a mesmerizing speaker and knew how to pull the heart strings of his listeners. He found scapegoats for the problems facing Germany, and promised solutions. As we have seen, he pulled Germany out of an economic swamp by launching massive public infrastructure projects and by improving the economic lot of the middle class. He won over conservatives and the military through programs of rearmaments. He completely outmaneuvered his foreign counterparts to the delight of the German people.

Hitler offered a plethora of objectives for his policy and virtually all fail, as we have seen, to stand up to close scrutiny. Even if they had been clearly laid out it would be unreasonable to think that they could be achieved. Some—such as the attitudes of the Finns and Swedes—could not be changed by German actions in the Baltic, but rather were the results of the broader military situation as correctly seen by those two countries. Others were unobtainable because of events well beyond German control.

By ruling the skies the Allies were able to frustrate the German efforts to bring new submarines into service in a timely manner and in quantities that could have had an impact on the flow of supplies and equipment from the United States. Stalin was right when he said that the war would be decided by industrial production. The production facilities in the Soviet Union and the United States were out of Germany's reach, while their own facilities and the fuel to keep the war machine operating were systematically demolished.

The dramatic transformation in the mobility of Soviet armies brought about by immense Soviet production and aid from the West created a situation for which the Germans were not prepared and could not cope. In addition to receiving Lend-Lease shipments, the Soviet Union produced a staggering 29,000 tanks and self-propelled assault guns, 122,500 guns and mortars, and 40,300 aircraft in 1944 alone. While German production of aircraft, tanks, and assault guns also reached new heights in 1944, experienced operators and adequate fuel were lacking.

This brings us inexorably to what may be an unanswerable question—what motivated Hitler to take the actions he did in the Baltic region? Hitler's star as a military leader began to fade during Operation *Barbarossa.* He had reached a point where he fully believed in his own infallibility as a military genius. Instead of listening to the advice of his military leaders he became more and more entrenched in his own views. Like most failing "geniuses" he could not admit to personal failings, but looked for those failings in others. When faced with setbacks for the first time in December 1941, he resorted to the mass firing of some of his best generals, giving no sign of taking any personal responsibility.

Hitler's increasing tendency to micromanage operations from afar robbed subordinates of all personal initiative and may well have overwhelmed his own capability to deal with problems in a rational manner. His actions became increasingly erratic and irrational at the very time when the opposite was required. Hitler's increasing resort to "hold at all cost" orders and the designation of "fortified places" may be a fallback to his own experience in the positional/trench warfare of World War I. It was a war where voluntary withdrawals and elastic defense were seldom practiced.

Hitler appears to have sunk into an illogical fantasy world towards the end, insisting that some kind of miracle would turn the tide of war and bring Germany victory despite the clearly insurmountable odds. This irrational behavior reached a crescendo toward the very end. According to Goebbels, Hitler maintained an "unquestioned belief in final victory."[3] Field Marshal Albert Kesselring (1885–1960) makes a similar observation after his last visit to Hitler in Berlin:

> Even on 12 April 1945, at my last meeting with Hitler he had an optimistic view: whether he was putting on an act is difficult to fathom. Looking back, I want to say that he was obsessed with the idea of any possible rescue like a drowning man clutching at straws. He believed with certainty in a successful ending to the campaign in the East, in a number of new weapons, and even in the collapse of the enemy coalition. All these assumptions were delusions. From the beginning of the Russian offensive Hitler lived increasingly in a self-imposed loneliness and progressively in an unreal world.[4]

Warlimont writes that in the last meeting he and Jodl had with Hitler in April: "Hitler still clung to the belief, for which there were no military grounds of any sort, that somehow the fortunes of war would turn."[5]

It would not be irrational to expect that the earlier "man of the people," who had correctly concluded as early as 1942—if we are to believe Jodl—that the war was lost if the Allies managed to break through the German defenses on a broad front in the West, would call it quits after the Falaise Pocket and the capture of Paris. However, there was now no place for him to go, since neither the Western Allies nor the Soviet Union would deal with him or his government. That was when he should have taken his life if he truly had the best interests of the German people in mind.

Instead he broadened the blame for his misfortunes from the military to the German people. Hitler's dogmatism made him incapable of making the logical decision to allow surrender—for him it was either total victory or total destruction. He decided to go out in the greatest Wagnerian Götterdämmerung in history, with the German troops and people on his funeral pyre. Maybe Hitler had read the less well-known short essay by Karl von Clausewitz titled "I Believe and Profess," mentioned in Chapter 1, and decided to follow his admonitions.

NOTES

1. Warlimont, *op cit.,* p.504.
2. Joseph Goebbels, *Final Entries 1945: The Diaries of Joseph Goebbels*, edited and Introduced by Professor Hugh Trevor-Roper (New York: Avon Books, 1979) p.94.
3. *Ibid*, entry for March 14, 1945, p.156. Goebbels and his wife Magda lived in the Führer bunker at the end of the war. On May 1, the day after Hitler and his wife Eva Braun (1912–45) killed themselves, Goebbels and his wife killed their six children and then committed suicide.
4. Walther Hofer (ed. and commentator), *Der Nationalsozialismus Dokumente 1933–1945* (Frankfurt am Main: Fischer Bücherei, 1959) p.257, my translation.
5. Warlimont, *op. cit.*, p.514.

APPENDIX

Code-names: Operations, Plans, and Studies

Aster—A map exercise that became an operation involving the withdrawal of Army Group North in the Baltic States in September 1944.

Aufbau Ost (Build-up East)—An estimate prepared by Oberstleutnant Lossberg in the National Defense Section (Section L) of OKW Operations Section.

Aufmarschanweisung Ost (Deployment Directive East)—OKH marshaling order against the Soviet Union, issued on January 31, 1941.

Bagration—The Soviet offensive in Belorussia, June–August 1944.

Barbarossa—Invasion of the Soviet Union.

Birke (Birch)—Plan for withdrawal of the Twentieth Mountain Army to northern Lapland in 1944.

Blau (Blue)—Army Group North's withdrawal to the Panther Line in late 1943 and early 1944.

Doppelkopf (Double Head)—German operation out of East Prussia in August 1944 that opened a corridor to Army Group North.

Fall Gelb (Case Yellow)—1940 German invasion of France and the Low Countries.

Fritz—A feasibility study for the invasion of the Soviet Union produced by Lossberg in the summer of 1940.

Lachsfang (Salmon Catch)—Proposed German–Finnish operations against Kandalaksha and Belomorsk in the summer and fall 1942.

Lituanian Positions—Switch positions behind Army Group North in July 1944.

Nordlicht (Northern Lights)—Planned operation against Leningrad in the fall of 1942.

Nordlicht (Northern Lights)—Withdrawal of the Twentieth Mountain Army from Finland in October 1944 to January 1945.

Operationsstudie Ost (Operational Study East) prepared by the OKW's National Defense Section in 1940.

Overlord—The Allied landings in Normandy in 1944.

Panther Positions or Line—Narva River–Lake Peipus line of fortifications, constructed in late 1943.

Parkplatz (Parking Place)—Proposed operation against Leningrad in the spring of 1943.

Regenbogen (Rainbow)—An unsuccessful German naval sortie against Arctic Convoy JW-51B in the Barents Sea in 1942.

Rollbahn Position—A German line paralleling the Leningrad–Moscow Highway, 1943–44.

Seelöwe (Sea Lion)—Planned German operation for a cross-Channel invasion of England.

Sonnenwende (Solstice)—German counterattack at Stargard in February 1945.

Studie Nord (Study North)—OKW feasibility study for the attack on Norway, prepared in January 1940.

Studie Schweden (Study Sweden)—German study in preparation for an invasion of Sweden in 1943.

Tanne Ost (Fir East)—1943 German plan for the occupation of Suursaari (Hogland) Island, carried out in 1944.

Tanne West (Fir West)—1943 German plan to occupy the Åland Islands in case of a Finnish withdrawal from the war.

Wesewrübung (Weser Exercise)—The attack on Norway and Denmark in April 1940.

Zitadelle (Citadel)—German operation against the Kursk salient in southern Russia in July 1943.

Bibliography

Adair, Paul, *Hitler's Greatest Defeat: The Collapse of Army Group Centre, June 1944* (London: Rigel Publications, 2004)

Alexander, Bevin, *How Hitler could have Won World War II: The Fatal Errors that led to Nazi Defeat* (New York: Three Rivers Press, 2000)

Baldwin, Hanson W., *Battles Lost and Won: Great Campaigns of World War II* (New York: Avon Books, 1968)

Becker, Peter W., "The Role of Synthetic Fuel in World War II" in *Air University Review* (July–August 1981)

Bellamy, Chris, *Absolute War: Soviet Russia in the Second World War* (New York: Alfred A. Knopf, 2007)

Beevor, Antony, *The Fall of Berlin 1945* (New York: Penguin Books, 2003)

Bergström, Christer, *Bagration to Berlin: The Final Air Battles in the East 1944–1945* (Buress Hill: Classic Publications, 2008)

Beschloss, Michael, *The Conquerors: Roosevelt, Truman and the Destruction of Hitler's Germany, 1941–1945* (New York: Simon & Schuster, 2002)

Blair, Clay, *Hitler's U-Boat War: The Hunted, 1942–1945* (New York: Random House, 1998)

Blücher, Wipert von, *Gesandter zwischen Diktatur und Demokratie* (Wiesbaden: Limes Verlag, 1951)

British Air Ministry, Pamphlet No. 248, *The Rise and Fall of the German Air Force 1933–1945* (London: Public Record Office, War Histories series, 2001)

Budiansky, Stephen, *Air Power: The men, machines, and ideas that revolutionized war, from Kitty Hawk to Gulf War II* (New York: Viking, 2004)

Bullock, Alan, *Hitler: A Study in Tyranny* (New York: Penguin Books, 1963)

Buttar, Prit, *Battleground Prussia: The Assault on Germany's Eastern Front 1944–45* (Oxford: Osprey Publishing, 2010)

Carell, Paul, *Hitler Moves East 1941–1943*, translated by Ewald Osers (New York: Bantam Books, 1966)

Carell, Paul, *Scorched Earth: The Russian-German War 1943–1944*, translated by Ewald Osers (New York: Ballantine Books, 1971)

Carlgren, Wilhelm M., *Swedish Foreign Policy during the Second World War*, translated by Arthur Spencer (New York: St. Martin's Press, 1977)

Carruthers, Bob and Erickson, John, *The Russian Front 1941–1945* (London: Cassell, 1999)

Chuikov, Vasily Ivanovich, *The End of the Third Reich*, translated by Ruth Kisch with an introduction by Alistair Horne (London: Panther Publishers, 1969)

Churchill, Winston S., *Closing the Ring* (New York: Bantam Books, 1962)

Churchill, Winston S., *The Hinge of Fate* (New York: Bantam Books, 1962)

Churchill, Winston S., *Triumph and Tragedy* (Boston: Houghton Mifflin Company, 1953)

Citino, Robert M., *Death of the Wehrmacht: The German Campaigns of 1942* (Lawrence, Kansas: University Press of Kansas, 2007)

Clark, Alan, *Barbarossa: The Russian-German Conflict 1941–45* (New York: The New American Library, Inc., 1966)

Clausewitz, Carl von, *On War*, edited with an introduction by Anatol Rapoport and translated by J. J. Graham (Baltimore: Penguin Books, 1968)

Clausewitz, Carl von, *On War*, translated by O. J. Matthijs Jolles (Washington, D.C.: Combat Forces Press, 1953)

Clausewitz, Carl von, *War, Politics, and Power: Selections from On War and I Believe and Profess*, translated and edited by Edward M. Collins (Chicago: Henry Regnery Company, 1970)

Creveld, Martin van, *Command in War* (Cambridge, Massachusetts: Harvard University Press, 1985)

Das Deutsche Reich und der Zweite Weltkrieg (Stuttgart: Deutsche Verlags-Anstalt, 1983–1984)

Devins, Joseph H. Jr., *The Vaagso Raid* (Philadelphia: Chilton Book Company, 1968)

Doenitz, Karl, *Memoirs: Ten Years and Twenty Days*, translated by R. H. Stevens in collaboration with David Woodward (New York: Da Capo Press, Inc., 1997)

Duffy, Christopher, *Red Storm on the Reich: The Soviet March on Germany, 1945* (Edison, New Jersey: Castle Books, 2002)

Dupuy, Richard Ernest and Dupuy, Trevor N., *The Encyclopedia of Military History from 3500 B.C. to the Present* (New York: Harper & Row, 1970)

Dupuy, Trevor Nevitt, *The Evolution of Weapons and Warfare* (Indianapolis: The Bobbs-Merrill Company, Inc., 1980)

Earle, Edward Mead (ed.), *Makers of Modern Strategy: Military Thought from Machiavelli to Hitler* (Princeton: Princeton University Press, 1973)

Eberle, Henrik and Uhl, Matthias (eds), *The Hitler Book: The Secret Dossier Prepared for Stalin from the Interrogations of Hitler's Personal* Aides, translated by Giles MacDonogh (New York: Public Affairs, a member of the Perseus Books Group, 2005)

Erfurth, Waldemar, *Die Geschichte des deutschen Generalstabes von 1918 bis 1945* (Göttingen: Verlag Musterschmidt, 1957)

Erfurth, Waldemar, *Surprise,* translated from the German by Stefan T. Possony and Daniel Vilfroy (Harrisburg, Pennsylvania: Military Service Publishing Company, 1943)

Erfurth, Waldemar, *The Last Finnish War*, written under the auspices of the Foreign Military Studies Branch of the Historical Division, Headquarters, European Command (Washington, D.C.: University Publications of America, Inc., 1979)

Erickson, John, *The Road to Berlin: Stalin's War with Germany* (London: Cassell, 2004)

Erickson, John, *The Road to Stalingrad: Stalin's War with Germany* (New Haven: Yale University Press, 1975)

Evans, Martin Marix, *Battles of World War II* (Shrewsbury: Airlife Publishing Ltd, 2002)

Evans, Richard J., *The Third Reich at War* (New York: The Penguin Press, 2009)

Farago, Ladislas, *The Game of the Foxes: The Untold Story of German Espionage in the United States and Great Britain During World War II* (New York: David McKay Company, Inc., 1972)

Feurstein, Valentin, *Irrwege der Pflicht 1938–1945* (München: Verlag Welsermühl, 1963)

Fleming, Peter, *Operation Sea Lion* (New York: Simon and Schuster, 1957)

Flower, Stephen, *Barnes Wallis' Bombs: Tallboy, Dambuster & Grand Slam* (Gloucestershire: Tempus Publishers, 2004)

Frederick the Great, *Instructions for his Generals*, translated by Thomas R. Phillips (Mineola, New York: Dover Publications, Inc., 2005)

Freiden, Seymour and Richardson, William (eds) *The Fatal Decisions: The inside stories of the six great European battles of World War II—written by the German generals who lost them* (Berkley, California: Berkley Publishing Corporation, 1966)

Fritz, Stephen G., *Ostkrieg: Hitler's War of Extermination in the East* (The University of Kentucky, 2011)

Fuller, J. F. C., *The Conduct of War 1789–1961* (New Brunswick: Rutgers University Press, 1962)

Gemzell, Carl-Axel, *Raeder, Hitler und Skandinavien: Der Kampf für einen maritimen Operationsplan* (Lund: C. W. K. Gleerup, 1965)

Germany, Army Group Center *Kriegstagebuch.*

Germany, Army Group North *Kriegstagebuch.*
Germany, Army of Norway *Kriegstagebuch.*
Germany, OKH *Kriegstagebuch.*
Germany, Third Mountain Division *Kriegstagebuch.*
Germany, Twentieth Mountain Army *Kriegstagebuch*
Germany, Wehrmachtfürungsstab, *Kriegstagebuch des Oberkommando der Wehrmacht 1940–1945.* Written by Helmuth Greiner and Percy Ernst Schramm; tasked by Arbeitskreises für Wehrforschung and issued by Percy Ernst Schramm (München: Bernard & Graefe, 1982.)
Germany, Seekriegsleitung, *War Diary of the German Naval Staff Operations Division* (Washington, D.C.: Office of Naval Intelligence, 1948–55)
Gilbert, Martin, *Churchill and America* (New York: Free Press, 2005)
Glantz, David M., *Operation Barbarossa: Hitler's Invasion of Russia 1941* (Gloucestershire: The History Press, 2011)
Goebbels, Joseph, *Final Entries 1945*, edited by H. R. Trevor-Roper (New York: Avon Books, 1978)
Goerlitz, Walter, *History of the German General Staff 1657–1945*, translated by Brian Battershaw (New York: Praeger, 1957)
Görlitz, Walter (ed.) *The Memoirs of Field Marshal Wilhelm Keitel Chief of the German High Command, 1938–1945*, translated by David Irving (New York: Cooper Square Press, 2000)
Greiner, Helmuth, *Die Oberste Wehrmachtführung 1939–1943* (Wiesbaden: Limes Verlag, 1951)
Grier, Howard D., *Hitler, Dönitz and the Baltic Sea: The Third Reich's Last Hope, 1944–1945* (Annapolis, Maryland: Naval Institute Press, 2007)
Guderian, Heinz., *Erinnerugen eines Sodaten* (Heidelberg: K. Vowinckel, 1951)
Guderian, Heinz, *Panzer Leader*, translated by Constantine Fitzgibbon, foreword by B. H. Liddell Hart, (Cambridge, Mass: Da Capo Press, 2002)
Haarr, Geirr H., *The German Invasion of Norway April 1940* (Annapolis, Maryland: Naval Institute Press, 2009)
Halder, Franz, *Kriegstagebuch* (Nuremberg: Office of Chief Council for War Crimes, Office of Military Government for Germany, 1946)
Hanfstaengel, Ernst, *Hitler: The Memoir of a Nazi Insider Who Turned Against the Führer*, translated by John Willard Toland (New York: Arcade Publishing, 2011)
Harding, Duncan, *Clash in the Baltic* (Surrey: Severn House Publishers Ltd, 2004)
Harrison, Mark, "Resource mobilization for World War II: The U.S.A., U.K., U.S.S.R. and Germany, 1938–1945" in *Economic History Review* (1988) pp.171–92
Hastings, Max, *Armageddon: The Battle for Germany, 1944–1945* (New York: Alfred A. Knopf, 2004)

Hastings, Max, *Winston's War: Churchill 1941–1945* (New York: Alfred A. Knopf, 2010)

Haupt, Werner, *Army Group North: The Wehrmacht in Russia 1941–1945*, translated by Joseph G. Welsh (Atglen, Pennsylvania: Schiffer Publishing Ltd, 1997)

Henderson, George Francis Robert, *Stonewall Jackson and the American Civil War* (New York: Barnes & Noble, Inc., 2006)

Hitler, Adolf, *Hitler's Secret Conversations 1941–1944*, translated by Norman Cameron and R. H. Steven, with an introductory essay by H. R. Trevor-Roper (New York: Farrar, Strauss and Young, 1953)

Hofer, Walther (ed. and commentator) *Der Nationalsozialismus Dokumente 1943–1945* (Frankfurt am Main, Fischer Bücherei KG, 1959)

Hoffmann, Peter, *The History of the German Resistance 1933–1945* (Cambridge, Massachusetts: MIT Press, 1977)

Holmes, Richard et. al. (eds) *The Oxford Companion to Military History* (Oxford: Oxford University Press, 2001)

Hugemark, Bo, *Neutralitet och försvar* (Stockholm: Militärhistoriska Förlag, 1986)

Huges, Terry and Costello, John, *The Battle of the Atlantic* (New York: Dial Press, 1977)

International Military Tribunal, *Trial of the Major War Criminals before the International Military Tribunal* (Volume 13)

Irving, David, *Göring: A Biography* (New York: William Morrow and Company, Inc., 1989)

Jackson, Robert, *Battle of the Baltic: The Wars 1918–1945* (South Yorkshire: Pen & Sword, 2007)

Jacobsen, Alf R., *Nikkel, jern og blod: Krigen i nord 1939–1945* (Oslo: Aschehoug, 2006)

Jacobsen, Hans-Adolf and Dollinger, Hans, *Der Zweite Weltkrieg: In Bildern und Dokumenten* (München: Verlag Kurt Desch, 1962–63)

Jodl, Alfred, *Diary, covering the period January 4, 1937 to June 29, 1942* (Volumes 2, 3, and 4, Nuremberg: International Military Tribunal, 1946)

Jomini, Antoine Henri Baron de, *The Art of War*, translated by G. H. Mendell and W. P. Craighill (Westport, Connecticut: Greenwood Press Publishers)

Jones, Archer, *The Art of War in the Western World* (New York: Oxford University Press, 1987)

Jones, Michael, *Leningrad: State of Siege* (New York: Basic Books, 2008)

Keegan, John, *Intelligence in War: Knowledge of the enemy from Napoleon to Al-Qaeda* (New York: Alfred A. Knopf, 2003)

Keegan, John, *The Face of Battle: A Study of Agincourt, Waterloo and the Somme* (New York: Penguin Books USA, Inc., 1976)

Keegan, John, *The Mask of Command* (New York: Penguin Books, 1988)

Keegan, John, *The Second World War* (New York: Viking Penguin, 1990)
Kershaw, Ian, *Fateful Choices: Ten Decisions that Changed the World 1940–1941* (New York: The Penguin Press, 2007)
Kershaw, Ian, *Hitler 1889–1936: Hubris* (New York: W. W. Norton & Company, 1999)
Kershaw, Ian, *Hitler: Nemesis* (New York: W. W. Norton, 1999)
Kershaw, Ian, *The End: The Defiance and Destruction of Hitler's Germany, 1944–1945* (New York: The Penguin Press, 2011)
Keskinen, Kalevi and Mantykoski, Jorma, *Suomen Laivasto Sodassa 1939–1945: The Finnish Navy at War* (Finland: Tietoteos Oy, 1991)
Khrushchev, Nikita S., *Khruschev Remembers*, with an introduction, commentary, and notes by Edward Crankshaw, translated and edited by Strobe Talbott (New York: Bantam Books, Inc., 1971)
Killen, John, *A History of the Luftwaffe 1915–1945* (New York: Berkley Publishing Corporation, 1967)
Kirchubel, Robert, *Operation Barbarossa 1941 (2): Army Group North* (New York: Osprey Publishing Ltd, 2005)
Koehler, Leif, *Fanget av krigen: Norsk ungdom, tysk soldat og russisk krigsfange* (Førde: Selja Forlag AS, 2009)
Kossert, Andreas, *Damals in Ostpreussen* (München: Deutsche Verlags-Anstalat, 2008)
Kurowski, Franz, *Bridgehead Kurland: The Six Epic Battles of Heeresgruppe Kurland*, translated by Fred Steinhardt (Winnipeg, Canada: J.J. Fedorowicz Publishing, Inc., 2002)
Kurzman, Dan, *Blood and Water: Sabotaging Hitler's Bomb* (New York: Henry Holt and Company, 1997)
Lewin, Ronald, *Hitler's Mistakes* (New York: William Morrow, 1984)
Liddell Hart, B. H., *History of the Second World War* (New York: G. P. Putman's Sons, 1971)
Liddell Hart, B. H., *Strategy* (New York: Praeger Publishers, 1972)
Liddell Hart, B. H., *The German Generals Talk* (New York, Quill, 1979)
Liddell Hart, B. H., *The Other Side of the Hill* (London: Cassell, 1951)
Lossberg, Bernhard von., *Im Wehrmachtführungsstab: Bericht eines Generalstabsoffiziers* (Hamburg: H. H. Nölke, 1949)
Lubbeck, William and Hurt, David, *At Leningrad's Gates* (Philadelphia: Casemate, 2010)
Lunde, Henrik O., *Finland's War of Choice: The Troubled German Finnish Coalition in World War II* (Philadelphia: Casemate, 2011)
Lunde, Henrik O., *Hitler's Pre-Emptive War: The Battle for Norway, 1940* (Philadelphia: Casemate, 2008)
Lundin, C. Leonard., *Finland in the Second World War* (Bloomington: Indiana University Press, 1957)

Luvaas, Jay (ed. and translator), *Fredrick the Great on the Art of War* (New York: The Free Press/Macmillan, 1966)

Luvaas, Jay., *Napoleon on the Art of War* (New York: Free Press, 1999)

Macksey, Kenneth, (ed.) *The Hitler Options: Alternate Decisions of World War II* (Mechanicsburg, Pennsylvania: Stackpole Books, 1995)

Magenheimer, Heinz, *Hitler's War: Germany's Key Strategic Decisions 1940–1945* (London: Cassell & Co, 1999)

Mann, Chris and Jorgensen, Christer, *Hitler's Arctic War: The German Campaigns in Norway–Finland, and the USSR, 1940–1945* (Hersham: Ian Allan Publishing, 2002)

Mannerheim, Carl Gustaf von., *The Memoirs of Marshal Mannerheim*, translated by Erich Lewenhaupt (New York: E. P. Dutton & Company, Inc., 1954)

Manstein, Erich von., *Lost Victories* (Minneapolis: MBI Publishing Company and Zenith Press, 2004)

Mayer, S. L., *Signal: Years of Triumph 1940–42* (Englewood Cliffs, N.J.: Prentice-Hall, Inc., 1978)

Medlicott, William Norton, *The Economic Blockade* (Volume 1, London: HMSO, 1952–59)

Megargee, Geoffrey P., *Inside Hitler's High Command* (Lawrence, Kansas: University Press of Kansas, 2000)

Meissner, Otto, *Staatssekretär unter Erbert-Hindenburg-Hitler* (Hamburg: Hoffmann und Campe Verlag, 1950)

Meretskov, Krill A., *Serving the People*, translated by David Fidlon (Moscow: Progress Publishers, 1971)

Merriam, Robert E., *The Battle of the Bulge* (New York: Ballantine Books, 1957)

Messerschmidt, Manfred and Wüllner, Fritz, *Die Wehrmachtjustiz im Dienste des Nationalsozialismus: Zerstörung einer Legende* (Baden-Baden: Nomos, 1987)

Miller, Nathan, *War at Sea: A Naval History of World War II* (New York: Schribner, 1995)

Mitcham, Samuel W. Jr., *The Men of Barbarossa: Commanders of the German Invasion of Russia, 1941* (Philadelphia: Casemate Publishers, 2009)

Montross, Lynn, *War Through the Ages* (New York: Harper & Row Publishers, 1960)

Muth, Jörg, *Command Culture: Officer Education in the U.S. Army and the German Armed Forces, 1901–1940, and the Consequences for World War II* (Denton, Texas: University of North Texas Press, 2011)

Newton, Steven H., *Retreat from Leningrad: Army Group North 1944/1945*, a compilation of articles written by German participants including Oldwig von Natzmer, Wilheim Heinemyher, Paul Hermann, Herbert Loch, and Paul Reichelt (Atglen, Pennsylvania: Schiffer Military History by Schiffer Publishing, Ltd., 1995)

Payne, Robert, *The Life & Death of Adolf Hitler* (New York: Barnes and Nobles Books, 1995)

Petrow, Richard, *The Bitter Years: The Invasion and Occupation of Denmark and Norway April 1940–May 1945* (New York: Morrow Quill Paperbacks, 1979)

Phillips, Thomas R., (ed.) *Roots of Strategy: A Collection of Military Classics* (Harrisburg, Pennsylvania: The Military Service Publishing Company, 1955)

Raeder, Eric, *My Life*, translated by Henry W. Drexel,(Annapolis: United States Naval Institute, 1960)

Raunio, Ari, *Sotatoimet: Suomen sotien 1939–45 kulku kartoin* (Kustantaja: GHenimap Oy, 2004)

Reid, Anna, *Leningrad: The Epic Siege of World War II, 1941–1944* (New York: Walker & Company, 2011)

Rendulic, Lothar, *Gekämpft Gesiegt Geschlagen* (Wels: Verlag Welsermühl, 1952)

Reynolds, David, *In Command of History: Churchill Fighting and Writing the Second World War* (New York: Random House, 2005)

Roberts, Andrew, *The Storm of War: A New History of the Second World War* (New York: Harper Collins Publishers, 2011)

Rogers, Duncan and Williams, Sarah (eds), *On the Bloody Road to Berlin: Frontline Accounts from North-West Europe and the Eastern Front 1944–45* (West Midlands: Helion & Company Ltd, 2005)

Ryan, Cornelius, *The Last Battle* (London: Collins, 1966)

Salisbury, Harrison E., *The 900 Days: The Siege of Leningrad* (New York: Avon Books, 1970)

Saxe, Maurice Comte de, *My Reveries Upon the Art of War*, edited and translated by General Thomas R. Phillips, and printed in his *Roots of Strategy*

Schramm, Percy Ernst, *Hitler: The Man and the Military Leader*, translated, edited, and with an introduction by Donald S. Detwiler (Chicago: Academy Chicago Publishers, 1999)

Schultz-Naumann, Joachim, *The Last Thirty Days: The War Diary of the German Armed Forces High Command from April to May 1945*, translated from the German by D. G. Smith (New York: Madison Books, 1991)

Schuster, Carl O., "What if? German Plans to Invade Sweden in World War II" in *Command Magazine*, Issue 9 (1991)

Sereny, Gitta, *Albert Speer: His Battle with Truth* (New York: Alfred A. Knopf, 1995)

Shirer, William L., *The Rise and Fall of the Third Reich: A History of Nazi Germany* (New York: Simon and Schuster, 1960)

Shtemenko, S. H., *The Last Six Months. Russia's Final Battles with Hitler's Armies in World War II*, translated by Guy Daniels (Garden City, New York: Doubleday & Company, Inc., 1977)

Shtemenko, S. H., *The Soviet General Staff at War 1941–1945*, translated from the Russian by Robert Daglish (Moscow: Progress Publishers, 1970)

Snyder, Louis L., *Fifty Major Documents of the Twentieth Century* (Princeton, New Jersey, D. Van Nostrand Company, Inc., 1955)

Speer, Albert, *Erinnerungen* (Frankfurt am Main: Ulstein Verlag,1969)

Speer, Albert, *Infiltration: How Heinrich Himmler Schemed to Build an SS Industrial Empire* (New York: Macmillan Publishing Co., Inc., 1981)

Speer, Albert, *Inside the Third Reich: The Memoirs of Albert Speer*, translated by Richard and Clara Winston (New York: The Macmillan Company, 1970)

Speer, Albert, *Spandau: The Secret Diaries*, translated by Richard and Clara Winston (New York: Pocket Books, 1977)

Steinweis, Alan E., and Rogers, Daniel E., *The Impact of Nazism: New Perspectives on the Third Reich and its Legacy* (Lincoln, Nebraska: University of Nebraska Press, 2003)

Strawson, John, *Hitler as Military Commander* (New York: Barnes & Noble Books, 1971)

Strutz, Henry and Thompson, Harold Keith (eds), *Doenitz at Nuremberg, a Reappraisal: War Crimes and the Military Profession* (New York: Amber Publishing Corporation, 1976)

Sundell, Olof, *9. April* (Stockholm: Sohlmans, 1949)

Sun Tzu, *The Art of War: Classic Edition*, translated and edited by Lionel Giles (El Paso Norte Press, 2009)

Tarrant, V. E., *The Last Year of the Kriegsmarine: May 1944–May 1945* (London: Arms & Armour Press, 1996)

Terraine, John, *Business in Great Waters: The U-boat Wars, 1916–1945* (London: Leo Cooper, 1989)

Thorén, Ragnar, *Ryska ubåtskriget i Östersjön 1941–1945* (Stockholm: Probus, 1992)

Thoresen, Knut Flovik, *En verden i flamer: Frontkjemperen Bjarne Dramstads egen historie* (Oslo: Forlaget Historie & Kultur AS, 2009)

Tippelskirch, Kurt von, *Geschichte des Zweiten Weltkriges* (Bonn: Athenaeum, 1956)

Tissier, Tony le, *Race for the Reichstag: The 1945 Battle for Berlin* (London: Frank Cass, 1999)

Tissier, Tony le, *Zhukov at the Oder: The Decisive Battle for Berlin* (Mechanicsburg, Pennsylvania: Stackpole Books, 2009)

Toland, John, *The Last 100 Days* (New York: Bantam Books, 1967)

Tooze, Adam, *The Wages of Destruction: The Making and Breaking of the Nazi Economy* (London: Penguin Books, 2006)

Trevor-Roper, H. R., (ed.) *Final Entries 1945: The Diaries of Joseph Goebbels* (New York: Avon Books, 1979)

Trevor-Roper, H. R., (ed.) *Hitler's War Directives 1939–1945* (London: Pan Books Ltd., 1966)
Trigg, Jonathan, *Hitler's Vikings: The History of the Scandinavian Waffen-SS: The Legions, The SS Wiking and the SS Nordland* (Glouchestershire: Spellmount, 2010)
USSR Ministry of Defense, *History of the Great Patriotic War of the Soviet Union, 1941–1945* (Moscow: Voennoe Izdat, 1962)
US Army War College, *Military Strategy: Theory and Application*, edited by Arthur F. Lykke Jr. (US Army War College, 1984)
US Army War College, *Military Strategy: Theory and Evolution*, a lecture by Arthur F. Lykke Jr. (US Army War College, undated)
US Army War College, *Principles of War*, an occasional paper from the Strategic Studies Institute (1981)
US Office of Naval Intelligence, *Fuehrer Conferences Dealing with the German Navy* (Washington, D.C.: Office of Naval Intelligence, Navy Department, 1947)
Valgma, Ingo, *Report on Latvian Shale Oil*
Vehviläinen, Olli, *Finland in the Second World War: Between Germany and Russia*, translated by Gerard McAlester (New York: Palgrave Publishers Ltd, 2002)
Veum, Eirik and Brenden, Geir, *De som falt: Nordmenn drept i tysk krigstjeneste* (Oslo: NRK Aktivum, 2009)
Waite, Robert G. L., *The Psychopathetic God Adolf Hitler* (New York: New American Library, 1978)
Wangel, Carl-Axel, (ed.) *Sveriges militära beredskap 1939–1945* (Köping: Militärhistoriska Förlag, Militärhögskolan, 1982)
Warlimont, Walter, *Inside Hitler's Headquarters 1939–45*, translated from the German by R. H. Barry (Novato, California: Presidio Press, 1964)
Weber, Thomas, *Hitler's First War: Adolph Hitler, the Men of the List Regiment, and the First World War* (USA: Oxford University Press, 2011)
Weintraub, Stanley, *11 Days in December* (New York: Free Press, 2006)
Westerlund, Göran, *Finland överlevde. Finlands Krig 1939–1945 i ord och bild* (Helsingfors: Schildts Förlag, 2007)
Wetterholm, Claes-Göran, *Dödens Hav—Östersjön 1945* (Stockholm: Prisma Bokförlag, 2002)
Wheeler-Bennett, John W., *The Nemesis of Power: The German Army in Politics 1918–1945* (New York: St. Martin's Press, Inc., 1954)
Williamson, Gordon, *Kriegsmarine U-boats 1939–45*, Volume 2 (Oxford: Osprey Publishing Ltd, 2002)
Williamson, Gordon, *Wolf Pack: The Story of the U-Boat in World War II* (Oxford: Osprey Publishing Ltd, 2006)

Winchester, Charles D., *Hitler's War on Russia* (New York: Osprey Publishing, 2007)
Woodman, Richard, *The Arctic Convoys 1941–1945* (London: John Murray Publishers Ltd., 1994)
Wuorinen, John H. (ed.), *Finland and World War II, 1939–1944* (New York: The Ronald Press Company, 1948)
Zhukov, Georgi K., *Marshal Zhukov's Greatest Battles*, translated by Theodore Shabad, introduction and explanatory comments by Harrison E. Salisbury (New York: Pocket Books, 1970)
Ziemke, Earl F., *Battle for Berlin: End of the Third Reich* (New York: Ballantine Books Inc., 1968)
Ziemke, Earl F., *Stalingrad to Berlin: The German Defeat in the East* (New York: Barnes & Noble Books, 1996)
Ziemke, Earl F., *The German Northern Theater of Operations 1940–1945* (Washington, D.C.: Department of the Army Pamphlet No. 20-271, 1959)

Index